BAY AREA WILD

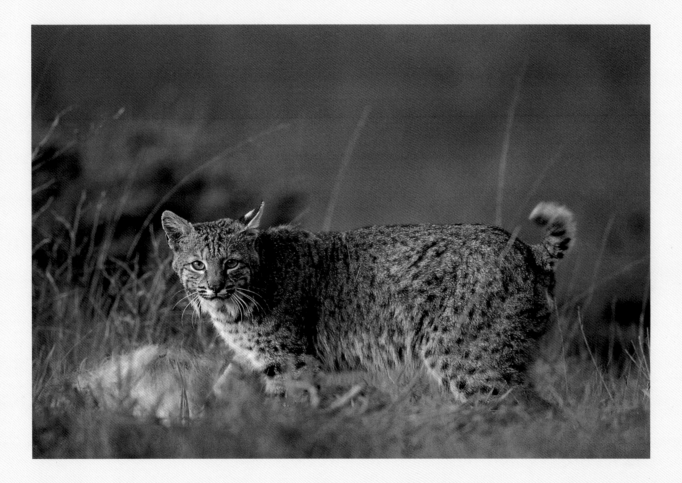

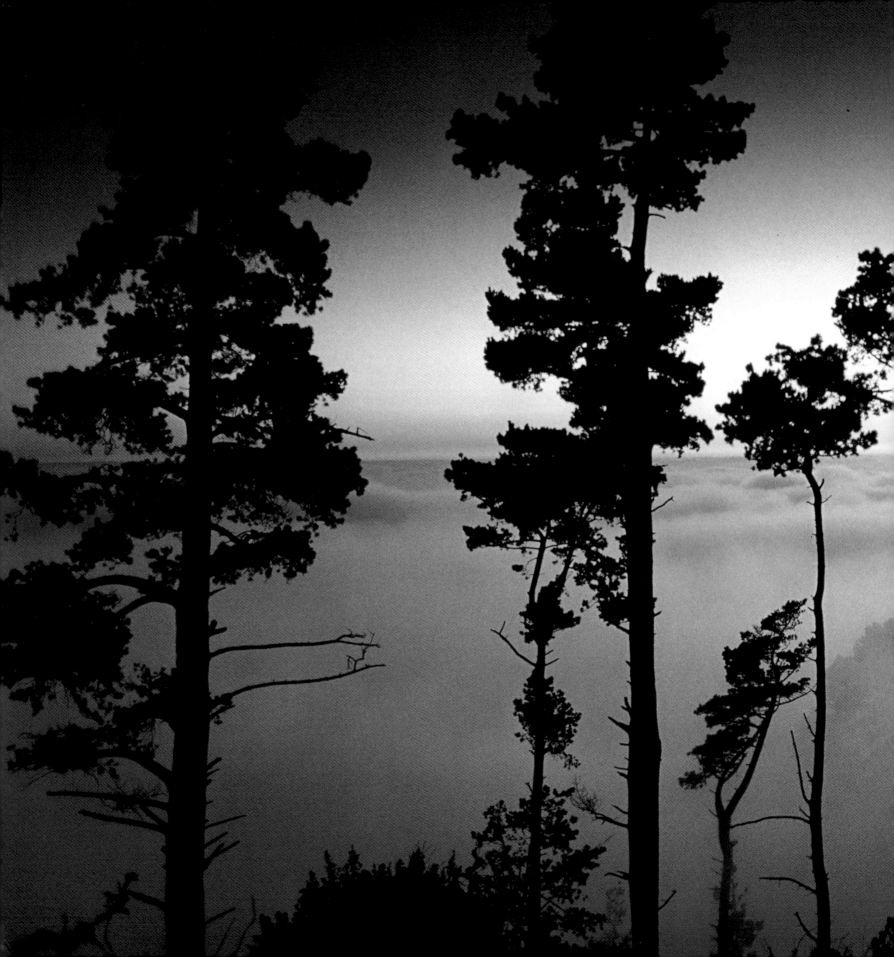

BAY AREA WILD

*A Celebration of the Natural Heritage
of the San Francisco Bay Area*

TEXT BY
GALEN ROWELL

PHOTOGRAPHS BY
GALEN ROWELL AND MICHAEL SEWELL

FOREWORD BY
DAVID R. BROWER

A MOUNTAIN LIGHT PRESS BOOK PUBLISHED BY
SIERRA CLUB BOOKS, SAN FRANCISCO

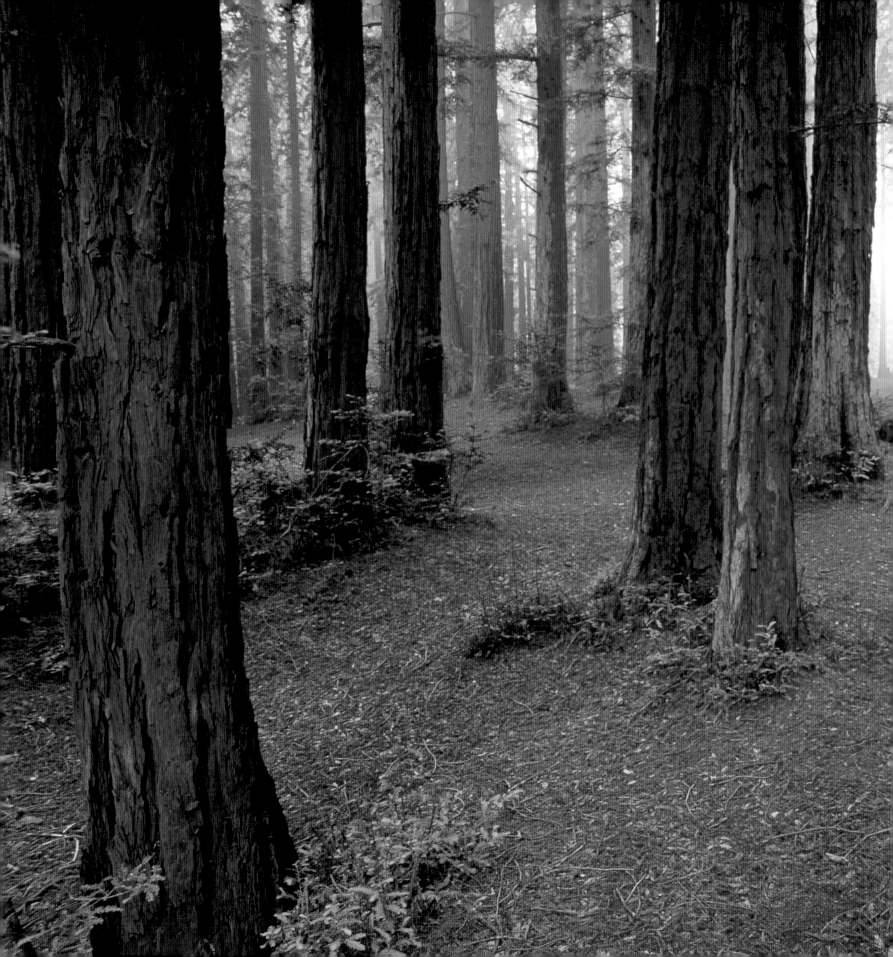

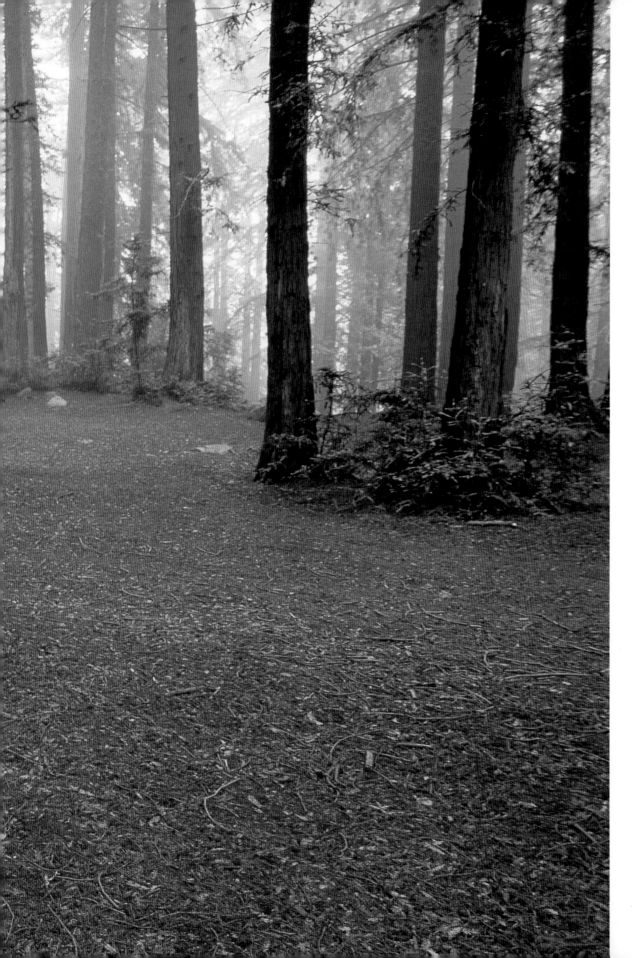

Coast redwoods in fog, Redwood Regional Park. This second-growth forest in the hills above Oakland stands near the site of two trees— more than 30 feet in diameter and 300 feet tall— reputed to be the world's largest of their species that were key navigational landmarks for sea captains sailing into the Bay. They were cut around 1860 for mine timbers, posts, railroad ties, and shingles.

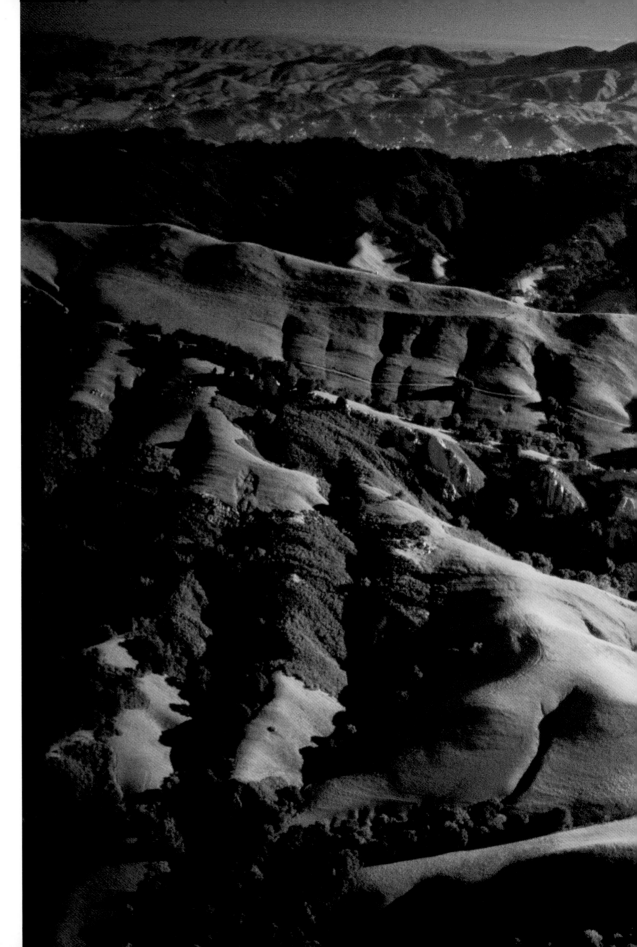

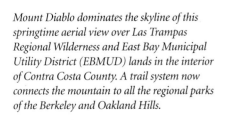

Mount Diablo dominates the skyline of this springtime aerial view over Las Trampas Regional Wilderness and East Bay Municipal Utility District (EBMUD) lands in the interior of Contra Costa County. A trail system now connects the mountain to all the regional parks of the Berkeley and Oakland Hills.

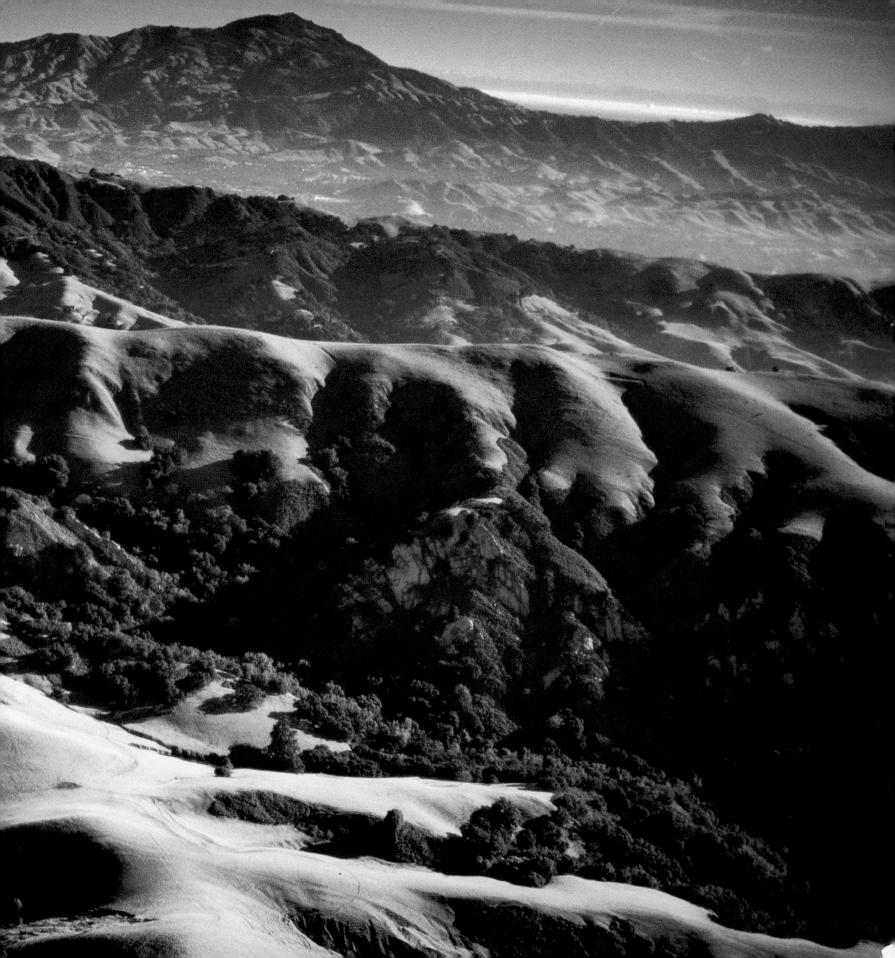

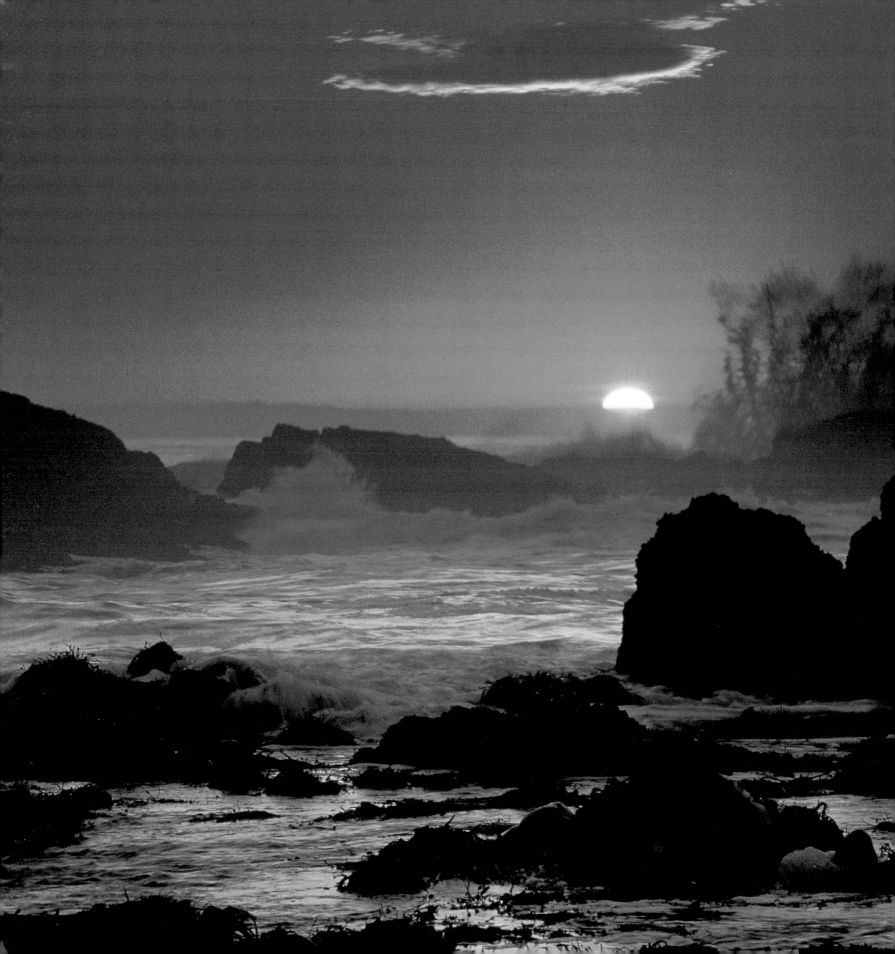

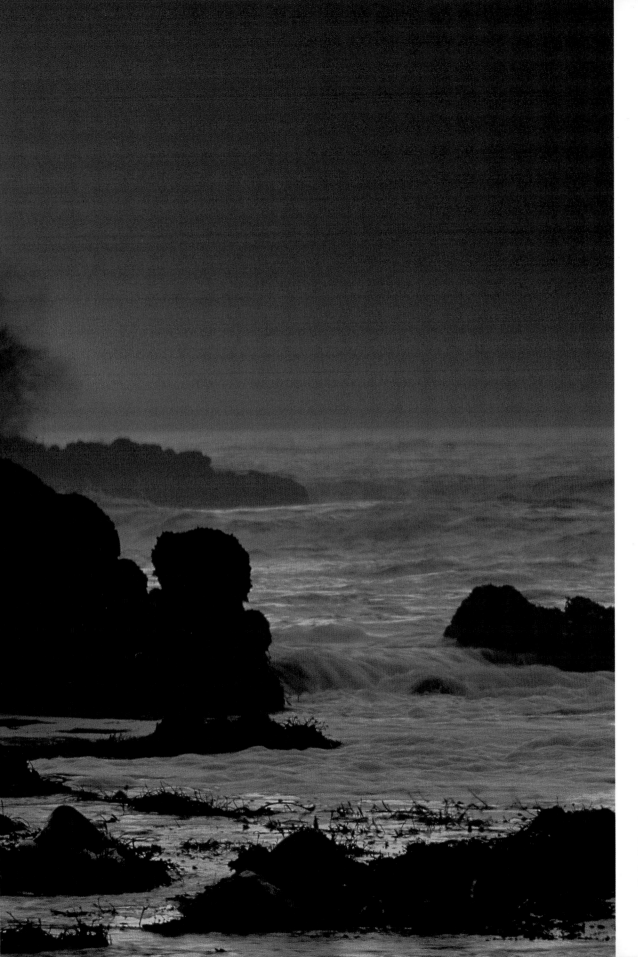

Winter storm waves crash against the rocky San Mateo coast at Pescadero State Beach in the last moments of sunset. The beach is south of Half Moon Bay along the twisting, scenic route of Highway 1.

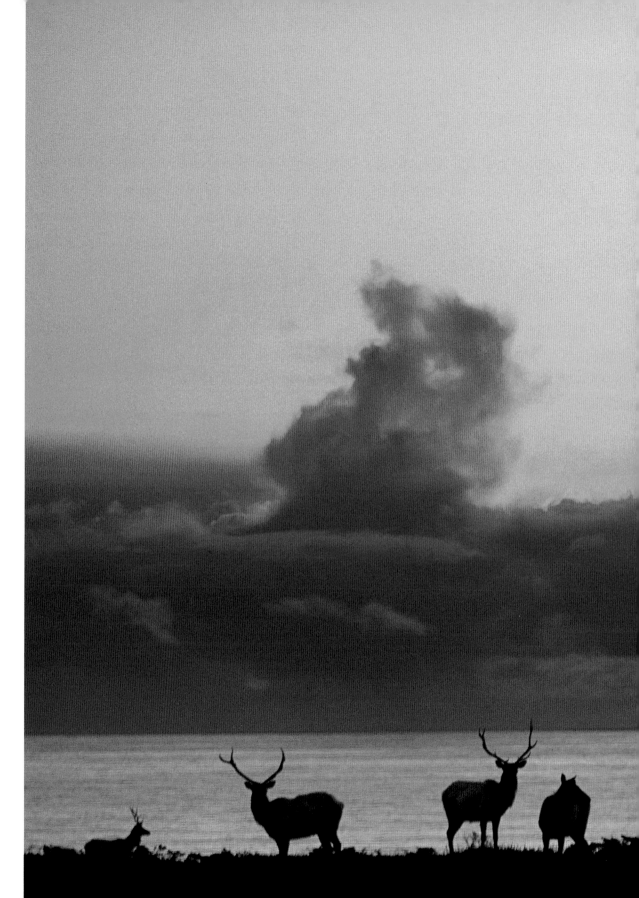

Tule elk graze near the northern tip of the Point Reyes Peninsula at sunset. Vast native herds, seen by every early explorer, were hunted to extinction on the peninsula just after the California gold rush of 1849. In 1978, the National Park Service reintroduced a small herd, which has thrived and multiplied into hundreds of animals.

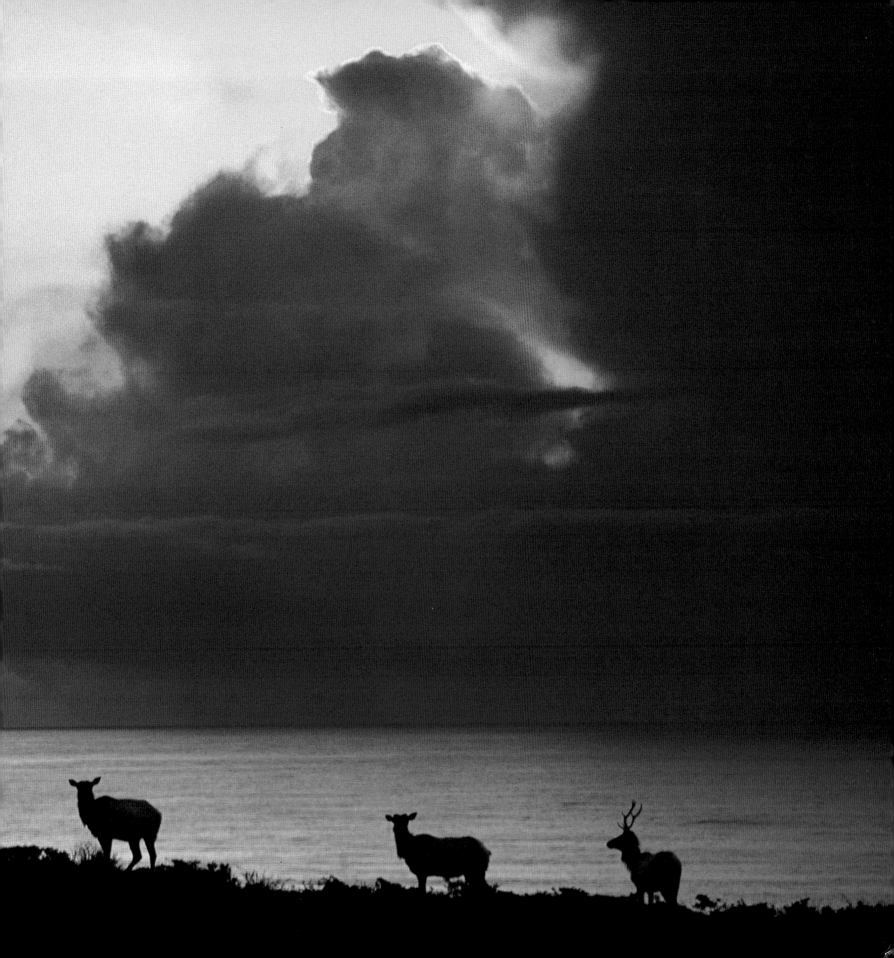

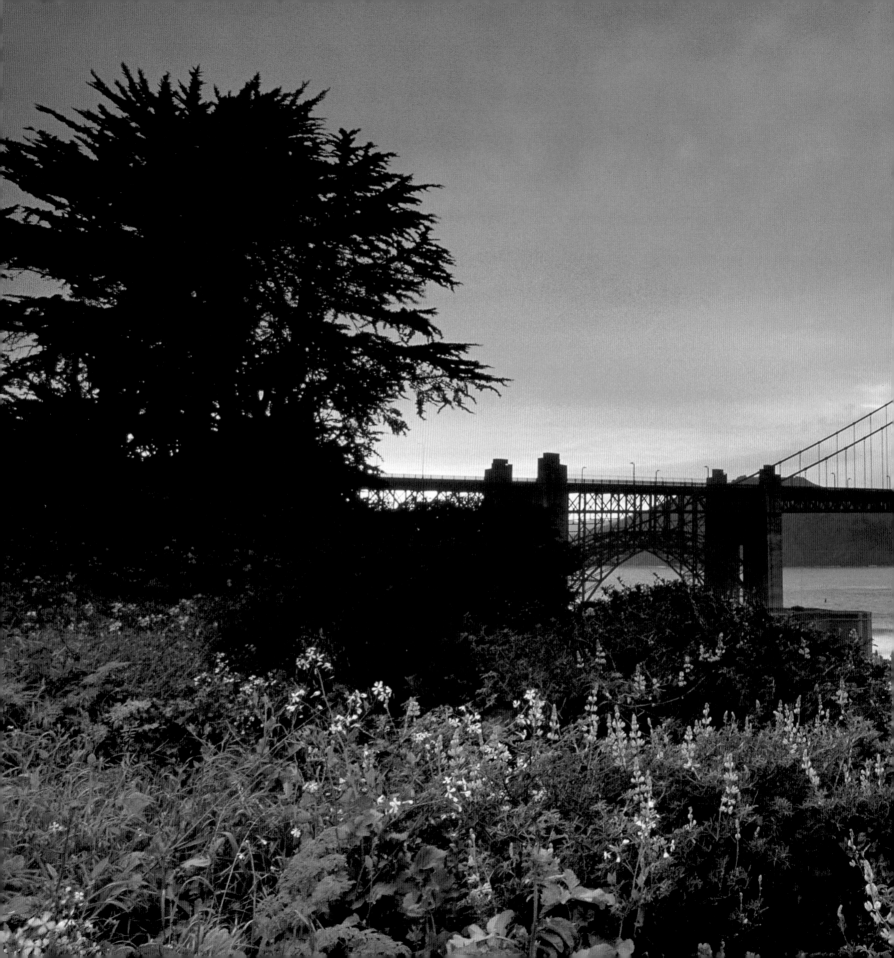

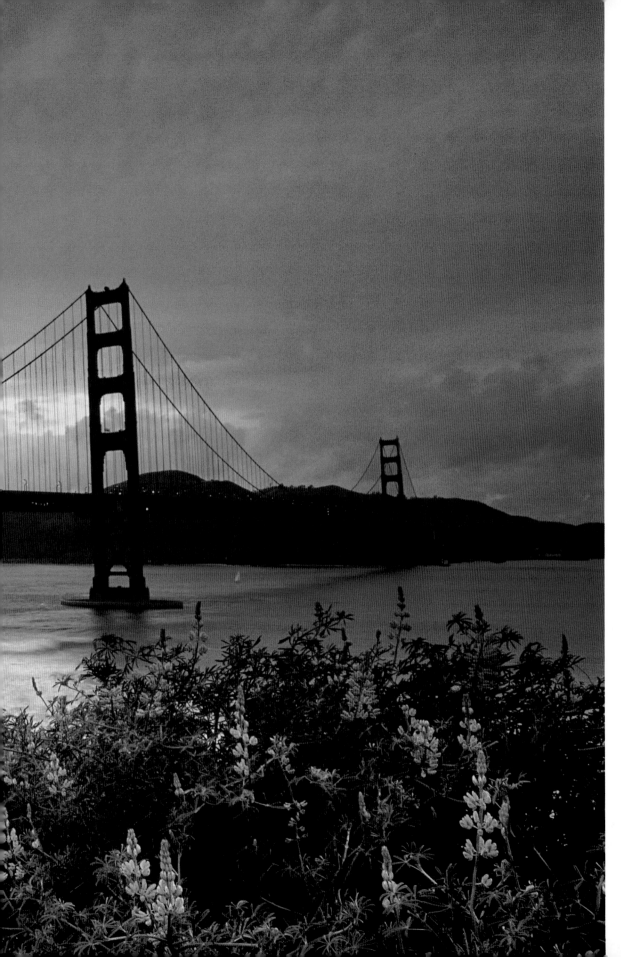

Wildflowers growing above the old bunkers of the Presidio of San Francisco in the Golden Gate National Recreation Area restore a degree of natural character to the Golden Gate—named for its original appearance by explorer Captain John C. Frémont shortly before the gold rush, not for the famous orange bridge completed in 1937.

13

"There is in some minds a tendency toward a wrong love of the marvelous
and mysterious, which leads to the belief that whatever is remote must be better than what is near."
—John Muir, *San Francisco Daily Evening Bulletin,* January 10, 1880

The Sierra Club, founded in 1892 by John Muir, has devoted itself to the study and protection of
the Earth's scenic and ecological resources—mountains, wetlands, woodlands, wild shores and rivers, deserts,
and plains. The publishing program of the Sierra Club offers books to the public as a nonprofit educational service
in the hope that they may enlarge the public's understanding of the Club's basic concerns. The point of
view expressed in each book, however, does not necessarily represent that of the Club. The Sierra Club has some
sixty chapters coast to coast, in Canada, Hawaii, and Alaska. For information about how you may participate
in its programs to preserve wilderness and the quality of life, please address inquiries to
Sierra Club, 85 Second Street, San Francisco, CA 94105.

www.sierraclub.org/books

First paperback edition 1999

Quotations are reprinted by permission from Harold and Ann Lawrence Gilliam,
Marin Headlands: Portals of Time (Golden Gate National Park Association, 1993); Malcolm Margolin,
The Ohlone Way (Heyday Books, 1978); and T. H. Watkins, *John Muir's America* (Crown Publishers, 1976).

Library of Congress Cataloging in Publication Data
Rowell, Galen A.
Bay Area wild : a celebration of the natural heritage of the San Francisco Bay area /
text by Galen Rowell ; photos by Galen Rowell and Michael Sewell ; foreword by David Brower.
p.   cm.
ISBN 1-57805-010-3 (paper)
1. Natural history—California—San Francisco Bay Area.
2. Natural history—California—San Francisco Bay Area—Pictorial works.
3. Natural areas—California—San Francisco Bay Area.
4. Natural areas—California—San Francisco Bay Area—Pictorial works.
I. Sewell, Michael, 1960–   . II. Title.
QH105.C2R69   1997
508.794'6—dc21   97-6191

10 9 8 7 6 5 4 3 2 1

Created and produced by Mountain Light Press in Emeryville, California,
in association with Sierra Club Books

Printed in China

Cover photo: San Francisco at dawn from Mount Tamalpais

Page 1 photo: Wild bobcat, Point Reyes Peninsula

Title page photo: Twilight fog over San Francisco Bay from the Berkeley Hills

CONTENTS

FOREWORD

My Geography of Hope

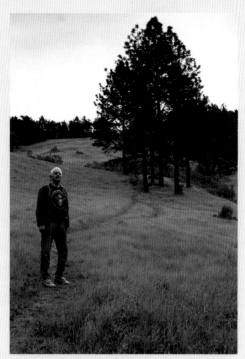

Though I've had eighty years to try, I haven't yet been able to forget my first adventure in the hills of San Francisco Bay. Born in Berkeley in 1912 in a Carleton Street house in better shape now than I am, I spent my youth on Haste Street in a house now almost hidden by a redwood I planted there in 1941, hoping we could mature together. I am now just over six feet tall and the tree is seventy-five feet taller. It was and is seven blocks below the foot of Dwight Way Hill, then steep and unsullied and still steep. There my parents joined my first hike.

On that adventurous day in 1916, my father showed me a tiny spring seeping from a little pool just a few inches above the trail. I was fascinated by what Wallace Stegner, years later, would call "the sudden poetry of springs." Indeed, without some poetry to filter it, how else can cool water come right out of dirt, yet be crystal clear? What I remember especially well about that very first day on a trail was attaining a summit and being delighted to discover that there was another hill beyond, and hills beyond it and beyond them. Stegner has described wilderness as part of the geography of hope. My geography of hope would need hills, endlessly wild.

My parents earned their bachelor's degrees beneath those hills, my father's in engineering in 1901 and my mother's in English in 1905. They earned their respective master's in Ann Arbor and Palo Alto but decided that Berkeley was the place in which to rear their four children, making sure that we got to the Sierra as often as possible. I would nevertheless become a sophomore dropout at the University of California, Berkeley, an editor at U.C. Press, and a Tenth Mountain Division combat veteran and would forever seek saddles under which to be a burr. Perhaps this was induced by the confidence my mother gave me. After she had lost her sight when I was eight, she allowed me to lead her all the way from Haste Street to Grizzly Peak, 1,750 feet above the Bay. Not seeing where she was going, she was willing to climb that high. The least I could do, seeing, was climb higher and steeper. I tried and became a world-class climber when that status didn't require much class. If it bothered her, she never let me know. Nor did my dad, who also tolerated my second-guessing engineers (which he was and I wasn't) before Congress to stop the damming of a river within a national monument. *Moral:* choose parents with care.

I developed a mapmaker's knowledge of Berkeley trails by making a map of them, then avoiding trails wherever I could. My off-trail travels were enriched by a fragrant sagelike native, the name of which I intend to learn soon. It pervaded my clothes each time I returned to Haste Street, and that aroma still reawakens earlier offbeat days for me. On one side trip in 1926 I discovered a variety of orange-tip butterfly that would later be named *Anthocharis sara reakerti* tr. f. *broweri* (Gunder); thus my name was in print on something more recent than my birth notice.

Today my hills of home remain as high as they were, and better cared for than most city hills—except for what has happened to the slopes that face the Bay. Far too much of the wildness has gone, scarred by Grizzly Peak Boulevard and the hill-climbing urge of the university buildings and redwood houses like ours, helping redwoods become endangered.

The distant views from my hills, and their eastern slopes, have fared remarkably well. Vast areas were originally left untamed to protect water supplies and a fort or two. Reserves envisioned in the days of Frederick Law Olmsted and his successors came to be established: a National Monument (Muir Woods), a National Seashore (Point Reyes), a National Recreation Area (Golden Gate), and scores and scores of state parks, open space preserves, and spacious regional parks. In Tilden Regional Park's botanic garden, a Brower Meadow was designated in the Sierra life zone area by James Roof, park botanist, who specialized in adapting native species from elsewhere to life in Tilden. The aspens he brought there helped nurture our kids.

Creeks that flow from the Berkeley Hills to the Bay are being nurtured too. For openers, Strawberry and Codornices Creeks are being restored. Who knows? Salmon may one day spawn again on the U.C. campus. Just liberate the Strawberry tunnel through downtown Berkeley and let the Hayward Fault reclaim the segment of Strawberry's south fork that was buried in 1920 by what was then touted as the Million Dollar California Memorial Stadium.

I was lucky. As a six-year-old I could explore, enjoy, and build ephemeral dams on Strawberry Creek's main stem and begin to acquire a passion for wilderness, rugged and dam-free. Had I not developed a taste for the wild places of my puppyhood, would I ever have become so hung up on the business of blocking dams or advocating parks; or fussing about clearcuts, human rights, justice, and war; or hammering away on Conservation, Preservation, and Restoration (global CPR), including the restoration of some open space to the U.C. campus?

It's fun to take a crack at redefining progress. Because we *can* do a thing, *must* we? Hell no! Better a taboo or two. An ultimate element of my geography of hope is this simple fact: we cannot create wildness, but we can spare it and celebrate it—in far-off, exotic places and at home.

In past books, Galen Rowell has focused on the exotic. Prepare to celebrate what he has to reveal near our homes!

—David R. Brower
Berkeley, California, November 8, 1996

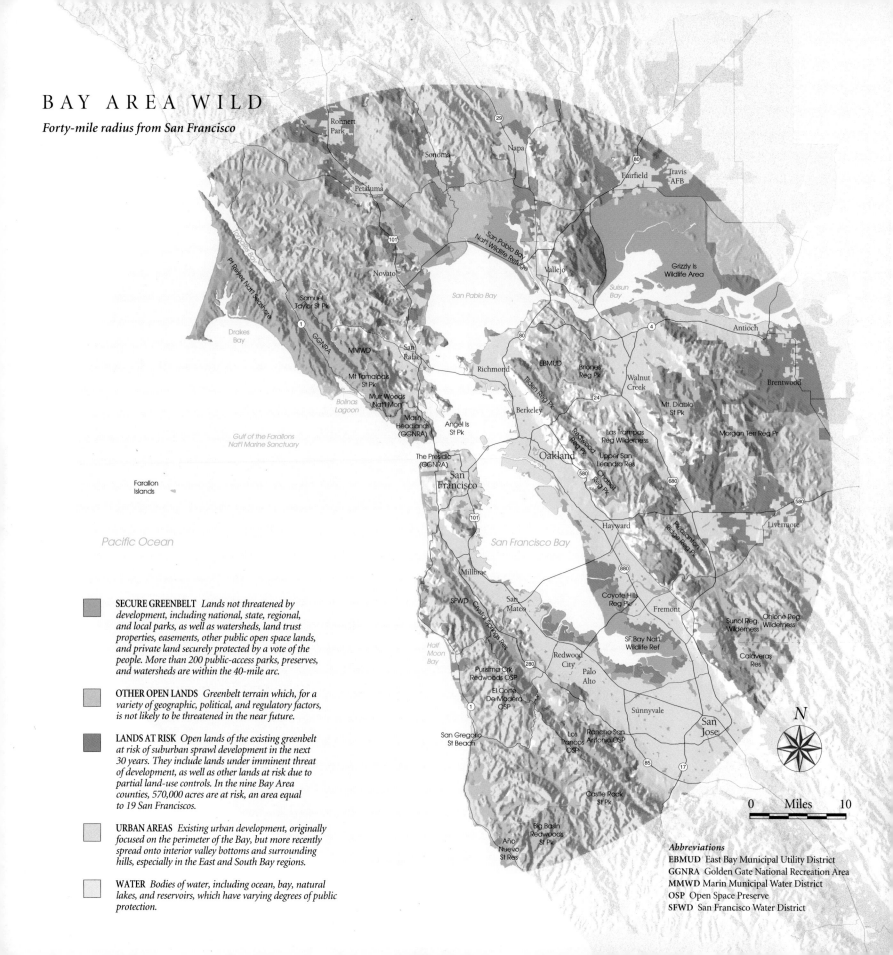

BAY AREA WILD
Forty-mile radius from San Francisco

SECURE GREENBELT *Lands not threatened by development, including national, state, regional, and local parks, as well as watersheds, land trust properties, easements, other public open space lands, and private land securely protected by a vote of the people. More than 200 public-access parks, preserves, and watersheds are within the 40-mile arc.*

OTHER OPEN LANDS *Greenbelt terrain which, for a variety of geographic, political, and regulatory factors, is not likely to be threatened in the near future.*

LANDS AT RISK *Open lands of the existing greenbelt at risk of suburban sprawl development in the next 30 years. They include lands under imminent threat of development, as well as other lands at risk due to partial land-use controls. In the nine Bay Area counties, 570,000 acres are at risk, an area equal to 19 San Franciscos.*

URBAN AREAS *Existing urban development, originally focused on the perimeter of the Bay, but more recently spread onto interior valley bottoms and surrounding hills, especially in the East and South Bay regions.*

WATER *Bodies of water, including ocean, bay, natural lakes, and reservoirs, which have varying degrees of public protection.*

Abbreviations
EBMUD East Bay Municipal Utility District
GGNRA Golden Gate National Recreation Area
MMWD Marin Municipal Water District
OSP Open Space Preserve
SFWD San Francisco Water District

0 Miles 10

N

INTRODUCTION

Of Unexpected Wildness

To the casual eye, the wildness of the greater San Francisco Bay Area is not nearly as evident as it appears between these covers. The region's numerous cities, counties, and disparate preserves managed by a host of public agencies veil the extraordinary amount of protected land around San Francisco Bay. No other major metropolitan center in the world boasts such an extensive system of wild greenbelts, though unlike the case in many preserved wild areas, this land is neither contiguous nor defined by a single name.

Until my wife, Barbara, expressed the idea for this book, I lacked a clear vision of the conceptual whole presented in *Bay Area Wild*. Though I had spent decades celebrating the grand design of natural areas around the world in words and photographs, I had looked right past the extraordinarily rich and varied wild hills, valleys, delta, bay, ocean, islands, and mountains in my own backyard. Because no one natural feature stands out—other than the Bay itself, so clearly girdled by civilization—the essential character of these lands and waters escapes simple description.

My frequent trail runs and photographic excursions in Bay Area preserves had served only to separate them in my mind, much as I had developed a sense of certitude that my hometown, Berkeley, known for the radical politics of its university community, was fundamentally different from nearby San Francisco, a world of big business, high-rise buildings, sprawling neighborhoods, and a vast Central Park clone of designed and planted open space that makes no pretense of being a preserved natural habitat. Nevertheless, the very proximity of these two distinct yet complementary cities is part of what makes each one unique.

As with the cities, so it is with the hundreds of the region's natural preserves, each contributing a certain character and thus shaping the overall quality of life in the Bay Area. Rather than influencing only the rugged few who venture there, these preserved areas not only define one another but also condition the urban experience in myriad ways. It is no coincidence that the Bay Area's infamously high residential property values reach their zenith near the edges of preserved wildlands and dip to their nadir at points farthest away, where views of wild horizons are obscured by inner-city skylines or treeless suburbs.

San Francisco's powerful cultural appeal is inextricably tied to its geography. Surrounded by open ocean or bay on three sides, the city has been held back from devouring its natural setting; its contained size and steep hills guarantee that one is never far from a view of open water or land. Indeed, some of the city's most attractive features are adaptations to this wild and rugged natural setting: cable cars climb streets that appear nearly vertical from afar, and aesthetic suspension bridges span the deep waters of one of the world's most ideal natural harbors.

Because the Bay Area lacks a monumental wonder in its natural state such as those that symbolize Yosemite and Grand Canyon National Parks, a monumental example of human endeavor—the Golden Gate

Bridge—has become the region's symbol by default. Without a bold, unique natural icon, many urban residents of the Bay Area simply fail to recognize the wealth of wildness right before their eyes.

I'm reminded of a park ranger's story about a couple visiting the Grand Canyon, lodging in a comfortable hotel a stone's throw from the rim. While chatting with the pair in a restaurant line, the ranger asked them if they were enjoying their visit. "I don't see what the attraction is here," the husband complained. "Why did they build this hotel in the middle of a desert? Everything looks the same in all directions."

"Have you had a chance to walk to the edge of the lawn and look over the railing?" the ranger inquired.

"Not yet," was the reply.

The idea for this book came to Barbara immediately after a Bay Area experience hauntingly similar to that of the Grand Canyon ranger. Barbara and I used to take it for granted that people who lived in the Bay Area had some degree of understanding of their wild heritage. We bought our Berkeley home a block from Charles Lee Tilden Regional Park so we could run, hike, ride, and bike the extensive trail system through this section of a thirty-mile greenbelt that rims the back of the East Bay hills from Richmond almost to Hayward. Viewed from San Francisco or from the Bay itself, these hills do not appear wild, but a glance at a map or from the window of an arriving flight reveals the vast tracts of undeveloped land hidden in their lee. For years we surprised out-of-town guests by taking them on wildland walks along our favorite trail, frequently seeing deer, foxes, and coyotes at dawn or dusk. Though we often had the trail to ourselves, we assumed that locals knew it was there and were consciously choosing to sit in front of their television sets or travel elsewhere.

During these same years, Barbara began volunteering her airplane and her services as a pilot to an environmental organization that specializes in giving influential people an opportunity for direct observation from the air. Her flights, as far north as the Yukon and as far south as Latin America, were carefully planned to allow passengers to quickly assess the character and condition of threatened wild landscapes. From the nearest airport to the problem area, Barbara would fly politicians, scientists, land managers, and members of the media who lacked the time, funds, or inclination for extensive travels on the ground. They would return with a vivid personal vision that would belie any rhetoric or photographs others might use to attempt to influence them for their own ends.

One day Barbara met a kindred spirit, a woman who also had lived in Berkeley for many years and flew her own airplane for the same organization. When Barbara invited her on a hike in the Berkeley Hills, she seemed as startled and suddenly uncertain of her surroundings as the deer we often catch in our headlights while driving home at night. She had never walked through the parklands that border her town, though she had flown over them en route to more exotic wildlands on countless occasions. Barbara took her on a long hike along the high

Hiker looking east from the crest of the Berkeley Hills on a winter morning.

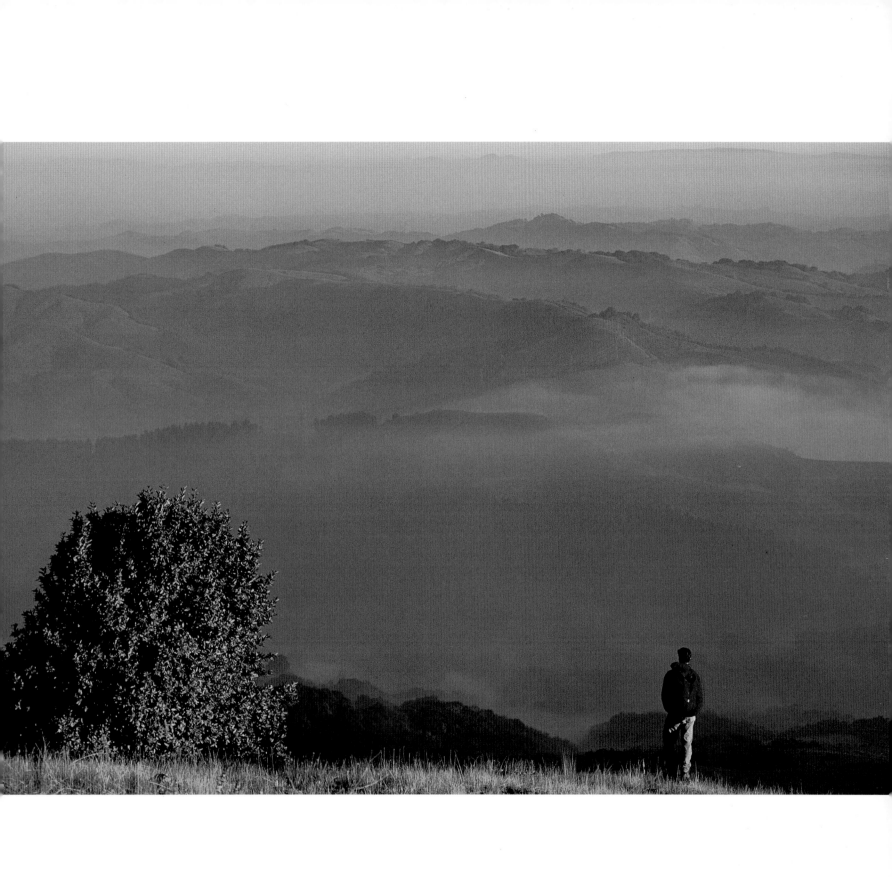

ridge of the Sea View Trail and returned with a vivid description of her new friend's amazement at the extent of wildness there—a wildness she had always gone elsewhere to experience.

After that, Barbara pondered the impact a properly conceived picture book could have in making people aware of the scope of wildlands around the Bay. Though she had conflicting feelings about the power of photography compared with that of direct observation, she also had good reason to believe that photographs of the wilds of the Bay Area could hold their own with those of any place in America. After all, a student in one of our photography workshops had won a *National Geographic* travel photography contest with a shot of a local scene— his image of a foggy Berkeley Hills forest, sensitively scaled down into a photographic icon, had won out over scores of Old Faithfuls, Half Domes, and Grand Canyons.

Carefully selected photographs can reveal hidden meanings in complex scenes and can freeze memorable moments for future contemplation, even though thumbing through a picture book or photo album at home can never equal the experience of watching the same landscape pass beneath the wing in real time or—better yet—of walking through it oneself. Only after I began showing people my favorite Bay Area photographs did I get past my doubts that a collection of images could engage the interest of people who so often looked right past the real thing.

When Barbara set my course toward producing this book, she also changed her own heading away from a steady diet of exotic environmental flights toward local flights for organizations such as Greenbelt Alliance, Save Mount Diablo, Save San Francisco Bay Association, and The Wilderness Society. Her turning point came that same spring she took her pilot friend for a hike, on an exceptionally clear morning after a storm.

She had grown used to seeing the Bay Area from the air in murky midday light, on urban approaches into Oakland Airport after a morning tour for a congressman over the northern coast's vanishing old-growth redwoods or a dawn flight over the High Sierra on assignment for *National Geographic*. One morning, however, I joined her on a more frivolous mission. She had just returned from an environmental flight in Costa Rica, and I had been climbing in the High Sierra. Rather than drive over a hundred miles of twisty roads to pick up our golden retriever from friends, we had decided to fly. The clarity of the air and the lush greenery of spring provided some of the most ideal conditions for aerial photography I had ever seen. The glistening ring of cities around San Francisco Bay resembled little clusters of diamonds surrounded by huge emeralds of open space. I found the verdant facets of Mount Tamalpais rising above Marin County especially compelling, so I asked Barbara to divert from her normal route and circle the peak at the level of the summit.

As we made a low pass over the north side of Mount Tamalpais with the window opened for photography, Barbara excitedly announced over the intercom: "This is incredible. It's all unbroken forest down there. I'm seeing more continuous forest right here in the Bay Area than in all my flights over the national parks of Costa Rica."

"That can't be possible," I replied. "Costa Rica is legendary for preserving its rain forests. Those forests are what people from all around the world go there to see."

"You'll just have to take my word for it—they don't look as wild as what's below us. Costa Rica's so-called protected lands have areas slashed and burned by squatters trying to cash in on our quest for perfect bananas and Big Macs. Ecotourism tours never show you these places; even forestry officials don't know about most of them until they see them from the air. The lands Costa Rica calls 'national parks' or 'biological reserves' have nowhere near the environmental protection those designations imply here."

Just as Barbara's firsthand knowledge of Costa Rica's blemished topography clashed with my idealized vision of continuous rain forests there, the wild, unbroken forests below us were in stark contrast with our mental images of distinct boundaries as drawn on Marin County maps. While our eyes told us we were looking at a single wild entity, the maps indicated we were above separate state park, national park, and local water district lands. From the air, all these natural preserves merged.

Among them, on the western flanks of Mount Tam, is a grove of old-growth redwoods given to the government by a wealthy landowner in 1908. Muir Woods National Monument has since become one of the eight main subregions of the Golden Gate National Recreation Area—the world's largest extent of urban national park lands. Though we flew directly over it, Muir Woods was not easy to single out from the air because its less than two square miles of redwood forest blend so perfectly into the surrounding twelve square miles of Mount Tamalpais State Park and forty square miles of Marin Municipal Water District forest. As Barbara made a higher circle over the mountain, even more protected lands came into view, including several other state parks, most of the twenty-seven Marin County Open Space preserves, the vast 130 square miles of Point Reyes National Seashore, and Audubon Canyon Ranch, a private preserve nestled where the forest meets the biologically wealthy Bolinas Lagoon, lying in the depression of the San Andreas Fault.

Farther in the distance, the entire expanse of Pacific Ocean within our view was encompassed by the Gulf of the Farallones National Marine Sanctuary, controlled by the National Oceanic and Atmospheric Administration. Rising like an apparition from the shimmering ocean twenty miles offshore from Point Reyes were the Farallon Islands themselves, a cluster of Matterhorn-like rock spires where the largest breeding colony of seabirds in the contiguous forty-eight states flourishes in total protection on terrain where even ecotourism is forbidden. The islands are strictly monitored by the Point Reyes Bird Observatory under a federal contract with the United States Fish and Wildlife Service, which controls the islands themselves.

When we returned home I checked some figures, which confirmed Barbara's aerial impressions. Whereas a significant 11 percent of Costa Rica is under national park designation, 27 percent of Marin County's land area is directly administered by the National Park Service. When other public-access natural preserves are added in, Marin's portion of protected land jumps to a whopping 44 percent.

The sense of wholeness and unity of Bay Area wildlands we gained from the air that day reminds me of the first lunar astronauts' surprise to see a whole, living Earth after a lifetime of looking at globes segmented

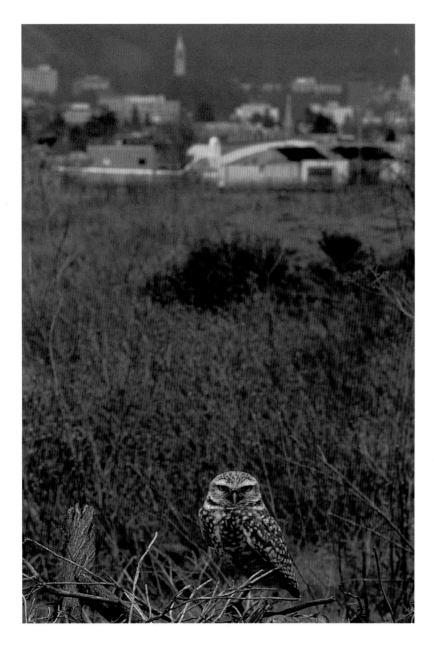

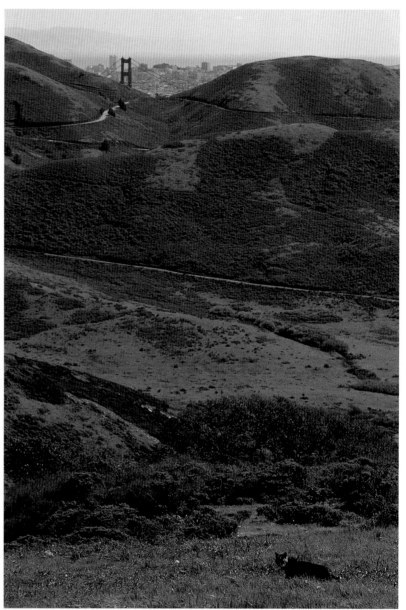

*A burrowing owl (**left**) makes a rare appearance in the grasslands of the Berkeley Marina; the campanile of the University of California can be seen in the distance. Across the Bay in Marin County (**right**), the world of a bobcat above Gerbode Valley in the Golden Gate National Recreation Area is so close to, yet so separate from, the city of San Francisco, peeking over the skyline ridge.*

into brightly colored political designations. Though they didn't expect to see a planet with national borders, the reality of their direct observation was overpowering.

Recalling our infinitely lower pass over Marin County, I wondered how the visual integrity that had so impressed me could be translated to the printed page, where disparate pieces of the whole are unlikely to strike readers as memorably as would images of a whole Earth or even a Yosemite Valley. Despite the wealth of wild scenes in the Bay Area, the uniquely sculpted landscapes people have grown accustomed to seeing on posters and book covers would be hard to come by here, I thought. Also, the more I considered it, the more impossible a task it seemed to bring together all the essential aspects of the wild Bay Area in one book. The photography would need to go well beyond aerial views and common scenes visible from roads and trails.

Just to document the elusive wildlife could take ten years. Truthful and evocative photographs of Bay Area creatures in their natural settings are not easily made, and I am dead set against some of the methods used in other regional books to close this gap in photographic documentation. I am not willing, for example, to print images of animals from other locations with vague captions, to present captive animals as wild, or—ever more prevalent in this computer age—to pass off digital illustrations of animals dropped into empty landscapes as photographic documentation of natural history.

Had this book's sole purpose been to celebrate preserved areas around the Bay, I might have undertaken the wildlife photography as a labor of love and put off publication until beyond the millennium. But the more I learned about local environmental issues, the more urgent production of *Bay Area Wild* became. I sensed that my initial optimism about the greater Bay Area's unusually large amount of protected land needed to be tempered with concern over issues such as the threat of imminent development of areas of open space nineteen times the size of San Francisco.

I felt strongly committed to produce a work that not only emphasized the importance of maintaining and expanding Bay Area preserves but also could serve as a guide for other rapidly expanding metropolitan areas. As a Berkeley native who came of age in the early sixties, I am not the least bit shy about predicting the continued spread of the social and political values that have resulted in our unique blend of urban and open space. As coming chapters will explain, the Bay Area has been an innovator in creatively preserving urban environmental values for more than a century. The question is whether this consciousness is arriving too late elsewhere.

I solved the problem of documenting Bay Area wildlife with integrity by inviting Michael Sewell to share in this book's photographic coverage. Michael, also a Berkeley native, had already spent ten years roaming wild parts of the Bay Area and photographing wildlife in some most unusual ways. I was especially impressed by the way he had captured a full-frame image of a wild bobcat at Point Reyes (page 1), for which he had been named Wildlife Photographer of the Year in 1990 by the California State Fish and Game Commission. The photograph captures the primeval stare of a stalking predator—strikingly different from the expression of a wild cat that is aware of human presence.

The bobcat had not stepped into a meadow in front of a camera in broad daylight by chance. Michael had mastered the Native American art of wildlife calling. He had imitated the sound of a rabbit in distress while sitting absolutely still in camouflage clothing, with skunk scent dabbed on nearby brush to mask his own scent. Several times during the making of this book I donned similar battlefield attire and joined Michael in the field as he called in bobcats, foxes, and coyotes, whose haunting expressions indicated their uncertainty about our true genus and species. Even a wary bobcat spooked by an inadvertent movement was likely to stick around at more of a distance to try to comprehend what we were.

Michael had also spent four years maintaining remote cameras placed along wildlife paths to be triggered by the tripping of an infrared beam. His thousands of slides from these endeavors include images of stray dogs, feral pigs, windblown branches, and a wealth of powerful candid moments in the lives of wild creatures from which to select the fine images on pages 90–91.

We agreed that though Michael's main emphasis would be on wildlife, we would both shoot new work for the book for two more years, with no firm dividing line between wildlife and landscape photography. Scenes in which animals become graphic figures in a landscape, for example, can be especially evocative of wild experience, with no need to place them in one category or the other. In other words, we would both continue to photograph whatever we believed was relevant, with no constraints on spontaneity. We were reasonably sure the majority of wildlife images would end up being Michael's and the majority of landscapes and close-up shots mine.

Our next decision was especially tough: which lands should we include? To cover all preserved lands in the nine Bay Area counties would unquestionably dilute our concept, yet to omit such key natural areas as the tip of Point Reyes National Seashore and the elephant seal breeding grounds at Año Nuevo State Reserve seemed even more problematic. Further, as soon as we began drawing circles on maps, the problem of choosing a central point arose. Should it be downtown San Francisco? The Golden Gate Bridge? The center of the Bay? We eventually settled on a rough circle extending about forty miles out from the perimeter of San Francisco. Though a number of fine areas are excluded by this boundary, it focused our attention on the places that most closely define the meaning of *Bay Area Wild*.

To keep the visual voltage of this book as high as possible, we decided from the outset to wholly avoid a guidebook approach. We had no intention of producing a visual inventory of every park, preserve, life zone, mammal, bird, reptile, insect, rare plant, or currently threatened piece of open space within our chosen area. Indeed, the number of photographs required to fully document the area's more than two hundred parks, preserves, and protected natural areas would have made this book prohibitively expensive and visually redundant.

Enduring bedrock mortars ground long ago by Ohlone Indians into hard Franciscan chert repose above preserved wetlands in the San Francisco Bay National Wildlife Refuge, near Newark. Adjoining Coyote Hills Regional Park holds 2,300-year-old Ohlone shell mounds and a replica of a traditional village.

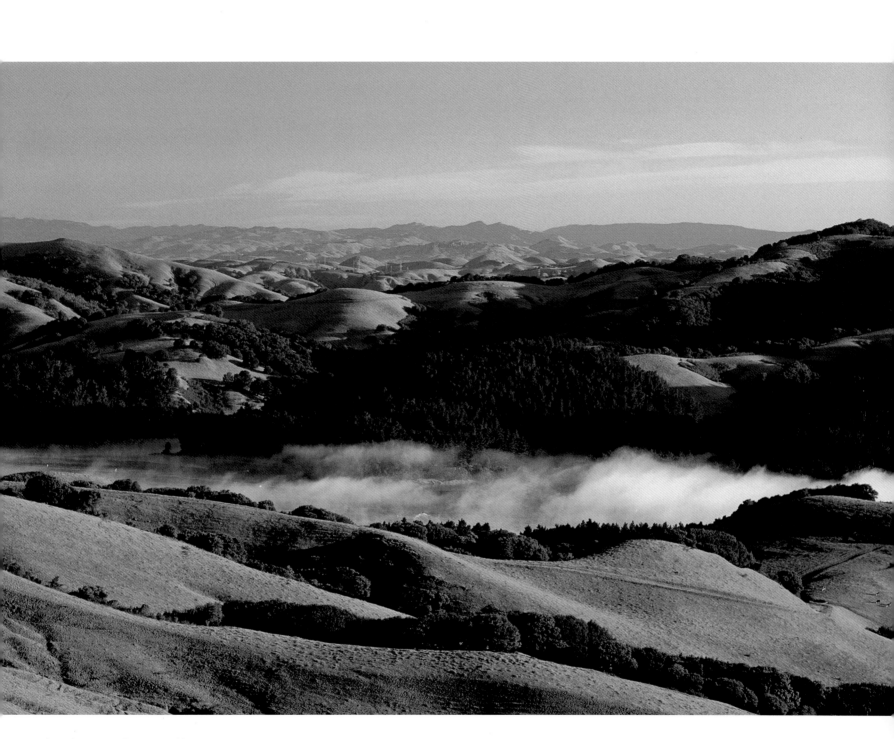

along the streams above San Pablo Reservoir on EBMUD lands. The view is from Inspiration Point, on the border of Tilden Regional Park in the Berkeley Hills.

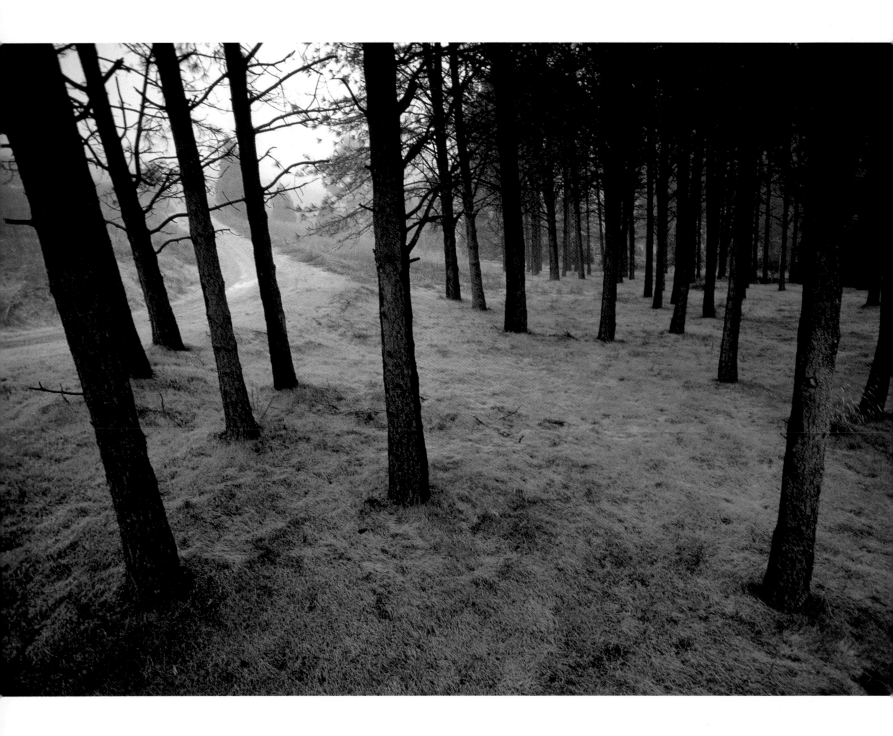

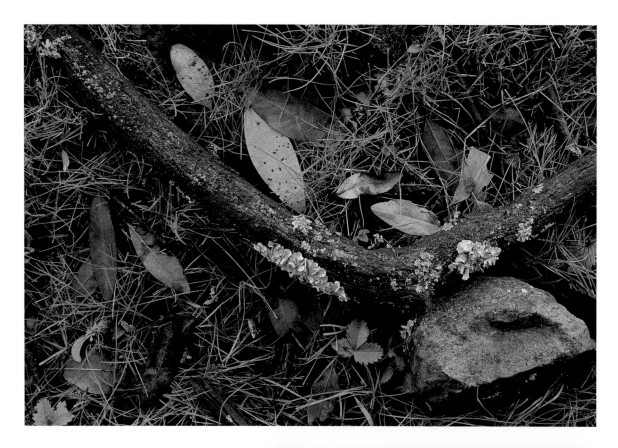

Bay Area winters tend to be lush and green, except in the uncommon years of freezes or droughts. After the long summer and fall dry season ends, a thin carpet of verdant grasses appears first on the forest floors, nurtured by dripping fog and early rains. The lawnlike December pine forest floor (**left**) is beside the Quarry Trail near Inspiration Point in Tilden Regional Park; the fallen leaves beneath a bay tree amidst November greenery (**above**) are alongside the East Bay Skyline National Recreation Trail between Tilden Regional Park and Sibley Volcanic Regional Preserve. Farther south, in the deeper shade of Huckleberry Botanic Regional Preserve (**right**), starry false Solomon's seal begins to bloom on the moist forest floor at winter's end.

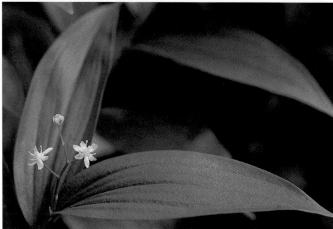

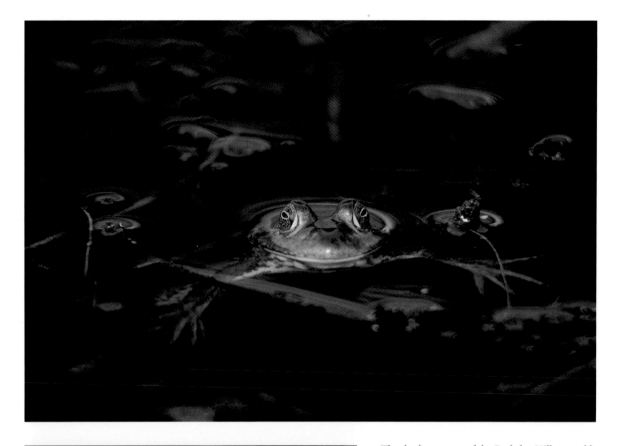

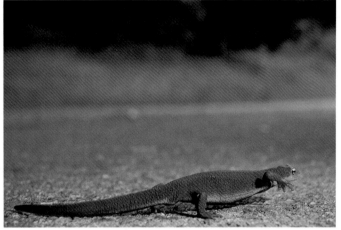

The shady canyons of the Berkeley Hills resemble tropical rain forests during the storms of winter and spring. Wildcat Creek's (**right**) importance to East Bay inhabitants traces from Ohlone Indians, who built villages beside it; to Spanish ranchers, who grazed livestock around it; to private companies that fought water wars over it; to the East Bay Regional Park District, which included this section below Lake Anza in its first acquisition, Tilden Regional Park. Here, 1.6 miles of South Park Drive are now closed during the wet months to allow California newts (**left**), a declining species, to slowly cross the wet pavement. The common bullfrog (**above**), an introduced species often seen in Bay Area ponds, has been displacing the more rare native frogs.

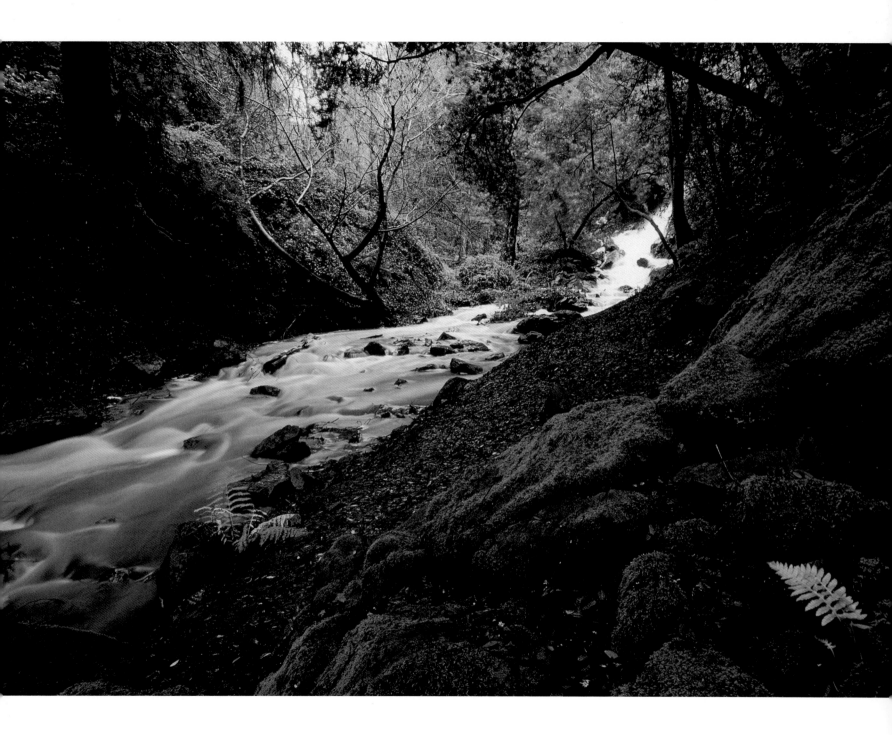

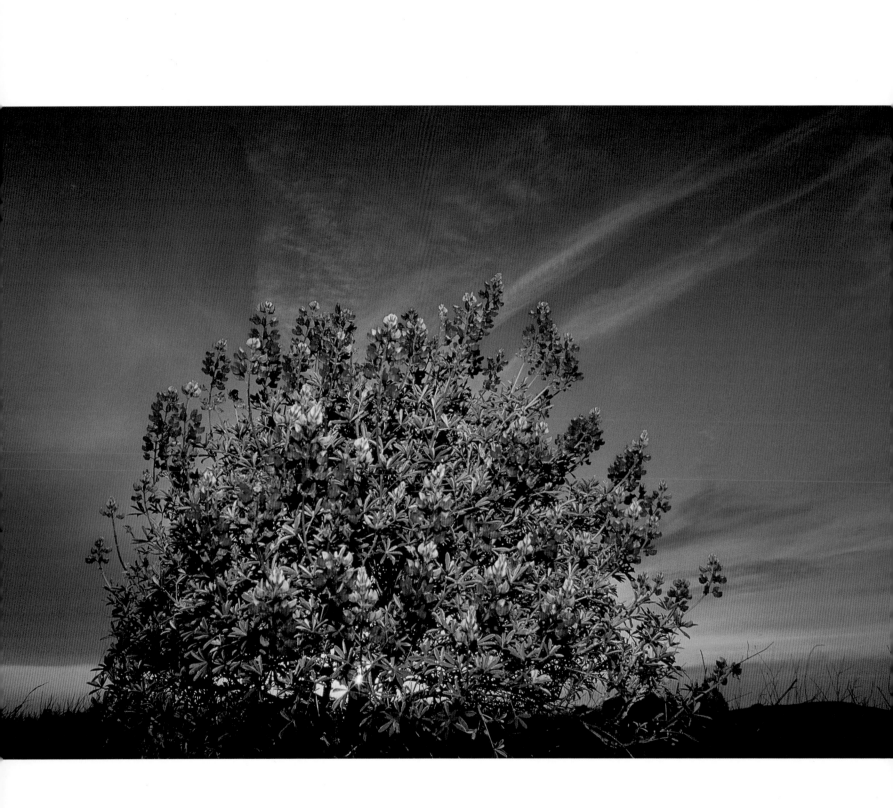

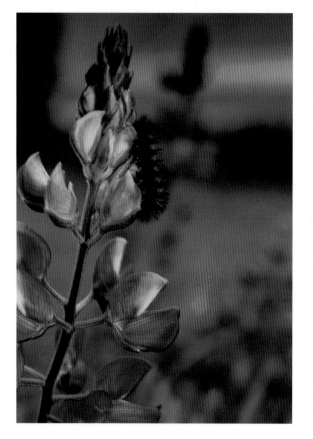

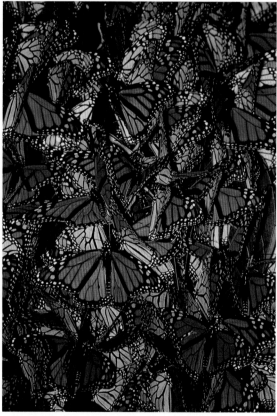

*A small bush of silver lupine (**left**) in full bloom fills the evening sky at sunset in this wide-angle view from ground level. On the same ridge in the Berkeley Hills, a closer view of another silver lupine (**above, left**) discloses a caterpillar. Most species of moths and butterflies stay reasonably close to where they were as caterpillars, but the entire western population of monarch butterflies (**above, right**) migrates to the mild, moist California coast to winter in trees at a few select locations, such as Ardenwood Regional Preserve in the southern East Bay.*

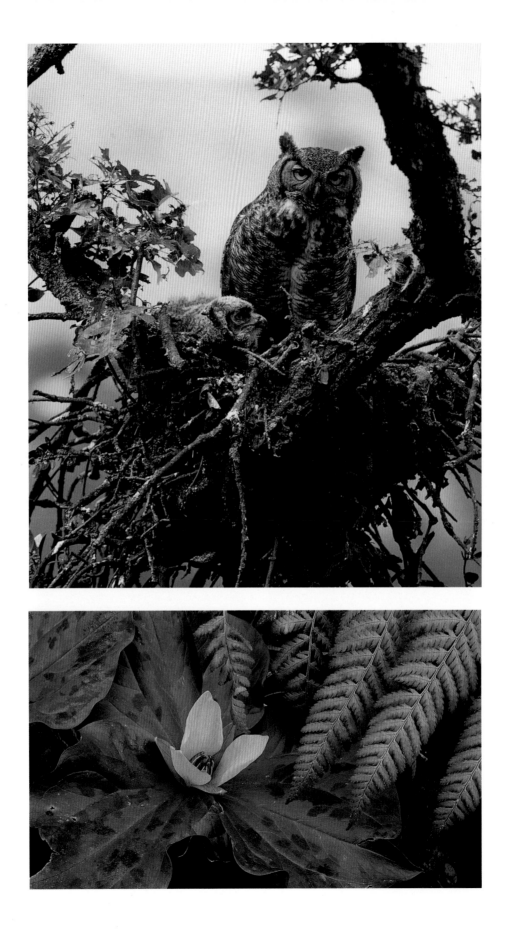

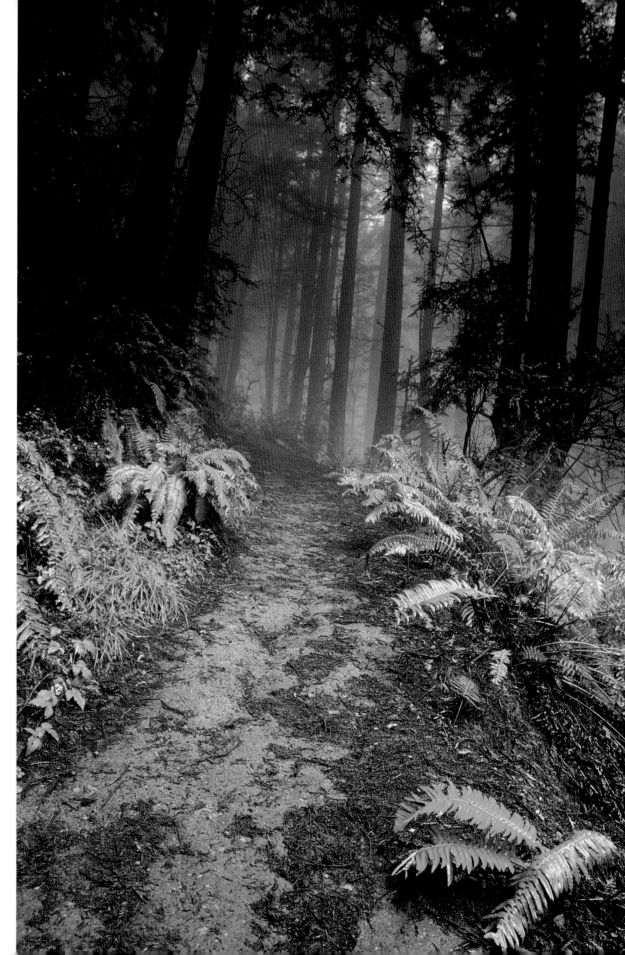

The narrow French Trail (**right**) wanders through miles of dense redwood forest carpeted with ferns in Redwood Regional Park, behind the city of Oakland. Three-leaved giant trillium (**left, below**) graces hidden spots in deep shade. Great horned owls (**left, above**) are frequently heard but less often seen on the high limbs of the forest canopy.

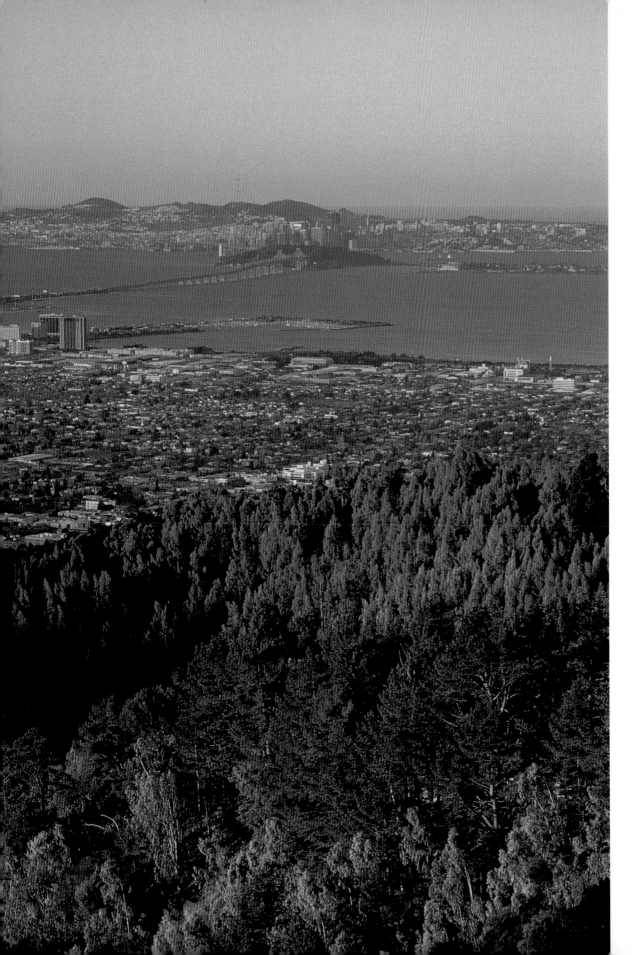

The view west on a clear morning from the crest of the Berkeley Hills (**left**) shows University of California open space lands in Strawberry Canyon dropping into the back of the campus in the city of Berkeley. Half of the San Francisco–Oakland Bay Bridge can be seen traversing the Bay to Yerba Buena Island en route to the city of San Francisco on the distant peninsula. The view facing east from the crest of the same hills (**right**) reveals San Pablo and Briones Reservoirs surrounded by the verdant open space of EBMUD lands.

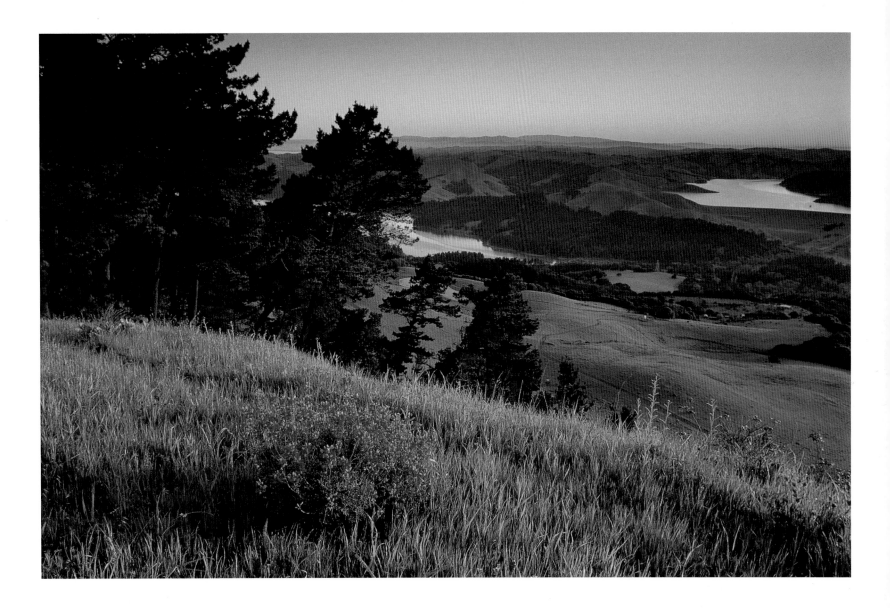

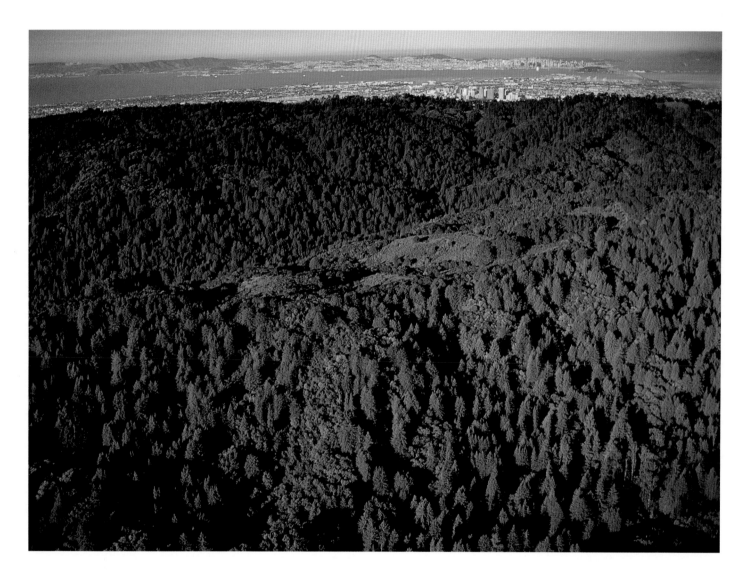

A surprising number of Oakland residents are unaware of the great expanse of preserved wild forest (**above**) just over the crest of the hills in Redwood Regional Park. This aerial view includes a strip of the city with San Francisco Bay in the distance. Mystical crepuscular rays, commonly called "god beams" (**right**), appear to radiate from a point of sunlight coming through a pine tree at the edge of a fog bank, though in reality they are parallel. The illusion is similar to that of railroad tracks appearing to meet in the distance.

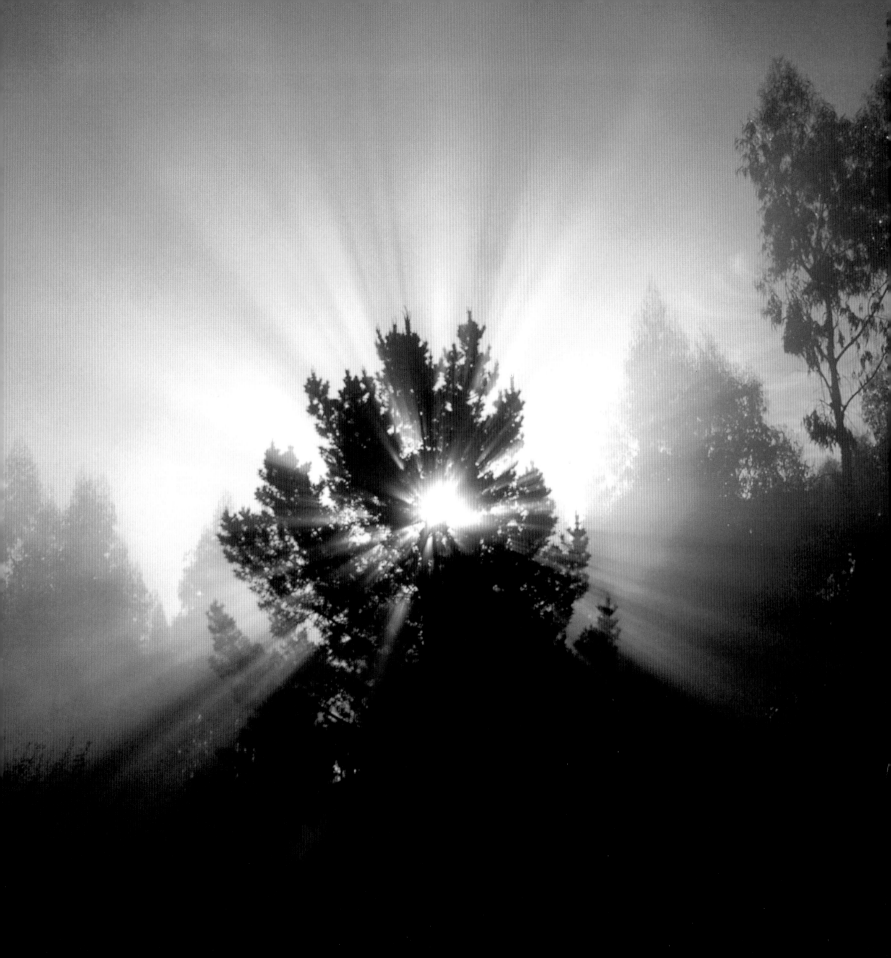

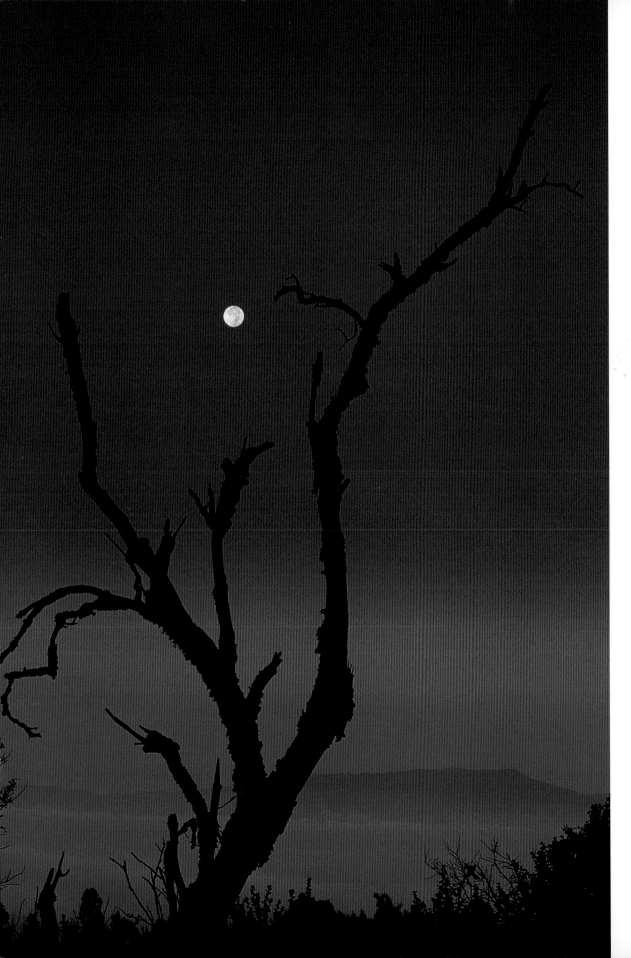

*A full moon (**left**) sets behind a dead tree over Mount Tamalpais. Viewed on a different morning from the same turnout along Grizzly Peak Boulevard in the Berkeley Hills, a blanket of fog (**right**) snakes through a eucalyptus forest beneath the pink glow of sunrise.*

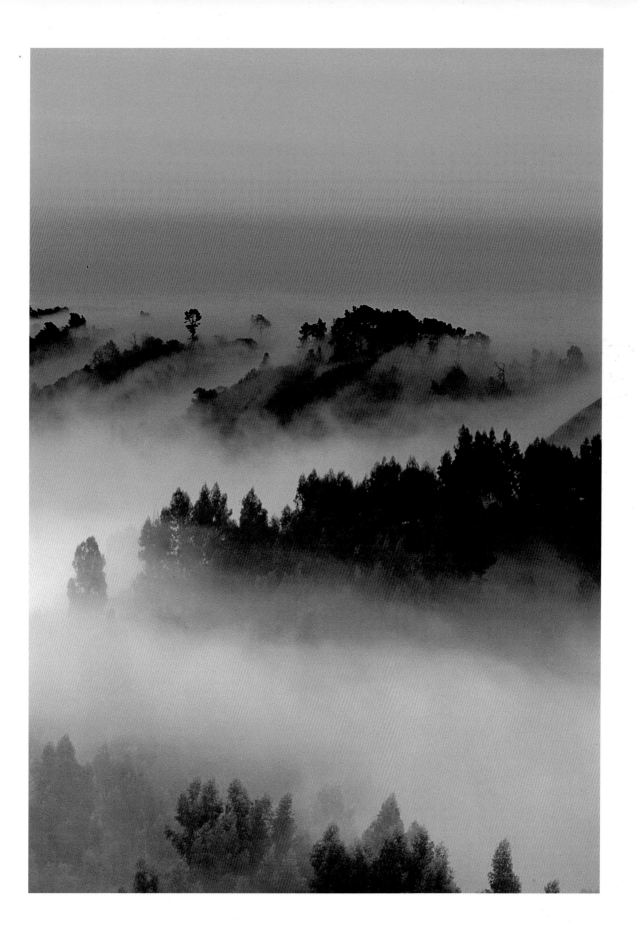

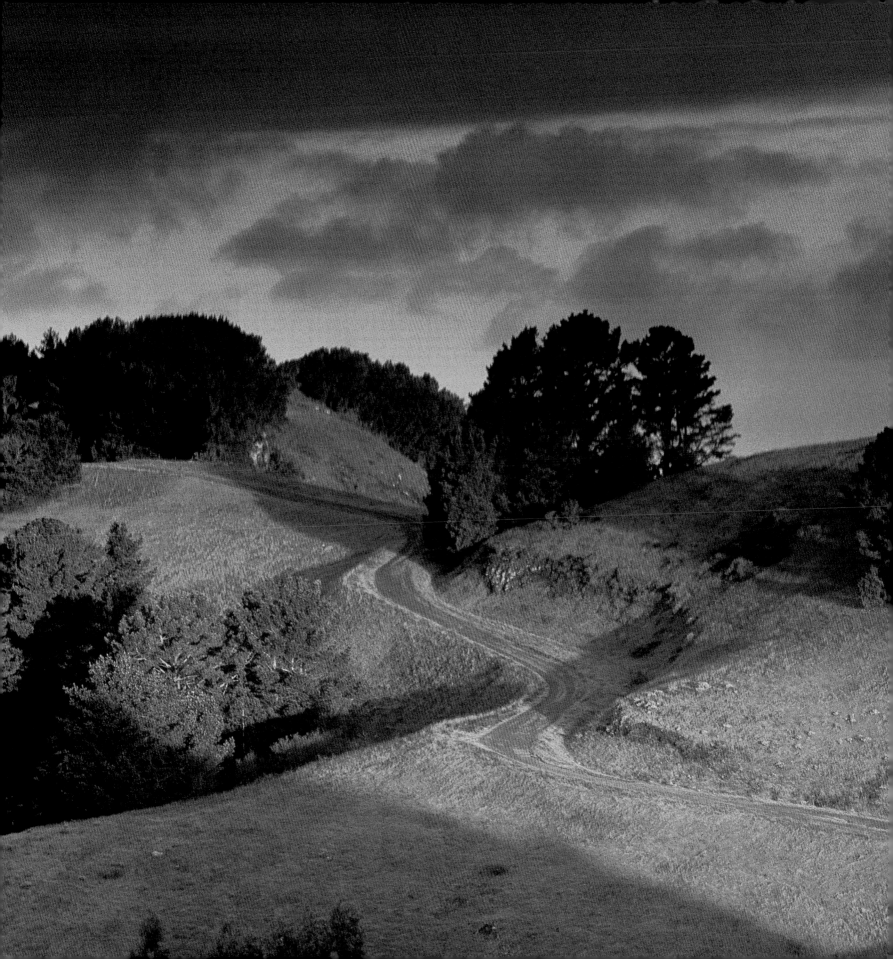

Romantic Notions

My father came to Berkeley in 1921 to teach at the University of California for a year. He returned to Chicago only to gather his belongings. View lots were available for a hundred dollars each in the undeveloped upper ramparts of the Berkeley Hills, and my father built a house on four of them. He carefully chose an almost level pocket of land protected from the brunt of the wind and situated just above a large slide area a hundred feet below the crest, where his real estate agent assured him no one would ever build. When the great Berkeley fire of 1923 roared across the hills, his new home with its special asbestos shingles was left standing alone on the scorched, bare earth.

I grew up in that house watching Berkeley rise up all around us—except in the deep brush of that slide area, where I cut my own private trails with an army surplus machete and watched birds, deer, foxes, and raccoons go about their daily lives. Crawling on my belly, I regained the sense of wildness that had lured my father to live in the hills beyond the city that now so nearly surrounded us. The rows of vacant lots on our street were disappearing, and homes already lined the crest of the hills above us.

Only many decades later, as my father was nearing ninety, did "the canyon," as we called the slide area, succumb to state-of-the-art deep foundations. My wife, Barbara, and I purchased one of those homes that had been built in the fifties, when I was growing up. It sits just a quarter-mile from my childhood home on the opposite side of the hills, without the view of San Francisco Bay. We wake up in the morning with a stronger sense of solitude as we look into the protected lands of Charles Lee Tilden Regional Park, where I often set out on a dawn trail run. Sometimes I crest out above the summer fog and find myself suddenly gazing into a bright, wild world devoid of other human beings. The curtain of swirling mist that shrouds the valleys as far as I can see steers my imagination back well beyond my father's first visit to Berkeley. It is as if I am witnessing some primeval era when the hills were lower, the seas higher, the air cooler, and the face of the land shaped entirely by natural design.

At these times when the civilized world is erased from my view, an especially powerful surge of attention tingles through my body if I happen to spot a wild creature. I feel compelled to stop running and watch that deer or coyote sharing my personal wilderness above the mist, though if I see a similar wild animal while driving through the same park in my car, I usually smile and keep going. Perhaps the heightened awareness I feel when on foot in the misty hills reflects an age-old affinity with the natural world buried deep in my psyche or an equally buried vestige of a primal instinct that would have me reaching for an arrow were I somehow transported back to the Bay Area of a thousand years ago.

When the mist parts to reveal a modern city, or when I pass back through it to take a hot shower and drink my morning coffee, conflicting emotions arise in me. I can't deny an unfathomable longing to have been

Stormy dawn on the Sea View Trail, Berkeley Hills

there on Grizzly Peak with the Ohlone Indians when antelopes, elk, wolves, and—yes—grizzly bears roamed the Berkeley Hills in abundance. Nor can I deny how that longing clashes with who I am: a citizen of the modern world, trapped in my allotted era by more than the calendar of history. As I daydream about what it would have been like to live in the Bay Area of the past, the notion becomes less romantic as I grapple with fundamental questions: If I could travel back in time, exactly when would I stop to get off? Would I want to stay, or would I want to return to the present?

I might choose to fulfill my desire to live with the Ohlone Indians a thousand years ago. Their lives were clearly more in tune with the natural world than is my own. Author and historian Malcolm Margolin deftly describes their lost world in *The Ohlone Way,* a book about a way of life that persisted in the Bay Area until about two hundred years ago, with very little change, before vanishing "with terrible rapidity." Margolin relates how the Ohlone "lived in a world where the animal kingdom had yet to fall under the domination of the human race and where (how difficult . . . to fully grasp the implications of this!) people did not yet see themselves as the undisputed lords of all creation. . . . The powerful, graceful animal life of the Bay Area not only filled their world, but filled their minds as well."

After exhaustively researching the accounts of early explorers and missionaries, Margolin created a vivid word-picture of the Bay Area in its natural state during Ohlone times:

> *Marshes that spread out for thousands of acres fringed the shores of the Bay. Thick oak-bay forests and redwood forests covered much of the hills. The intermingling of grasslands, savannahs, salt- and freshwater marshes, and forests created wildlife habitats of almost unimaginable richness and variety. . . . "There is not any country in the world which more abounds in fish and game of every description," noted the French sea captain, la Perouse. Flocks of geese, ducks, and seabirds were so enormous that when alarmed by a rifle shot they were said to rise "in a dense cloud with a noise like that of a hurricane." Herds of elk . . . grazed the meadowlands in such numbers that they were often compared to great herds of cattle. Pronghorn antelope, in herds of one or two hundred, or even more, dotted the grassy slopes. Packs of wolves hunted the elk, antelope, deer, rabbits, and other game. Bald eagles and giant condors glided through the air. Mountain lions, bobcats, and coyotes—now only seen rarely—were a common sight. And of course there was the grizzly bear. . . . These enormous bears were everywhere, feeding on berries, lumbering along the beaches, congregating beneath oak trees during the acorn season, and stationed along nearly every stream and creek during the annual runs of salmon and steelhead. . . . To the Ohlones the grizzly bear must have been omnipresent, yet today there is not a single wild grizzly bear left in all of California.*

Yes, I would love to visit the Bay Area of Ohlone times, but would I really want to live my entire life there? According to Margolin's estimate of Ohlone life expectancy, I would already have been dead for sixteen years. Were I an Ohlone Indian of old, who saw as many wild animals in a day as I now see buildings, would the magic I feel on spotting a wild bobcat in Marin County's Tennessee Valley be nearly as strong?

Equally important, if I really believe in emulating Ohlone ways, shouldn't I be living in some distant backwater of the Bay Area on the wildest piece of property I can find? One reason I don't is that I already dread the grueling drive to San Francisco International Airport, which enables me to explore and document distant and exotic places. I'm not willing to give up these travels or to have my airport commute become unbearably long. In fact, I'm convinced that my unabashed appreciation of Bay Area wildness is based on my direct experience of such places as Alaska, Hawaii, the Galápagos Islands, the polar regions, and Tibet: only after visiting areas touted by the media do I really know how favorably my home wildlands compare.

My next choice might be to have been here with the first European party to discover the Bay. I'm not at all convinced that this would place me at José Ortega's side in 1769 as a member of the Portolá Expedition, along with forty-five other bedraggled Spaniards. Just as we now know that Columbus was preceded by a number of other Europeans who visited North America, the fact that the Spanish recorded the Portolá Expedition as discoverers of the Bay doesn't mean that no explorer had set eyes on it before. As early as 1579, a British pirate later to be knighted Sir Francis Drake spent a month in the Bay Area repairing the *Golden Hinde* in what is now called Drakes Bay at Point Reyes National Seashore.

The notion of being the Bay's European discoverer loses its luster when I contemplate the possibilities of returning home with a story no one believes, never returning home alive, being a pirate, or being a hero of the times who shares the worldview of the Spanish conquistadores, which led to the virtual enslavement of the Ohlone people and the destruction of their ancient culture. Instead of reaching for that Ohlone arrow when I spotted wildlife, I would have reached for my musket. Indiscriminate shooting of wildlife was the norm for the well-armed European explorers of the period; the invention of firearms came centuries before the spread of an ethic of respect for other forms of life.

Nor would I choose to have explored northern California with any of the mountain men of the early nineteenth century, whose shooting sprees were legendary. One small band of Hudson's Bay Company trappers proudly tallied 395 elk, 148 deer, 17 bear, and 8 antelope as they crossed the Sierra Nevada. During the 1860s, however, two men of a different breed—who were to become major players in the preservation of wild places—arrived in the Bay Area, five years apart. To have been here with either of them is a far more tempting proposition.

Experiencing the wild Bay Area through the eyes of the great landscape architect Frederick Law Olmsted has enormous appeal. However, to have accompanied this visionary in 1863 would have meant sharing dreams that were not fully realized until well after his death. California was caught up in the gold rush, and setting aside tracts of public land to remain undisturbed was the furthest thing from most people's minds.

Olmsted was essentially a city person. Fresh from conceiving Central Park in Manhattan, Olmsted founded his career on creating aesthetic urban parks rather than on exploring and savoring wild places. When he envisioned what was to become San Francisco's Golden Gate Park as a vast "pleasuring ground second to none," he viewed a landscape that was becoming "more and more artificial day by day" and imagined a park designed to serve the needs "not merely of the present population, or even of their immediate successors, but of many millions of people."

Being at Olmsted's side at the height of his career would have meant having virtually no time to explore wildlands, though, because he was so engaged in emerging land-use projects. He split his time between Berkeley, where he planned the University of California campus; San Francisco, where he created the city's park system; Palo Alto, where he designed the Stanford University campus; a ranch near Sacramento, where he planned an estate for the wealthy Whitney family; and Mariposa, where he served as the original commissioner of Yosemite after it was designated as the nation's first federally mandated preserve to protect land in its natural state. Creation of the National Park Service was still more than half a century away in 1864, when Abraham Lincoln signed the bill passed by Congress to set aside Yosemite Valley as a grant to the state of California.

Olmsted was asked to write a charter for this first American wilderness park that would declare its purpose and serve as a "solemn compact" between the federal and state governments to hold these wildlands in their natural state for public use. In 1866, the California legislature ratified Olmsted's charter, which clearly spelled out the government's "duty of preservation" and the inherent differences between artificially landscaped urban parks and nature preserves. Olmsted described the new preserve's central purpose as to prevent "the otherwise insurmountable . . . selfishness of individuals" from destroying essential natural values and to conserve these values for future generations to enjoy.

A quarter-century later, in 1890, when Yosemite was being considered for full federal national park status, Olmsted pulled no punches in describing to Congress the rare type of person needed to manage such a place:

> *Integrity, general education, business experience, and what is comprehensively called good taste do not in themselves qualify men to guard against the waste of such essential value, much less do they fit them to devise, with artistic refinement, means for reconciling with its development and its exhibition. . . . There are thousands of estimable men who have no more sense in this regard than children, and it must be said that those most wanting in it are those least conscious of the want.*

Just after writing the Yosemite charter in 1865, Olmsted drafted plans for the University of California that included the first public preservation of Bay Area wildlands. As he looked up into the Berkeley Hills in 1866 from the site of the future campus, he marked out Strawberry Canyon to be held in its natural condition. He also publicly stated that extensive "scenic lanes" should be set aside in their natural condition well beyond the jurisdiction of the university, in the upper wildlands of the Berkeley Hills. But more than sixty years passed before Olmsted's sons—also landscape architects—helped turn his enlightened vision into the reality of the East Bay Regional Park District, a unique agency created to procure and manage parklands for the multiple cities and counties of the East Bay.

Olmsted's impressive conservation efforts laid the groundwork for John Muir, who came to California five years later. Muir arrived in San Francisco by steamer from Panama on March 28, 1868, at age twenty-nine. He found the city ugly with commercialism and asked the first person he encountered to tell him the quickest way out of town. Asked where he wanted to go, Muir replied, "Anywhere that is wild!" He took a ferry to Oakland and "set out afoot for Yosemite" through hills of the East Bay and the Santa Clara Valley "so covered with flowers that they seemed to be painted." When he reached the crest of the Diablo Range at Pacheco Pass, "a landscape was displayed that after all my wanderings still appears as the most beautiful I have ever beheld. At my feet lay the Great Central Valley of California, level and flowery, like a lake of pure sunshine . . . one rich furred garden of yellow Compositae. And from the eastern boundary of this vast golden flower-bed rose the mighty Sierra."

Decades later, as a resident of the Bay Area, Muir received the lion's share of credit for founding Yosemite National Park. Indeed, Muir became the most important conservationist of the century at the same time he was a fruit rancher in Contra Costa County. Curiously, though he wrote many books on his favorite wild places, Bay Area wildlands were conspicuously absent in his writings and preservation work. His extensive journeys into wild places around the Bay are mentioned only briefly in accounts of his travels into the mountains of California and in his personal letters.

Among Muir's tantalizing brief descriptions of the region's natural features are strong indications that what is now Muir Woods National Monument in Marin County was not his favorite Bay Area redwood grove. He was more attracted to Big Basin in the Santa Cruz Mountains; in fact, he was not personally involved in efforts to preserve Muir Woods. William Kent, an influential Marin landowner, gave the old-growth forest to the federal government just before it was to be condemned for a reservoir site by the local water district in 1908. He asked that it be named for Muir only after President Theodore Roosevelt wanted to call it "Kent Woods." Soon afterward, as a U.S. congressman, Kent used his donation of Muir Woods for political leverage in lobbying for a dam in Yosemite's Hetch Hetchy Valley to supply water and power for the city of San Francisco. Muir considered

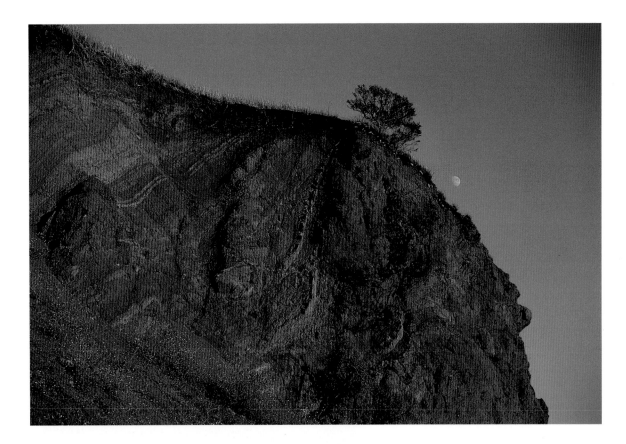

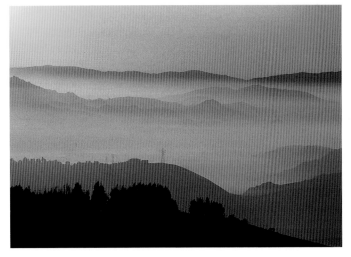

*Crimson tuff (**above**), composed of solidified volcanic ash, glows beneath a rising moon at sunset on Round Top Peak in the Berkeley Hills. Until the 1970s, geologists did not realize that the source of this violently extruded rock was the nearby high point of what was then called Roundtop Regional Park. The area was renamed Sibley Volcanic Regional Preserve after the peak was confirmed to be the East Bay's most prominent volcano. At least eleven eruptions about 10 million years ago mixed debris into a widespread geological stew called the Franciscan Complex. These rock types stand out on the crests of the ridges of the interior Coast Range (**left**), seen in this dawn telephoto view from farther north in the Berkeley Hills, culminating in the Ohlone Regional Wilderness on the skyline.*

the construction of this dam in his favorite park as his life's greatest defeat, writing, "Dam Hetch Hetchy! As well dam for water-tanks the people's cathedrals and churches."

After Muir had spent about four years in the High Sierra, his mentor, Jeanne Carr, offered him the use of her Oakland home as a base from which to explore the Coast Ranges. Muir wrote back that he would come and spend a month or so at most, but when the time approached, he canceled out and returned to the high country. A year later he did come to Oakland; he spent most of 1874 there, writing and taking only occasional forays into local wildlands. Though Muir called this period in his life "the strange Oakland epoch," he was well on his way to making the Bay Area his primary place of residence. At first he spent several months each year living in friends' homes in Oakland and San Francisco and taking breaks from his writing to hike through the redwoods of the Santa Cruz Mountains and Marin or the more open wild hills of the East Bay.

In an 1877 letter to his sister in Wisconsin, Muir casually mentioned going "across the top of Mount Diablo" in a brief description of walking home to Oakland after his first visit to the Strentzel family's ranch in Martinez. A few days later, he gave more details in a letter thanking the Strentzels for their hospitality. He described sleeping out under the stars on the windy 3,849-foot summit, watching a "truly glorious" sunrise, and spending an hour observing and taking notes before heading down. Reaching the crest of the Berkeley Hills that evening, he "beheld the most ravishingly beautiful sunset on the Bay I have ever yet enjoyed."

Mrs. Strentzel had previously confided in her diary, "How I would love to become acquainted with a person who writes as he does. What is wealth compared to a mind like his!" Her wish came true as Muir courted and eventually married her daughter, Louie Wanda Strentzel. The parents gave the newlyweds their ranch house and twenty acres of fruit orchards and moved into a new mansion farther down the Alhambra Valley on the large estate. Muir, a trained botanist, took to fruit growing with an obsession. He leased more lands from his father-in-law and greatly increased their productivity, growing sixty-five varieties of pears, which he shipped off to market by the ton, and converting pastures into vineyards.

In the evenings Muir sometimes took his young daughter, Annie Wanda, for strolls up Alhambra Creek, often continuing up the winding, cool canyon into the hills of what is now Briones Regional Park. He clearly came to explore, know, and love many natural areas around the Bay, yet his extensive writings and conservation efforts were always focused on places farther afield. Perhaps Muir, the nineteenth century's greatest conservationist, was dealing with a conflicting inner dialogue about his roles as protector of remote wildernesses and cultivator of Contra Costa County open lands in the tradition of California ranching.

I suspect that if John Muir were to return to the Bay Area today, he might not agree with having his old estate held out of productivity as a National Park Service historic site. I recall commenting twenty years ago that I was spending two-thirds of my time writing and one-third photographing, yet my financial rewards were vice versa. For Muir, too, the financial rewards of his long labors with a pen were far less than those of managing productive crops on his ranch.

In 1974 a friend of mine, Dewitt Jones, asked me to write the text for a book to be called *John Muir's America,* illustrated with photographs he had taken for a similar *National Geographic* story. When I declined because of a busy schedule, Jones enlisted a mutual friend who had a well-deserved reputation as a productive and creative environmental writer. T. H. Watkins dared to risk the conceit of crawling into John Muir's head and inventing first-person dialogues between himself and Muir. One of these imagined conversations takes place in an elegant Victorian house described as being perched "like a brown mushroom" at the end of the Alhambra Valley above a freeway that leads to the bridges across the Bay:

> *I worked here on this land every bit as hard as ever I did in Wisconsin as a boy, back on the old farms. You canna see it now, but perhaps you can imagine it . . . peach trees, cherry trees, olives, pomegranates, tamarisks, quince, figs, oranges, pecans, pears, plums, lemons, and grapes. Some were planted by Father Strentzel—a dear, guid mon—but most by myself. For ten years I worked here like a dray horse. All in good cause, lad. Money. It meant freedom. It seemed worth it at the time. I look at it now and wonder.*

Watkins's imagined dialogue suggests one reason why Briones Regional Park, which protects the lands through which Muir so frequently walked, was not created until 1967, three decades after similar regional parks laced the hills of Berkeley and Oakland. Profit-conscious Bay Area ranchers were rarely in favor of creating nature preserves.

When the California legislature passed a state law in 1933 to authorize the establishment of a wholly innovative East Bay Regional Park District, county initiatives were required to levy taxes to raise the funds needed to create and finance the parklands. Alameda County voters in and around Berkeley and Oakland passed their initiative by more than a two-to-one majority in 1934, but the Contra Costa County Board of Supervisors refused to put the initiative on the ballot. Ranchers in the mostly rural county objected to being taxed for parks. They believed they had plenty of nature right outside their doors and were concerned that their "Keep Out" signs would be metaphorically replaced by "Come In" signs as parklands were created. Additionally, they feared their taxes would go up when the new public lands were removed from the rolls. After several failed attempts over the years, Contra Costa County finally joined the park district in 1964 as urban voters began to outnumber the rural contingent.

Muir's balancing act between his career and his wilderness adventures would probably be no less a problem for him today. I have always believed that if Muir were alive now, he would be a wilderness photographer, and a very good one. Had I been alive in his day, however, I would *not* have been a wilderness photographer:

I wouldn't have compromised my core experience—enjoying nature—to cart around the cumbersome photo equipment of the times. I'm hooked on traveling light with 35mm equipment; I enjoy hiking, biking, and running Bay Area trails with either a light camera or none at all. However much I might fantasize about exploring the High Sierra or Alaska at Muir's side, there's no way I would give up my Bay Area life for the one he lived. In terms of choices, opportunities, and easy access, for me the present wins hands down.

Unlike T. H. Watkins's imagined conversations about an era long past, some very real ones with my mother and aunt are indelibly stamped in my mind. As teenagers in 1916, they traveled into Yosemite Valley with my grandfather in an open touring car, during the first year the road into the valley was open. (Muir had died just two years before.) My insatiably curious grandfather also drove his family over practically every back road into the wild corners of the Bay Area. My aunt went on to conduct field research with Yosemite naturalist Ansel Hall, who later became the first chief naturalist of the National Park Service. My mother, who had spent several summers in Yosemite, virtually worshiped the valley as a natural shrine and often took me there to hike and explore. As a result, however, our frequent walks through the parks of the East Bay hills and our weekend camping trips to Mount Diablo, Big Basin, and Point Reyes took on the aspect of rehearsals for greater events to come in Yosemite and other national parks. I grew up viewing Bay Area preserves as parks with training wheels—places to learn self-sufficiency for use in adventures elsewhere. It was only after I had traveled extensively in remote areas of the world that I truly began to appreciate the nature outside my back door—and that I began to realize how much concerned Bay Area citizens had accomplished in setting aside the region's two hundred–plus preserves and natural areas, most of which were established during my lifetime.

I believe my sense of being at home and wholly present in the moment in Bay Area wildlands relates to the awakening of some sort of cellular memory of my youth, something I am unable to express in words—something not present in me when I stand on a Himalayan summit or look at the endless wildlife of the Serengeti, however magnificent such experiences are in their own right. Though I deeply appreciate the wildness of faraway places, the feeling is more diffuse and metaphorical than the special affection I have for Bay Area experiences that mirror those of my youth. For example, if I walk up to a local crag I climbed as a teenager, my hands naturally grab just the right ledges and cracks in the rock; the process is at least as much mental as physical. Though I have no conscious memory of those particular holds, using them to climb is somehow distinctly different from, and far easier than, using equally good holds to ascend an unknown crag. Similarly, my eyes flow easily across even the most complex Bay Area landscapes in a way that satisfies my soul.

Ultimately, when I consider when and with whom I would want to have experienced the Bay Area in the past, I realize I already have the best of both worlds: I'm very much here in the present, yet walking beside me are my visions of times when the wild parts of the Bay Area were less populated—and less protected and appreciated. Given the chance to travel backward in time, I wouldn't.

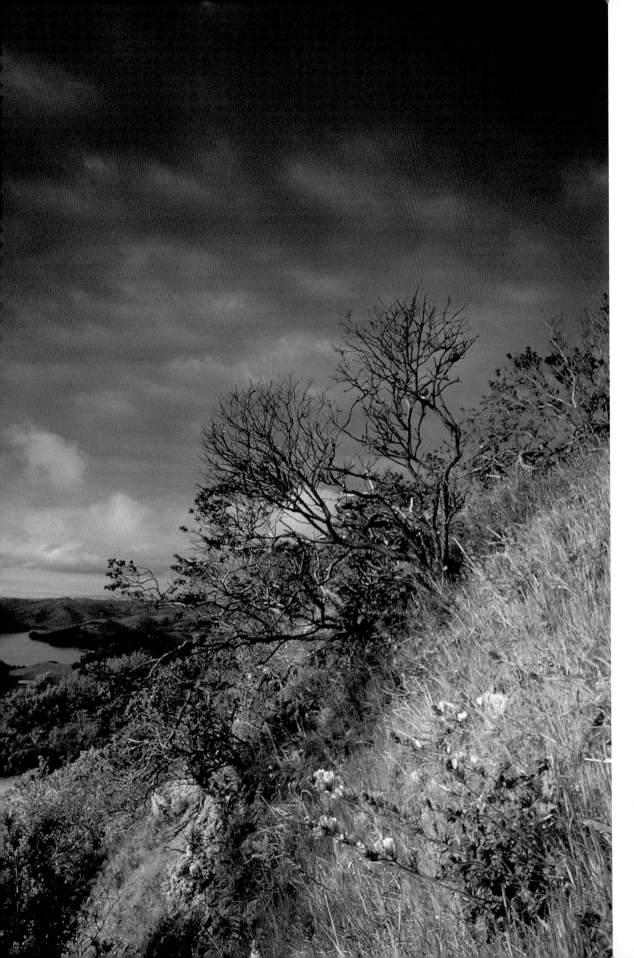

A ray of sunlight illuminates spring wildflowers (**left**) in the Berkeley Hills while San Pablo Reservoir, on EBMUD lands, remains shadowed by clouds. Among the showy blooms of the East Bay hills are (**right, clockwise from top left**) red columbine, Douglas iris, western leatherwood, and Indian paintbrush (here, sporting a caterpillar).

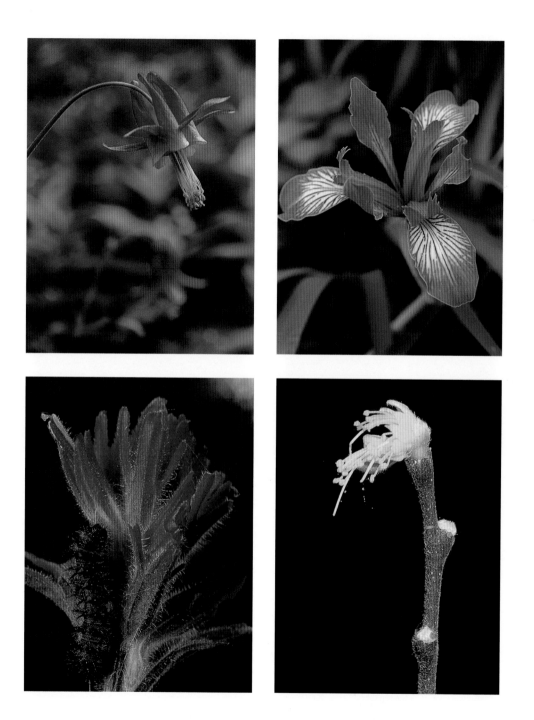

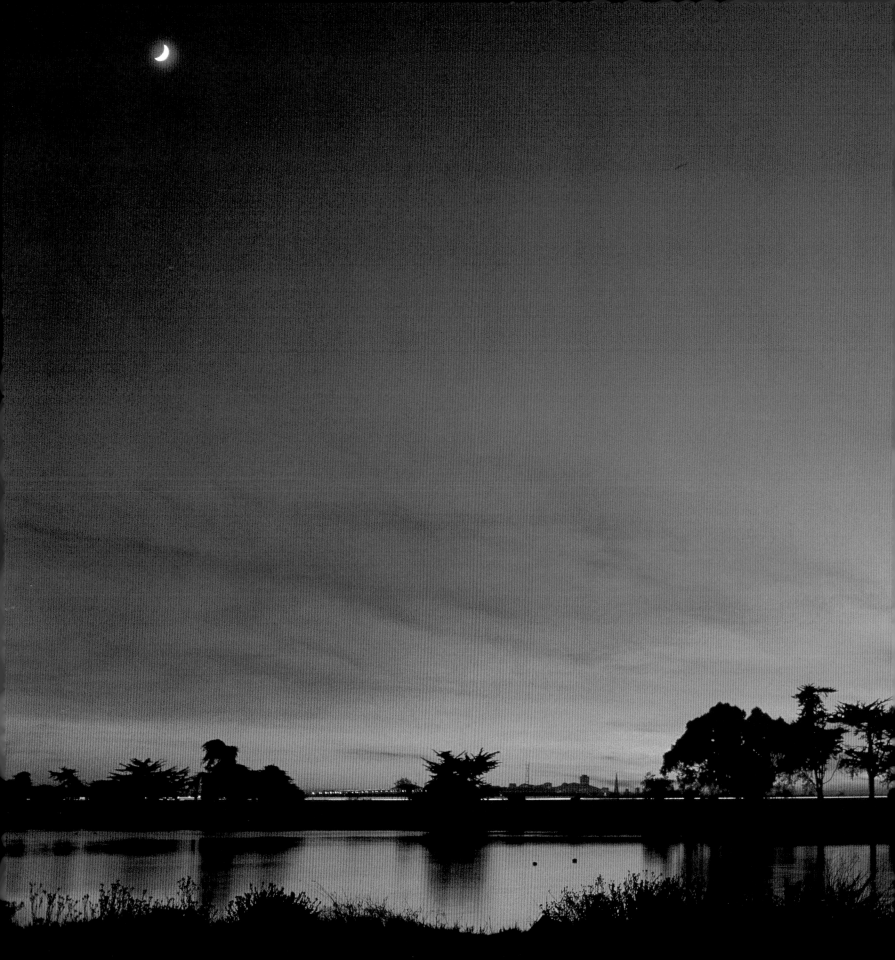

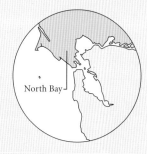

North Bay

N O R T H   B A Y

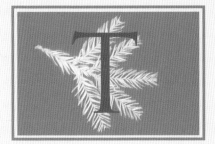

The supremely varied geography of the North Bay runs the gamut from its islands and shorelines to the Sacramento–San Joaquin Delta (the nation's largest inland river estuary); the agricultural lands of Napa and Sonoma Counties; the rugged peaks and forested canyons of Mount Tamalpais; the Marin Headlands, above the Pacific Ocean; Bolinas Lagoon and Tomales Bay, in the rift of the San Andreas Fault; and the wilderness of the Point Reyes Peninsula.

Marin County's natural preserves and other public-access lands account for a whopping 44 percent of its area. They trace back to William Kent's 1908 gift of Muir Woods as a national monument to avoid condemnation of his valley-bottom redwood forest for a reservoir. Originally a "Pinchot conservationist" who favored setting aside land for future resource use rather than for nature preservation, Kent evolved into a founding father of the National Park Service, the Save-the-Redwoods League, and Mount Tamalpais State Park (begun with another Kent land grant in 1928).

Preservation of almost all of western Marin came to pass with the creation of Point Reyes National Seashore in 1962 and the Golden Gate National Recreation Area (the world's largest urban national park) a decade later. The county's complex quilt of federal parks, state parks, county open space preserves, and municipal watershed must be seen firsthand for a full appreciation of the sum of its parts. Here, a person can truly perceive that Bay Area wildlands exceed those of Yosemite National Park in area.

The Coastal Trail section of the Bay Area Ridge Trail on Mount Tamalpais

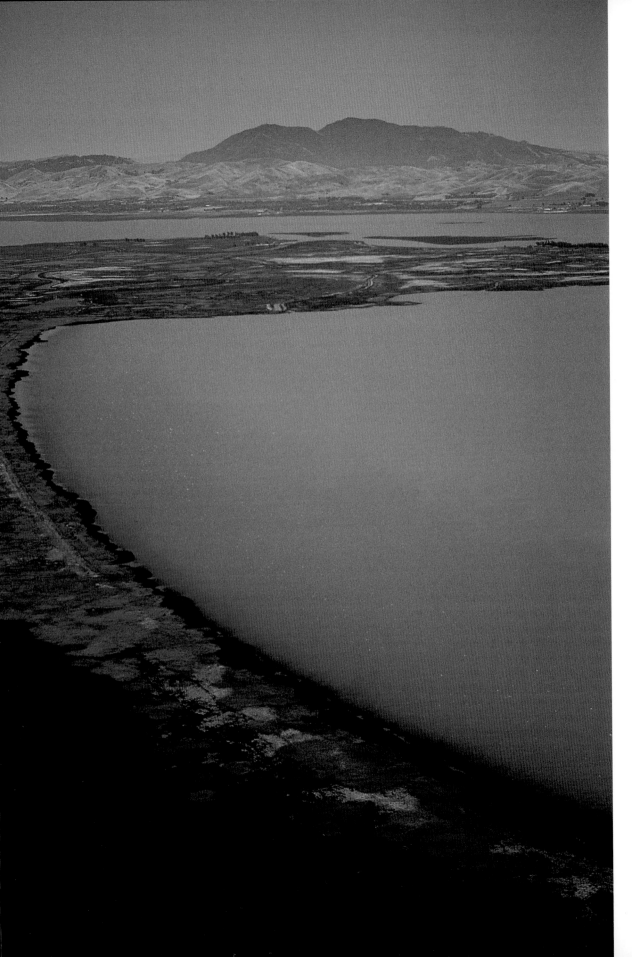

Mount Diablo rises over the bay front of Grizzly Island (left) in this aerial view of the Sacramento–San Joaquin Delta in Solano County. The Grizzly Island Wildlife Area, administered by the California Department of Fish and Game, has a winter population of more than a million ducks and geese (right)—only a fraction of the number that once inhabited the nation's most extensive system of tidal wetlands.

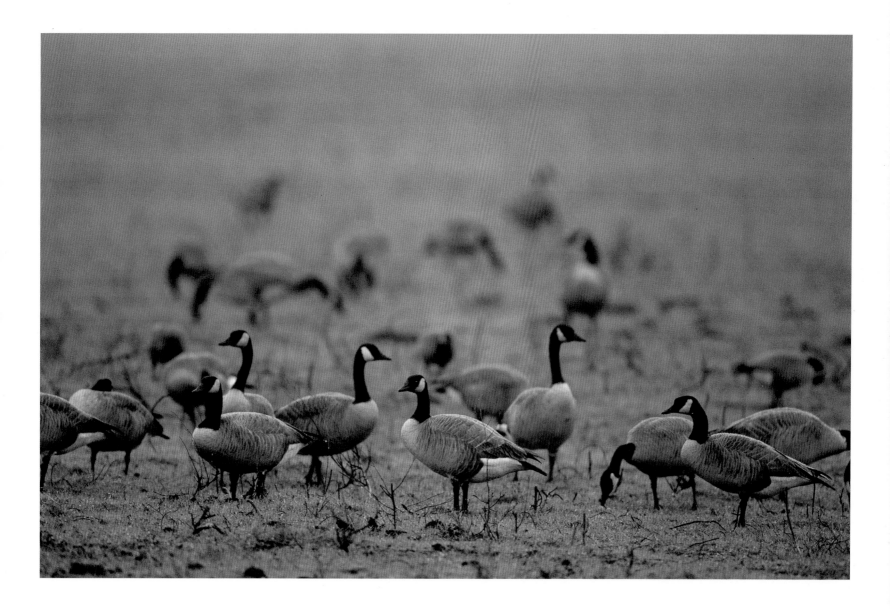

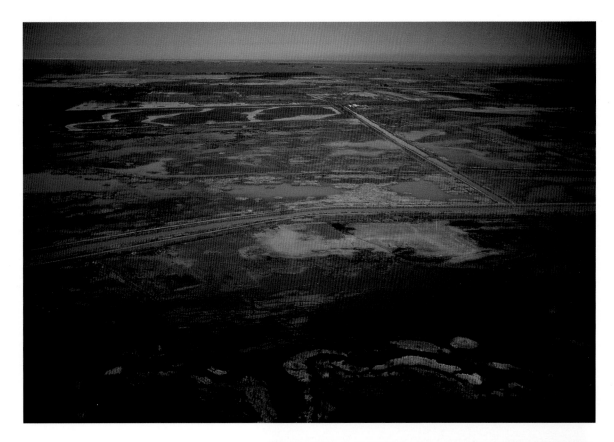

The reflection of a winter sunset (**left**) in the waters of the Sacramento–San Joaquin Delta profiles two fishermen near the Grizzly Island Wildlife Area. The 8,600-acre state wildlife reserve constitutes a small fraction of the Delta's vast wetlands (**above**). Levees for roads, rice paddies, and developments have greatly reduced the original thousand square miles of wetlands that existed here a century ago. From the air, Tubbs Island (**right**), on the northern edge of San Pablo Bay, forms a rich mosaic of agricultural lands fringed by a strip of wetlands that became part of the San Pablo Bay National Wildlife Refuge in 1974.

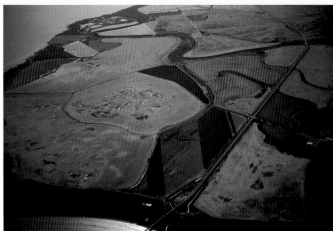

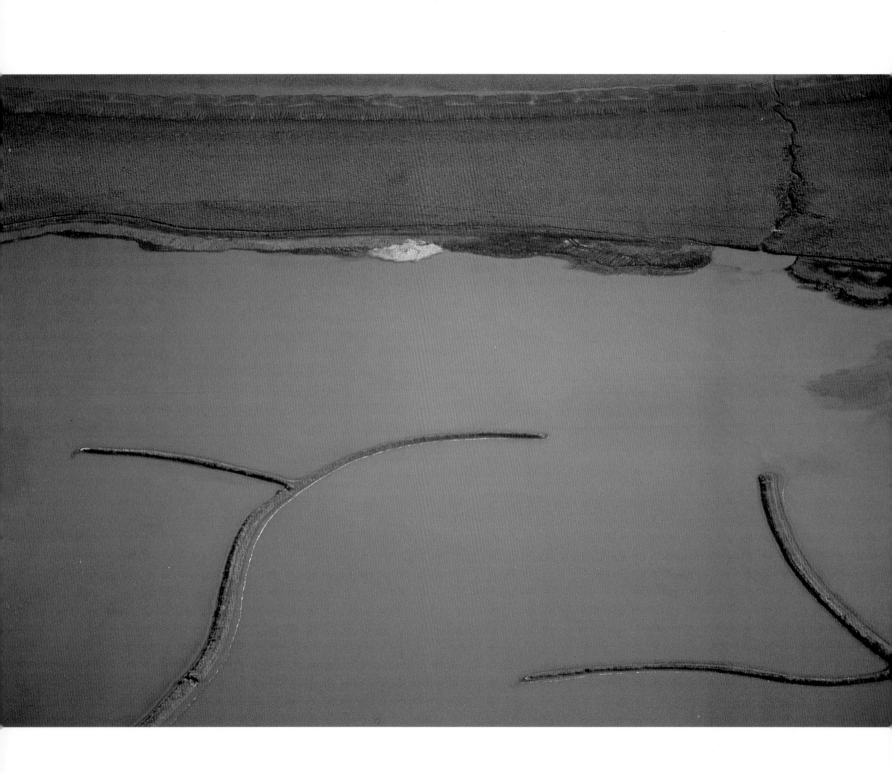

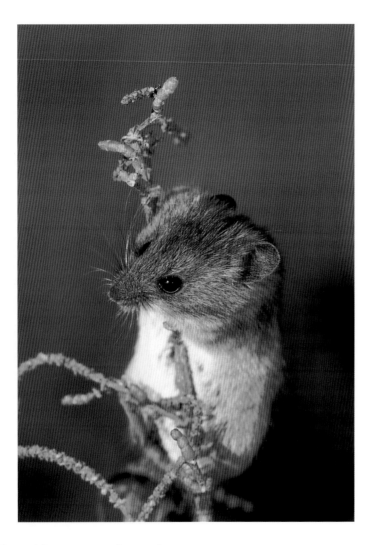 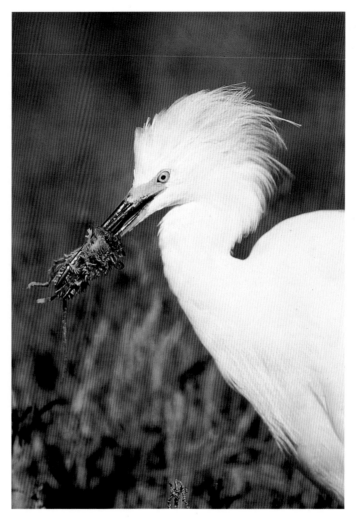

*In 1994, the state's largest-ever marsh restoration project (**left**) used sediments dredged from the Port of Oakland to fill the sunken Sonoma Baylands near the mouth of the Petaluma River. Historical wetlands were recreated in 1996 when a channel was cut to the bay, visible at the upper right. The endangered salt marsh harvest mouse (**above, left**) is adapted to brackish water and is found only in marsh habitat around San Francisco Bay. In somewhat sparse vegetation, one of the rare mice (**above, right**) falls prey to a snowy egret.*

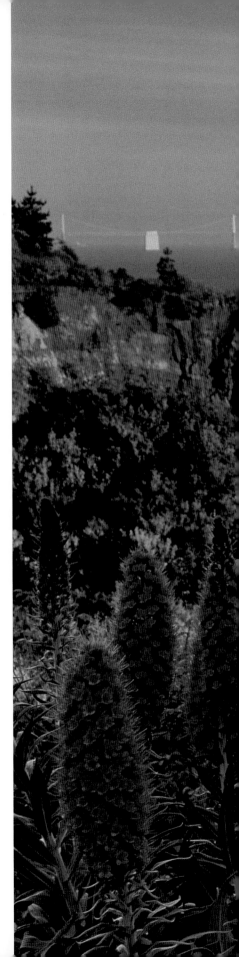

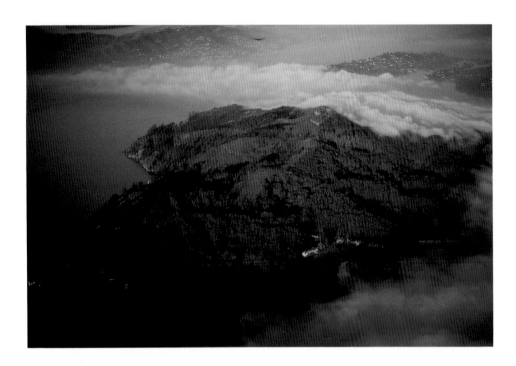

*In Angel Island State Park (**above**), off Tiburon Peninsula in Marin County, a spectacular field of flowers (**right**) erupts from the landscape in a pattern that mimics that of tall buildings rising from the distant city of San Francisco.*

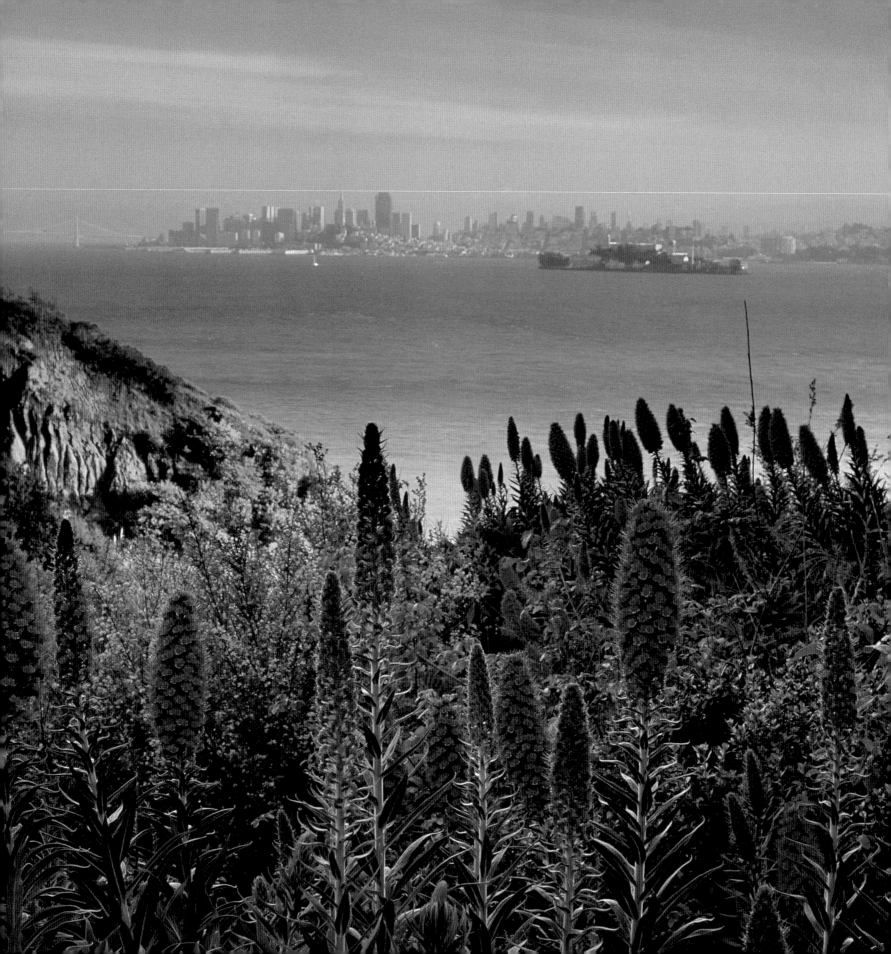

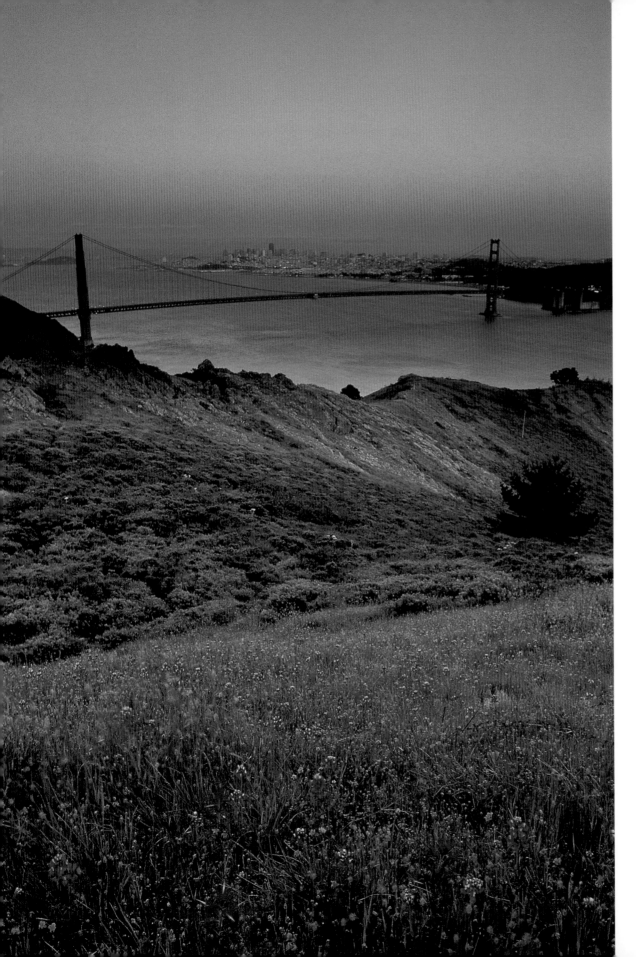

On a spring evening in the Marin Headlands (**left**), *native wildflowers tint the meadows as twilight hues tinge the sky over the Golden Gate and San Francisco. Numerous species of birds, such as this California quail (***right***), find the open coastal scrub of the headlands to be ideal habitat.*

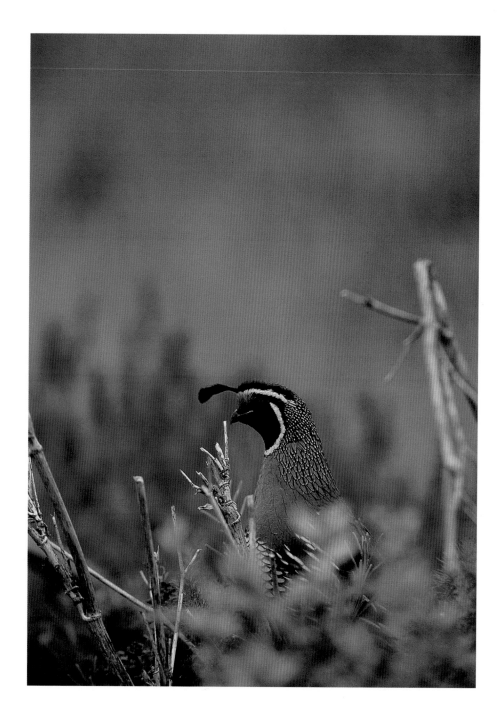

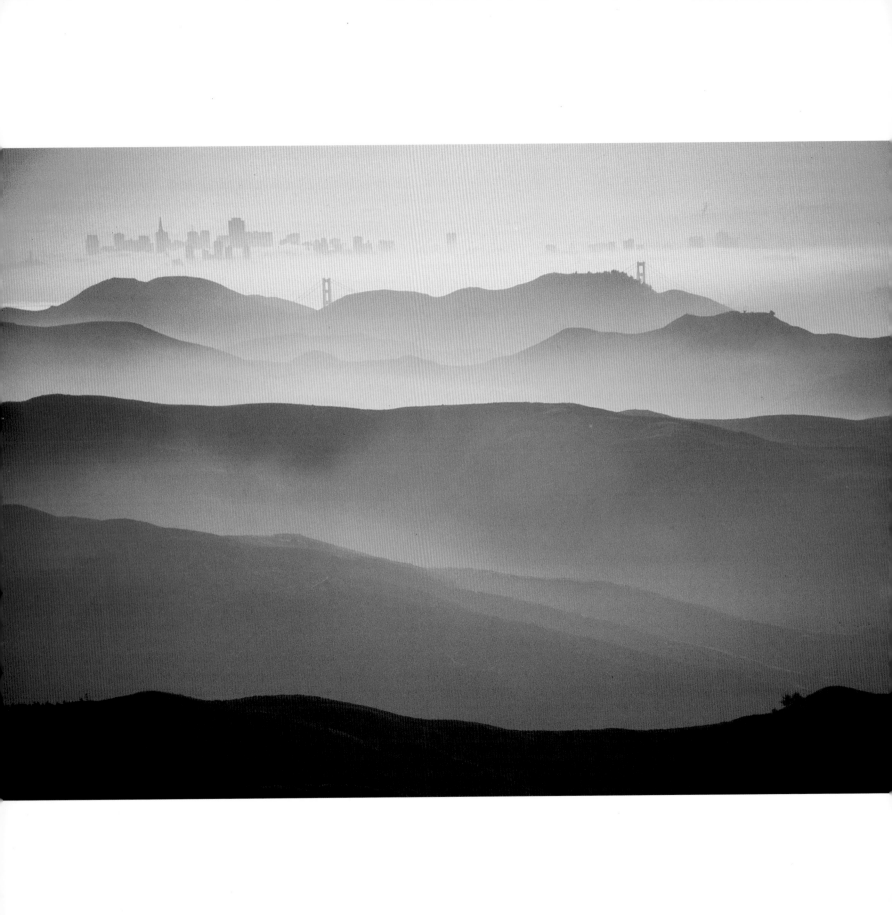

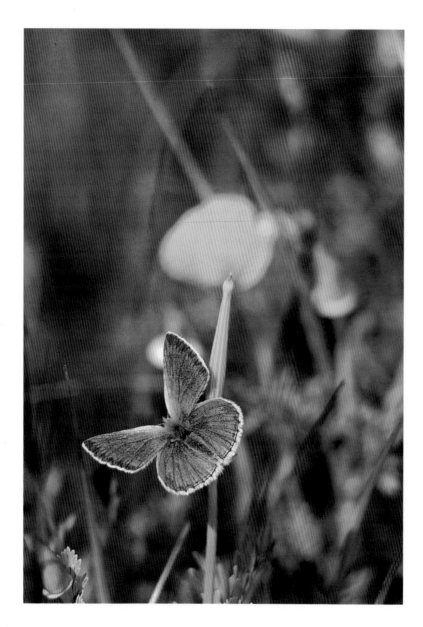

*In this aerial telephoto view across the vast wild-lands of western Marin County (**left**), the city of San Francisco and the Golden Gate Bridge appear to float in the sky. The foreground ridges of Mount Tamalpais State Park merge into the world's largest urban national park—the Golden Gate National Recreation Area (GGNRA). The park is home to twenty-seven rare and endangered species, including the mission blue butterfly (**above**), which lays its eggs only on certain species of lupines.*

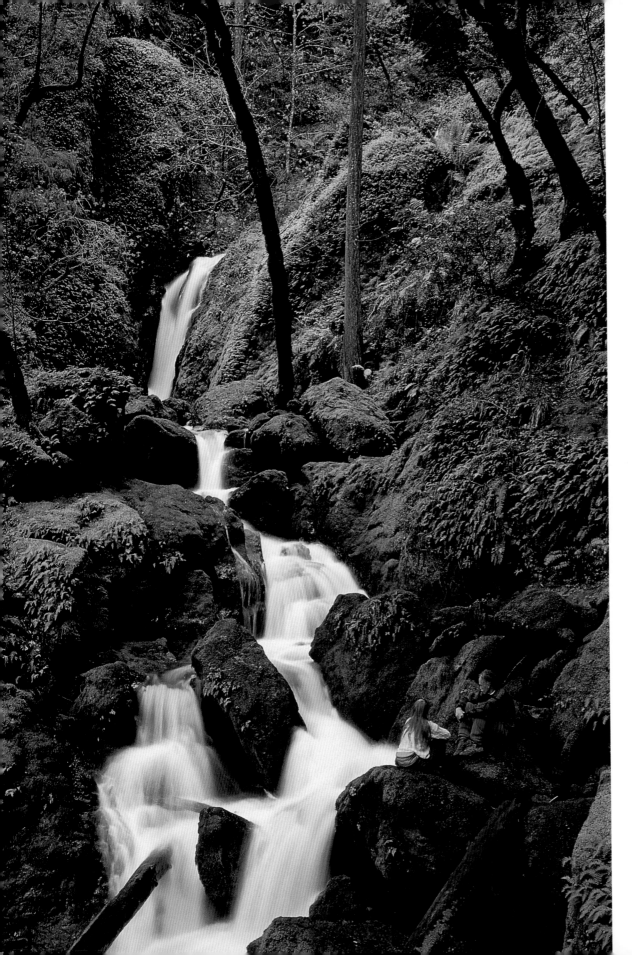

Hikers rest beside Cataract Falls (**left**) along the Cataract Trail, on the north-facing slopes of the Mount Tamalpais Watershed of the Marin Municipal Water District. These protected lands extend well to the north (**right**) through some of the Bay Area's thickest and most continuous forest.

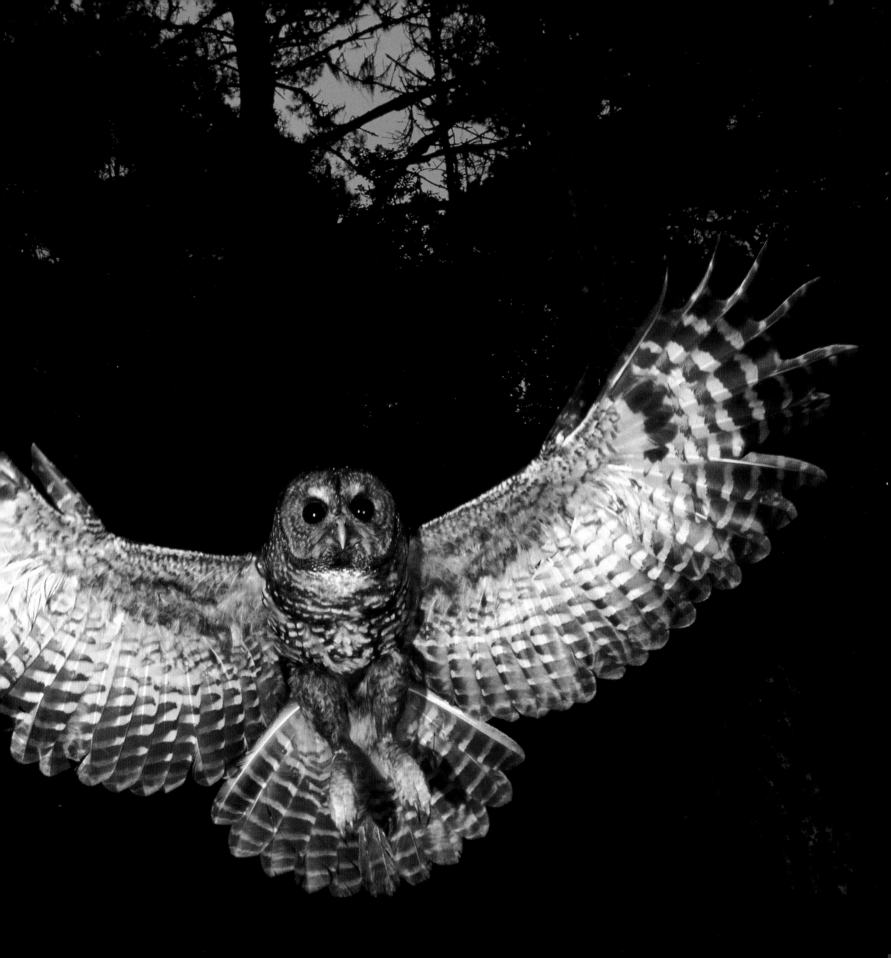

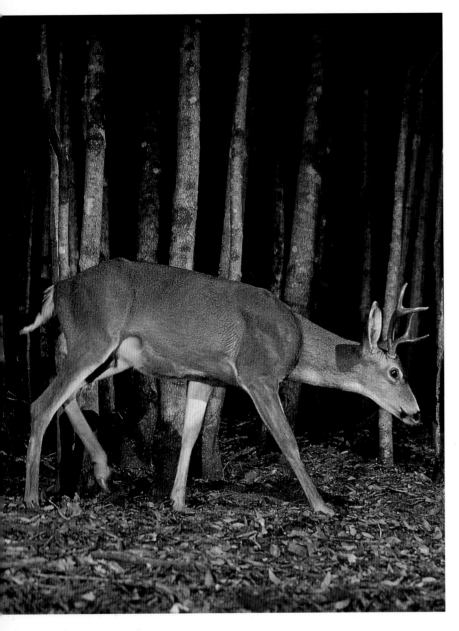

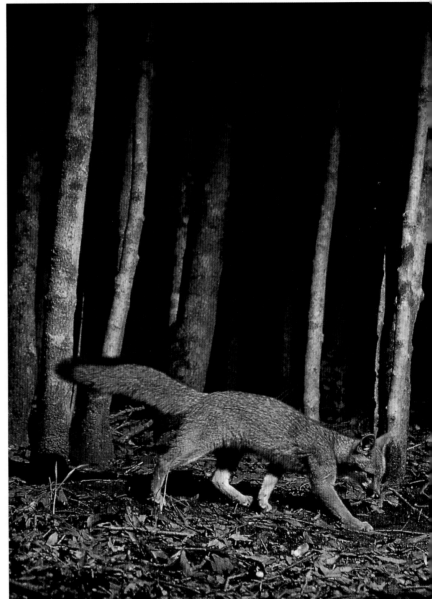

Beside an obscure animal trail on the wild slopes of Mount Tamalpais, Michael Sewell set up a remote camera with an infrared beam and a solar charger connected to two flashes. Hoping for an image of a mountain lion, he kept his gear at the ready miles from the road for two years, visiting the site occasionally to change film. Among the

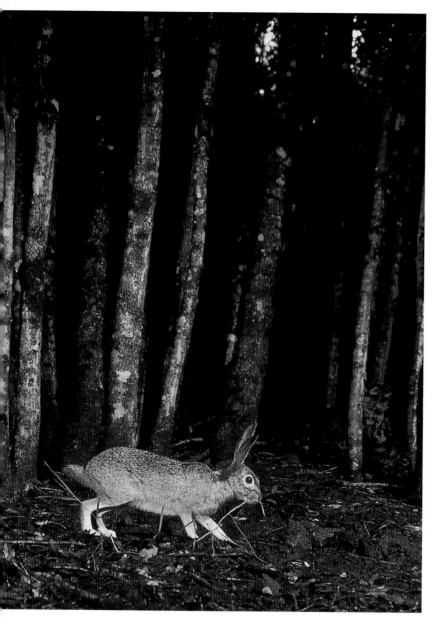
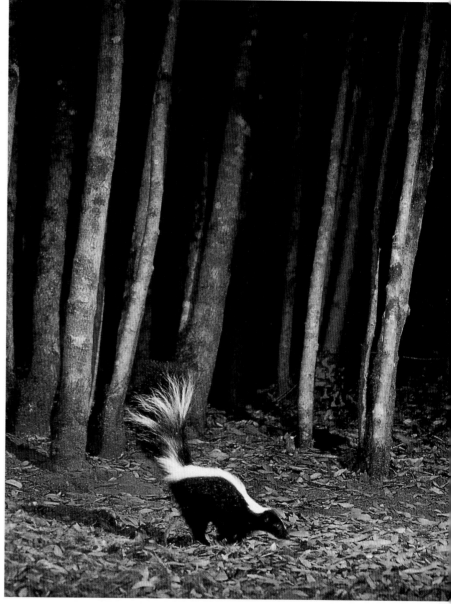

creatures caught on their nightly rounds are
(**left to right**) *a black-tailed deer, a gray fox,*
a black-tailed jackrabbit, and a striped skunk.
Other images not shown depict bobcats,
coyotes, opossums, a vulture, and a screech
owl, but not the elusive mountain lion.

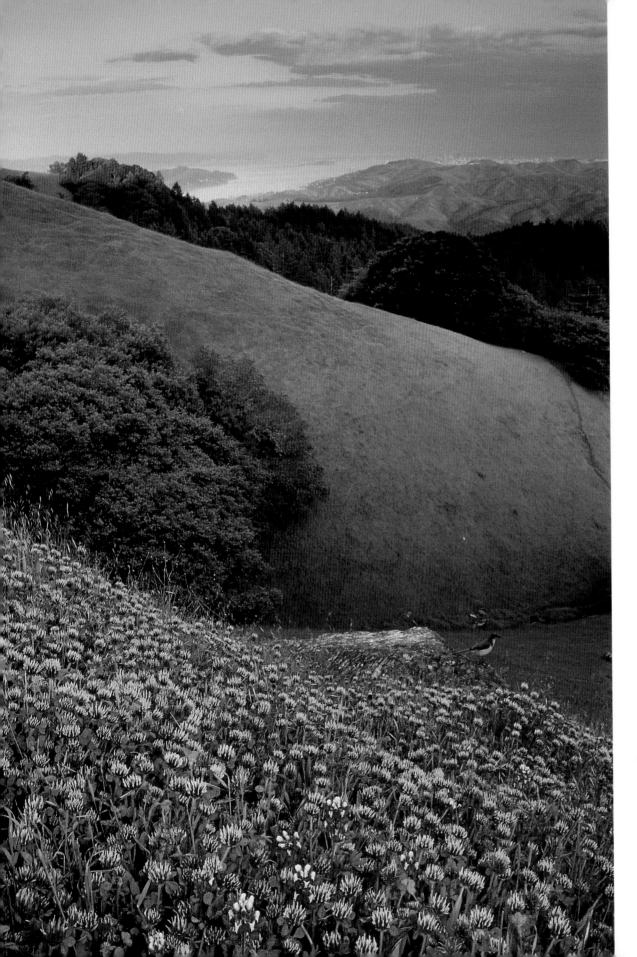

*A scrub jay stands out against a carpet of clover
(**left**) on the rolling hills of Mount Tamalpais
State Park. Higher on the mountain at sunset
along Bolinas Ridge above Stinson Beach (**right**),
a northern Pacific rattlesnake basks on a warm
rock to accumulate body heat before hunting
small mammals in the early hours of the night.
At dawn on a cool fall morning on the same
ridge (**following pages**), stringers of fog pour
down parallel ravines toward the ocean.*

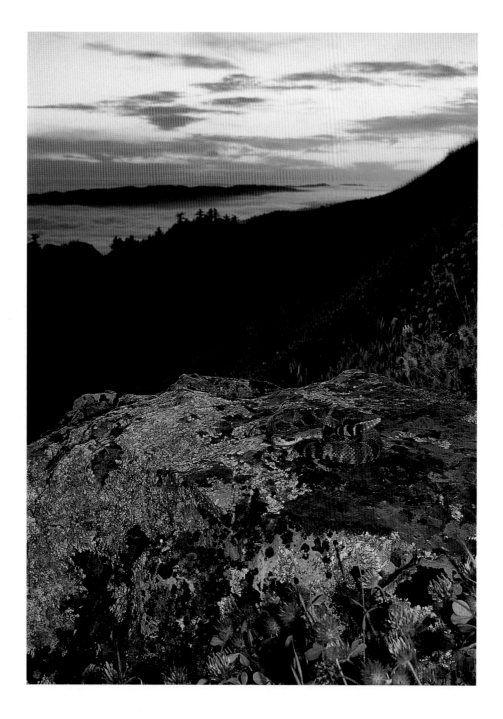

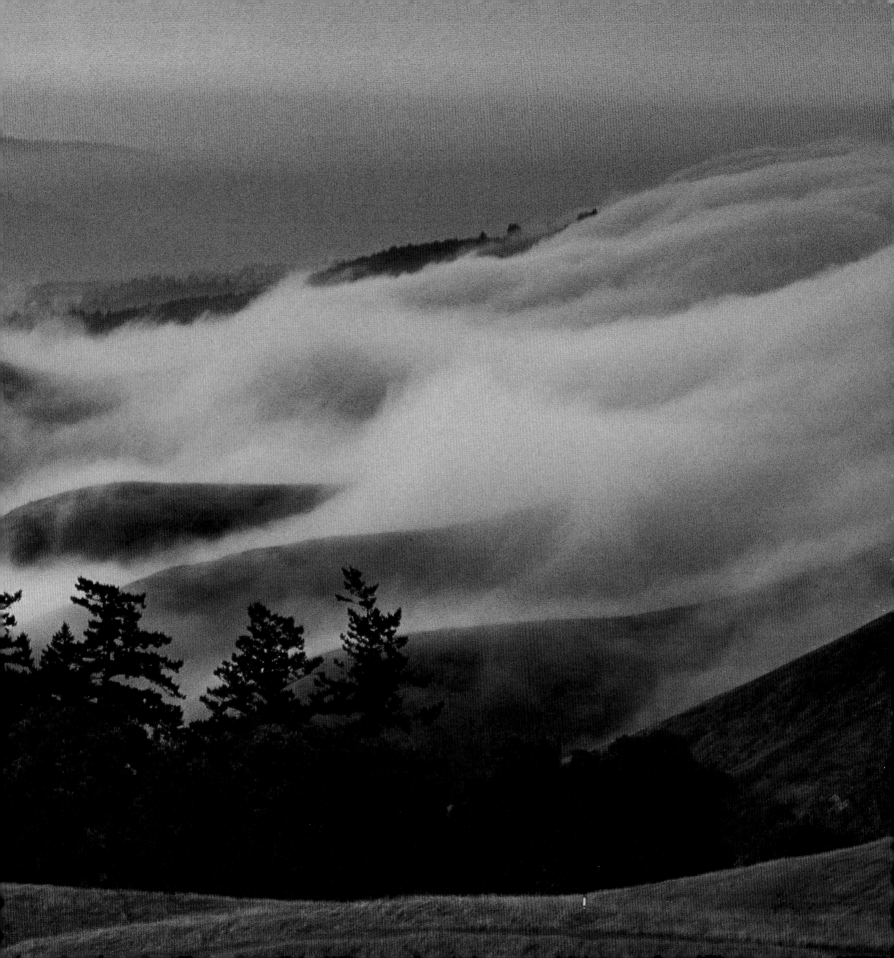

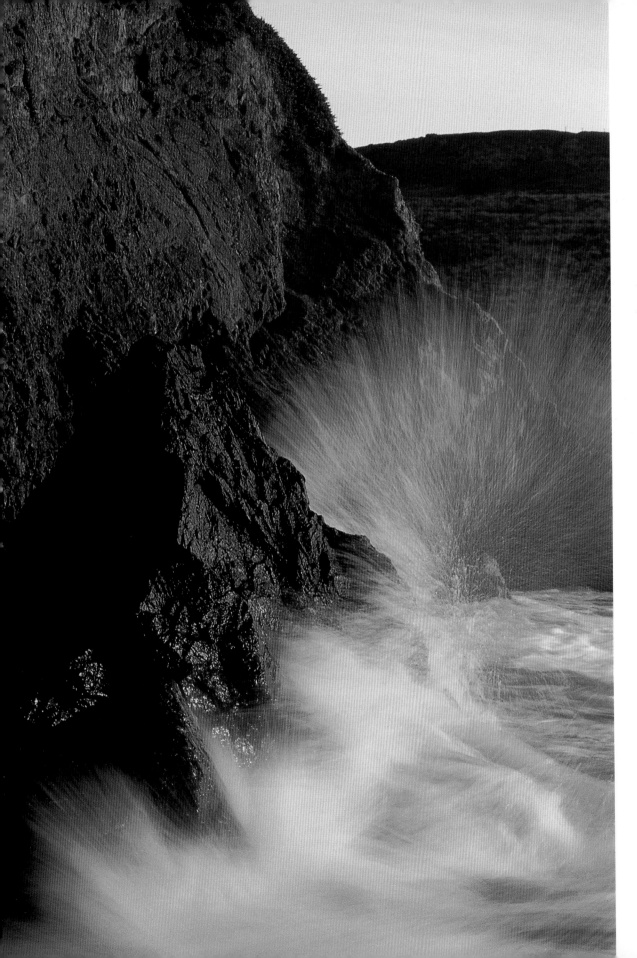

*During the last moment of sunset (**left**), a wave crashes against the rugged cliffs of the Marin Headlands in the GGNRA. At first light on Bolinas Ridge (**right**), a ravine between shadowed mists and sunlit ground forms a window looking out onto the Pacific Ocean.*

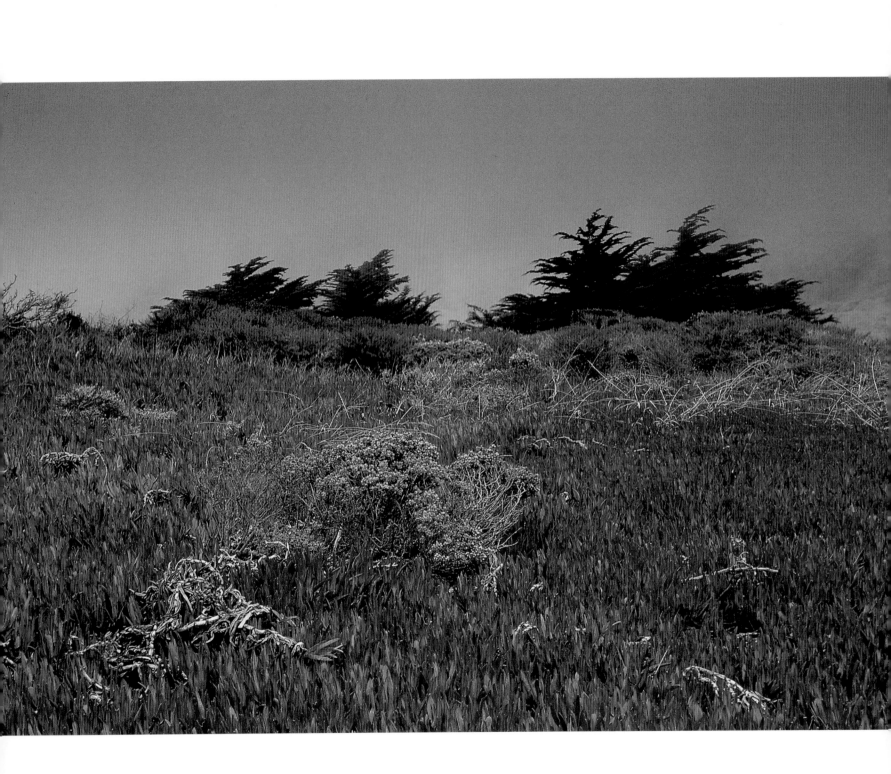

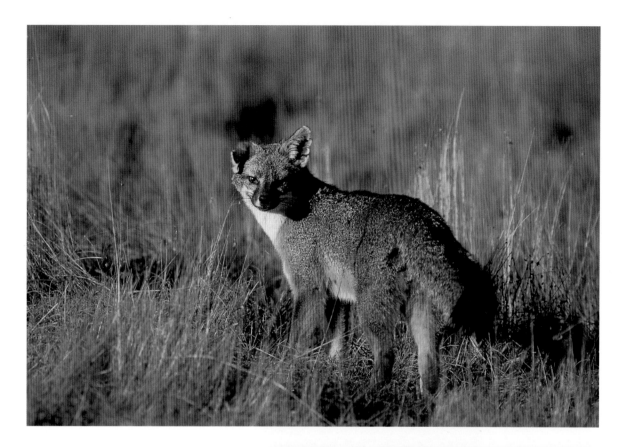

Mats of what Californians call iceplant and South Africans call a weed (**left**) cover many coastal bluffs and lap at the edges of sandy beaches. In the middle of the field is a coyote bush in bloom; in the background is a grove of cypress trees. Lack of moisture in late summer and fall causes many of the plants to turn red (**right**), accentuated here by backlighting from the evening sun. Although the sea fig family to which iceplant belongs is native to South Africa, one species found along the Marin Headlands—Carpobrotus chilensis—was probably here before the first European explorers. Similarly, the gray fox (**above**) of the coastal hills is native, whereas the ever-more-common red fox is an introduced species.

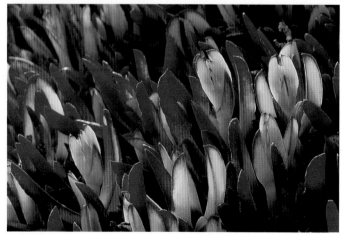

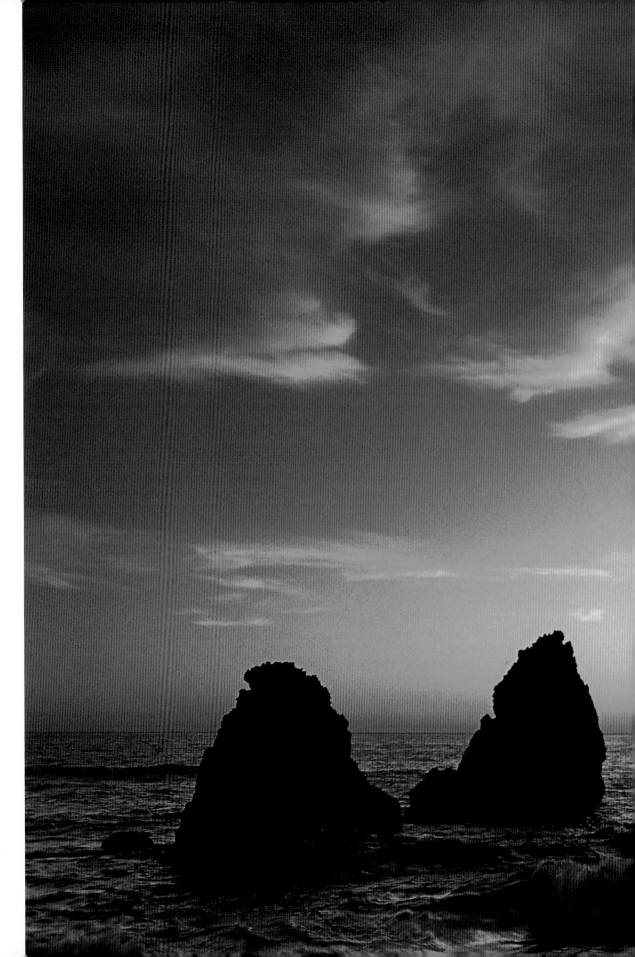

A group of sea stacks merges into the pattern
created by flowing clouds at sunset off Rodeo
Beach in the Marin Headlands, in the GGNRA.
The chaotic motion of the tides, sands, and clouds
virtually guarantees that no two evenings here
will look the same.

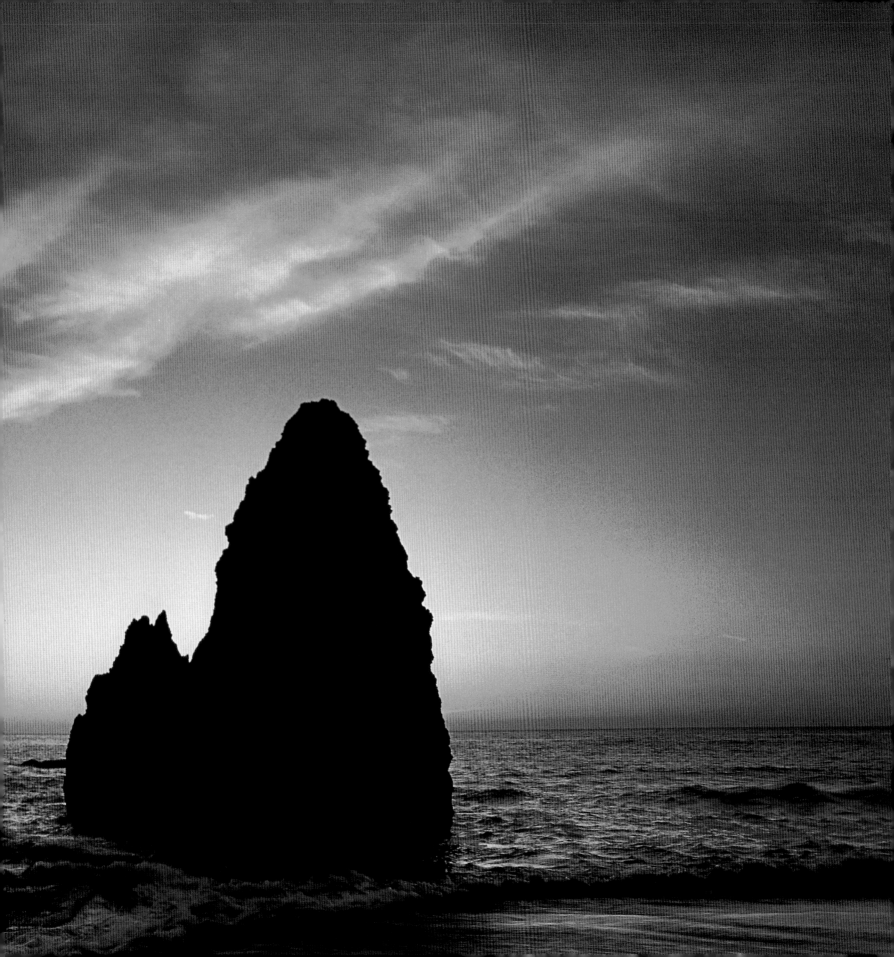

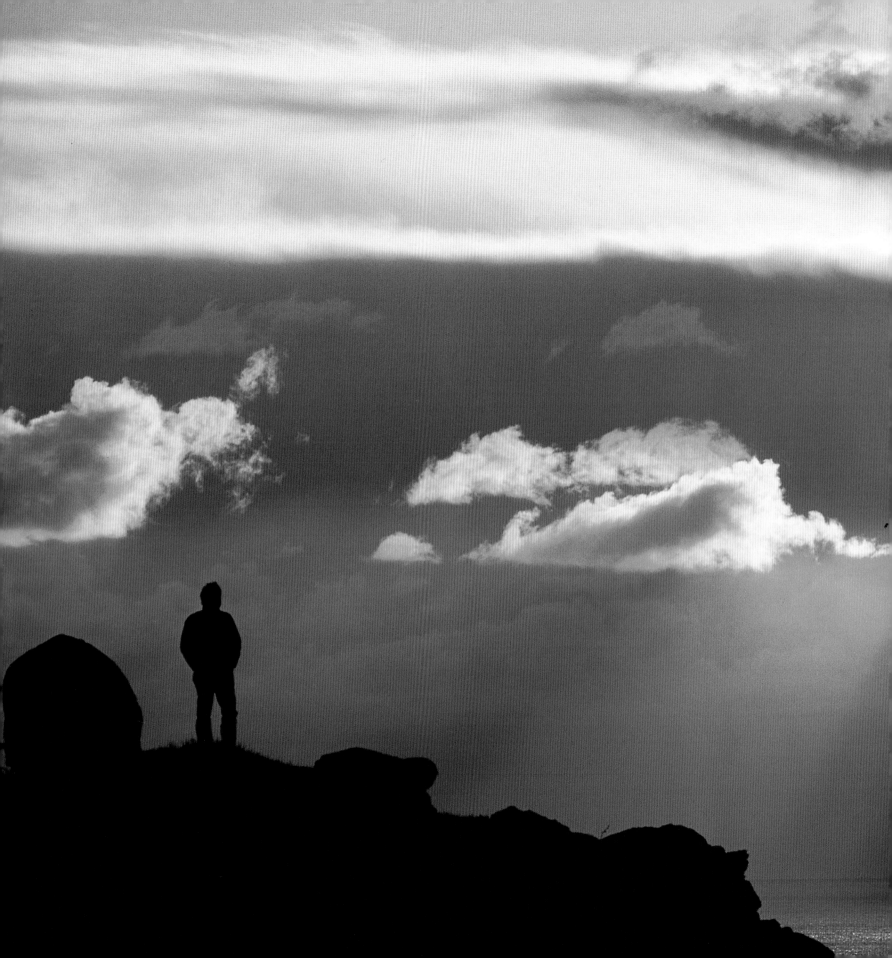

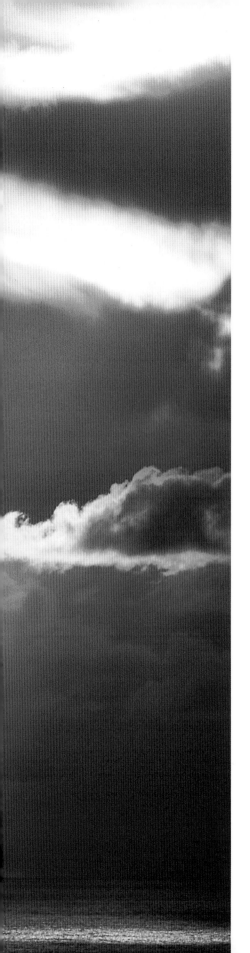

Urban Wildness and the Human Spirit

Before I began work on this book, I thought I knew quite a bit about the Bay Area's wild places. Over the course of several decades, I had made thousands of visits to parks and preserves to run or hike wild trails. Yet in a basic way, my experience was limited. Like a commuter, I tended to follow the same routes over and over.

I soon discovered that I was in good company. As I talked with veteran users of local wildlands, it became clear that virtually all of us had major gaps in our experience. We knew a few places well but rarely ventured beyond our favorite local haunts. The exceptions were notable: we were far more likely to have spent three days in wilds across the oceans than to have visited those on the opposite shore of the Bay. We didn't expend the same effort in planning visits to places we thought we could see anytime we wished, and therefore we never got to know them well. Interestingly, many of our brief journeys to remote parts of the Bay Area had not been self-initiated; rather, they were prompted by the presence of out-of-town visitors. This pattern had become familiar to me in my travels as a photographer—often my brief jaunts in a new region exceeded the lifetime local excursions of residents—but now I was witnessing the phenomenon from the other side.

I decided to begin approaching even the most mundane of my Bay Area journeys as if I were traveling abroad. Instead of choosing the fastest way to get from one point to another, I kept trail maps and natural history guidebooks in my car and, whenever possible, planned my road trips to include visits to new wild places. For example, on a recent Monday morning drive to a business appointment in Palo Alto, I gave myself more time than usual to buck the rush-hour traffic and arrived a full half-hour early. Instead of reading the morning paper over coffee in a restaurant or studying the wallpaper in my client's waiting room, I drove two minutes off the freeway and took a walk through the Palo Alto Baylands Nature Preserve. Here, sandwiched between the busy city airport and the waters of the Bay, are more than two thousand acres of restored marsh and wetlands, first set aside in the sixties. When I pulled into the nearly empty parking lot I was concerned about the preserve's juxtaposition with the airport, where private pilots were landing a stone's throw away every couple of minutes. Yet the hundreds of ducks, geese, egrets, and gulls in the tidal channels seemed completely unfazed by all the activity; nor were they bothered by an elderly gentleman playing a trombone on a bench overlooking the marsh.

As I strolled self-consciously along the elevated boardwalk in my coat and tie, no one, human or animal, even gave me a second glance. Within minutes, I began to feel at ease in my new surroundings. At first, I needed to remind myself that I had come with no expectation of stalking a rare bird or witnessing a fabulous sunrise: I was here simply to soak in a touch of wildness before facing office walls for the remainder of the day.

A hiker stops to watch a sunset on the Point Reyes Peninsula.

I sensed that these few minutes spent at the tidewater marsh with the birds would make my hours of meetings more bearable. And they did.

On another occasion, instead of entering a stream of bumper-to-bumper traffic on the Bay Bridge after a late-afternoon meeting in San Francisco, I drove in the opposite direction, into the cypress groves of the Presidio, a historic military base managed as urban open space by the National Park Service. Trading dress shoes for running shoes, I enjoyed an hour's walk on dirt trails high over the Bay before heading home in considerably lighter traffic.

These little journeys have a strong cumulative effect on my soul. The more often I take them, the more habit-forming they become, and the more they affect my urban experience. When I pass some little piece of wild terrain along the freeway that I've previously explored on foot, I'm keenly aware of a warm spot in my heart. For me, such experiences are the perfect answer to Gertrude Stein's famous put-down of Oakland—that there is no "there" there. Wherever I am in the Bay Area, there *is* a "there" there when I can connect the land I'm observing through my car window with a special memory of active involvement. As a side benefit, I am thrust into the flow of the present and out of whatever mental wanderings I might have been engaged in. I can only assume that Gertrude Stein failed to venture out and form a personal connection with the natural areas of the East Bay, which, in her time, around the turn of the past century, had yet to be formally preserved.

I can't drive along the crest of the Santa Cruz Mountains on Highway 280 without feeling a special pleasure when I pass the edge of Pulgas Ridge Open Space Preserve. I remember hiking from a trailhead a couple of miles away only to come face to face with a tall cyclone fence topped with barbed wire overlooking the freeway. My initial frustration with the dead end gave way to a sense of wonder when I noticed a series of footprints as large as my fist following the fence for a full hundred yards. It had rained recently, and these pugmarks, perfectly cast in the bare strip of mud alongside the fence, were those of an adult mountain lion. I imagined that the great cat, too, must have been frustrated by the fence (which might have saved its life by keeping it off the freeway). I feel a similar magic when I pass by a particular ranch on the outskirts of Walnut Creek. One night almost a decade ago, Barbara turned her car around in a driveway beside a corral as we were heading home from a party. Caught for a split second in her headlights was the tawny flash of a large cat with a long tail.

Though locations of unusual wildlife sightings provoke the most predictable responses in me, anyplace where I have seen a memorable sunset or moved through nature under my own power is likely to trigger pleasurable feelings for years to come. In a very real sense, I now perceive a far wilder Bay Area than I did in my youth. Even though much more open space existed here half a century ago, I was oblivious to its significance, except in the few areas around my home I regularly visited. Over time, as I've tuned my senses to spot edges of wildlands and have set out to explore them, my view of the Bay Area has been enhanced beyond the merely personal or visual. I would not be experiencing this, however, were it not for the fact that events during my lifetime have changed the essential nature of what I am observing.

A good example of a place that has a continually evolving meaning for me is a section of trail near our Berkeley home. Though it remains about as wild as it was when I first walked it with my parents during World War II, it is no longer just that old fire road tracing the crest of the Berkeley Hills below Vollmer Peak. When I was ten, I walked it as a member of the Tilden Regional Park Junior Rangers, wearing a uniform with a shoulder patch as I learned the names of its trees, flowers, birds, rocks, reptiles, and mammals from a full-sized ranger named Jack Parker. These names gradually began to take on meaning beyond simply identifying the specimens Jack pointed out along the trail. They became keys that unlocked the doors to a deeper sense of place. Yes, the buckeye tree I saw in the canyon in Tilden was also there beside a redwood in Muir Woods. No, I did not find one in Sequoia National Park beside a different species of redwood in a quite different habitat.

Decades later, the fire trail became known locally as "the Dog Run" because visitors were allowed to be unleashed from their dogs (as I prefer to state it). Sometime in the sixties trail signs appeared, with something of a misnomer: Sea View Trail had become the official name. "Bay View Trail" would have been more appropriate because splendid views of the Bay are commonplace all along it, whereas the far more distant waters of the sea are rarely seen through the narrow Golden Gate. The fog and low clouds that appear almost every month of the year often obscure the ocean view.

In 1979, a new set of signs joined the Sea View placards. The trail had become a section of the East Bay Skyline National Recreation Trail, which traverses thirty-one miles of the East Bay hills through several regional parks and water district lands. Though acquisitions and rights-of-way took more than a decade to complete, the trail was the very first to be designated under the National Trails System Act of 1968, as well as one of the only ones outside national park lands.

Just seeing the new name on these signs was an instant reminder to me that the fire road of my youth is now part of a long greenbelt that extends from behind the city of Richmond almost all the way to Castro Valley. Only after the name appeared did I hike "my" trail's continuation into Oakland's Redwood Regional Park and, eventually, along its entire length.

In 1989, yet another emblem appeared among the trailside signs. The new Bay Area Ridge Trail merged the Sea View Trail into a 400-mile circuit that roughly follows the rim of the entire basin surrounding the Bay. As of 1997, slightly more than half of the Ridge Trail was completed. It will eventually connect more than seventy-five parks and preserves around the Bay.

The very act of linking these places has changed public perceptions of them. Early on, planners conceived of both the Ridge Trail and a separate Bay Trail loop around the inner shoreline as strings of pearls.

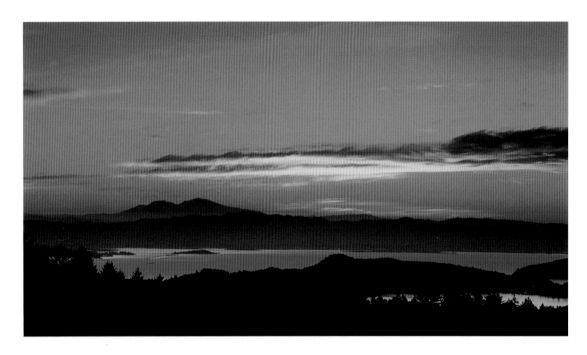

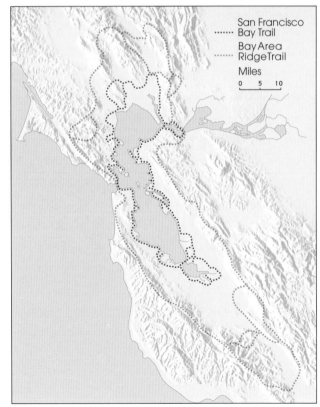

San Francisco
Bay Trail
Bay Area
RidgeTrail
Miles
0   5   10

Predawn shadows veil the cities and emphasize the landscape in this 1996 photograph taken from a knoll just above a section of the Bay Area Ridge Trail on Mount Tamalpais. On the opposite side of San Francisco Bay, another section of the half-completed 400-mile loop follows the crest of the East Bay hills along the long ridge in front of the twin summits of Mount Diablo. The separate Bay Trail, also about half completed, will trace an equally long inner loop near the convoluted shore-line. As seen more distinctly on a map (**left**), both of these projected trail routes follow the natural topography as they circle the Bay. They link together more than a hundred natural preserves, which appear in green on the larger map on page 18. Fittingly, the Bay Area Ridge Trail was the dream of the late William Penn Mott near the end of his illustrious career. He first managed Oakland city parks; then the East Bay Regional Park District; later on, the California State Park System; and finally, the entire National Park Service. Mott envisioned connector trails that would tie all the Bay Area communities together physically and spiritually. When the trails are completed, at least one segment of them will be within half an hour's drive or public transit ride from any Bay Area city.

The preserves were the pearls, and the trails were thought of merely as strings to thread them together. The strings, however, have taken on a character indistinguishable from that of the pearls. Despite the "Entering . . ." and "Leaving . . ." signs that mark the official borders of the preserves, walking either of these trails feels similar to walking through continuous wildness.

Though they form outer and inner pathways, respectively, around San Francisco Bay, the Ridge and Bay Trails are not entirely separate. They touch at the "top," as would two real strings of pearls draped around a woman's neck. The common ground they share is near the town of Benicia; here, at the Sacramento–San Joaquin Delta, the Bay's high ridges disappear. And though the two trails do not connect at the "bottom"—the South Bay end—an extension of the Stevens Creek Trail past the city of Sunnyvale will soon join them. On a map, the Ridge Trail appears, at first glance, to be a much larger circle and a longer route than the Bay Trail. In reality, however, the length of the inner loop, with its intricate curves and coves, almost equals that of the 400-mile Ridge Trail.

Thus the Berkeley Hills fire trail of my youth has evolved into part of a far greater whole that now includes even the Palo Alto Baylands I visited on a whim. The single wild entity I now perceive—San Francisco Bay and its environs—has become far more compelling to me than the captivating night scene out my parents' window that I took for granted long ago. That dark body of water girdled by twinkling city lights now has a far wilder, more natural, and more holistic character—not only for me but also for all those who have witnessed how well the democratic process has worked to preserve great parts of it in recent decades. Indeed, the urban Bay of my youth was rapidly shrinking in size and diminishing in both wildness and natural beauty. In the fifties, when I was in high school, 85 percent of the rich wetland wildlife habitat surrounding the Bay had been destroyed. Thousands of acres of new land were being created each year by filling in the shoreline to build new freeways and industrial parks or simply to expand the boundaries of cities as part of the unmitigated growth ethic of the times.

In much the same way parents fail to see a child's growth as clearly as do relatives whose glimpses are interrupted by long periods of time, most local citizens were oblivious to the shrinking of the large body of water they saw each day. The U.S. Army Corps of Engineers inadvertently provided the vision that turned the tide toward protection of the Bay. In late 1959, the agency published a map that projected its conception of the Bay in the year 2020, after sixty more years of filling. Only a narrow channel of open water remained between massive areas of landfill that virtually joined San Francisco, Oakland, and Marin County. Most of the Bay's remaining marshes were due to be "reclaimed" before 1990.

Catherine Kerr, wife of the president of the University of California, happened to see the map published the following year in the *Oakland Tribune*. She soon found two other Berkeley faculty wives—Esther Gulick and Sylvia McLaughlin—who shared her outrage and her passion to do something about it. None of the women was a political or environmental activist before the three formed a grassroots action group to wage what was to become one of the nation's most dramatic and successful environmental struggles. The powerful Save San Francisco Bay Association evolved out of an informal meeting at the Gulick home, overlooking the Bay from the Berkeley Hills. State legislators soon began receiving not only sacks of letters and telegrams about preserving the Bay but also sacks full of dirt with notes that read: "You'll wonder where the water went when you fill the bay with sediment."

Beyond grassroots activism, the association gathered solid facts about the Bay from the university and urged a comprehensive study by Mel Scott of the Institute of Governmental Studies. This information proved crucial to the creation of the San Francisco Bay Conservation and Development Commission, formed in 1965 by the state legislature with a mandate to protect the Bay, regulate development, and do long-term planning. By the end of the sixties, the Save San Francisco Bay Association had 18,000 members, and the Sierra Club had described the Bay as "the most significant open space within any major metropolitan area in the United States or abroad."

As of 1997, filling of the Bay has virtually stopped, and more than 180 miles of bay shore are open to public access. With the Bay protected by law, cities now gain civic pride by trying to outdo one another in preserving their shorelines rather than by extending their urban boundaries through landfill.

Regardless of the changing public perception of the Bay, its appearance depends on the viewer's state of mind. In terms of natural wonders, it no longer stands out as it did for members of the Portolá Expedition in 1769. The singular natural integrity they witnessed from what is now Sweeney Ridge of the Golden Gate National Recreation Area must have struck them as powerfully as a wild Half Dome, Grand Canyon, or Old Faithful captivate the modern imagination and serve as defining symbols of wild America.

Today, our eyes are too easily distracted by the metropolitan ring surrounding the Bay, seemingly divided into separate cultural and physical entities. Yet if the wild parts of the Bay Area could be designated as a single national park, it would be among the grandest in the nation. Its total land area would fall between those of Yosemite and Yellowstone National Parks, and its biodiversity—its wealth of plant, bird, and animal species—would exceed their combined total. Its annual rate of visitation, the traditional lever for prying loose federal funding for parks, would rank at the very top. The existing national park lands of the Golden Gate National Recreation Area—accounting for a mere fraction of the total area of the Bay Area's more than two hundred protected parks and preserves—currently draw twice the number of visitors as do Grand Canyon, Yellowstone, and Yosemite National Parks combined.

The natural wonders that define each of these great national parks were all created by the action of waters. The Colorado River carved the Grand Canyon over eons. The glacier-filled tributaries of the Merced River sculpted the bold features of Yosemite Valley during the last ice age, laying the groundwork for its magnificent waterfalls. Underground hot springs created the distinctive geysers of Yellowstone.

Similarly, the action of waters is the unifying feature that links the great diversity of Bay Area wildlands. The huge Sacramento and San Joaquin Rivers pour their waters into San Francisco Bay to merge with tidal currents that regularly exceed the flow of the Amazon River as they pass through the narrow Golden Gate into the Pacific Ocean.

To the observant scientist, these waters are an ever-changing dynamic system, but to the average person, San Francisco Bay simply is. Whereas visitors to a national park are deluged with information about the park's natural history, providing them with a strong sense of place over time, a modern Bay Area resident may briefly reflect on the 1906 earthquake or the gold rush era, but the idea of an evolving landscape is rarely, if ever, contemplated. It's quite refreshing, therefore, to hear someone comment on the Bay's meaning without taking its existence for granted. Bob Hansen, a Bay Area resident who has lived and done environmental work in various parts of the state, reflects: "If the Bay had been another valley, we would be another Los Angeles. Our geography has saved us."

Compared with the way it looked twenty thousand years ago, the Bay Area has changed at least as much as has Yosemite Valley. The ice then carving Yosemite's features and those of most other mountain areas of the world had locked up a great percentage of our planet's fresh waters that would otherwise have run into the oceans. Even after the first people arrived in North America, sea level was so much lower that there was no San Francisco Bay waiting to be discovered until the last ice age ended. The shoreline of the Pacific Ocean was beyond the Farallon Islands, now visible on exceptionally clear days as tiny dots twenty-seven miles out to sea from the Bay.

Viewed through time, the distant Farallon Islands—now seemingly so far removed from the rest of the Bay Area—are an integral part of the region's landscape. Today, places without automotive access are virtual blanks on our road maps, but the Farallones were important landmarks for Spanish sea captains before the discovery of the Bay in 1769. Following their sixth sense about the nature of the landscape, they always sailed outside the islands to ensure safe navigation, missing the chance to realize the significance of the tiny opening of the Golden Gate from afar and postponing the discovery of the Bay for centuries.

Just as Charles Darwin noticed the relatively recent evolution of species on the remote Galapagos Islands, a present-day visitor to the Farallon Islands is struck by the profusion of bird life there, which includes species rarely seen along the California coast. When first setting foot on these unique islands, even the most veteran observer of Bay Area wildlands experiences a clear sense of the exotic, of being a traveler in a foreign place. The Farallones are indeed a refuge for species that could not live in such numbers along California's mainland coast, where predators—including humans—would rapidly destroy colonies that depend on isolation for survival.

The Farallones hold many species, such as the tufted puffin and Cassin's auklet, that are most often associated with the subarctic waters of Alaska, Iceland, and Norway. Great numbers of northern elephant seals and two different species of sea lion also make their homes on these windblown, treeless islands. All these creatures have a good chance of surviving, locked in their separate island world, until the interglacial period in which we are now living ends and the ocean drops away to merge the Farallones with the mainland once more. When that happens, in the not-so-distant geological future, the islands will no longer serve as separate habitats, protected from mainland predators by the ocean and from curious humans by federal edict.

The distinctive geography of the Farallon Islands forces the few Bay Area residents lucky enough to view them at close range to adopt the perspective of an adventure traveler, but the islands are far from alone in this regard. The mountains that rim most of the Bay Area, though not particularly high, are just wild and remote enough to bring out the innate curiosity and urge to explore that lurks under the skin of even the most jaded urban dweller. To drive along a high ridge, perhaps to a summit, often is not enough to awaken such inclinations, but to get out and walk a trail on a clear day is to have the best of both worlds. One can experience the fresh new world of a traveler in an exotic land yet still hold on to the familiar and comfortable one of the local resident.

I feel this duality especially strongly when I am at the top of Mount Diablo, which rises to a modest elevation of 3,849 feet on the eastern edge of the Bay Area. Because of the mountain's unique situation above flat valleys and far from significantly higher mountains, the land area visible from its summit is vast; in fact, it is estimated to be the largest in the United States. The entire Bay Area is spread out below, and on a clear winter day the snowy crest of the High Sierra stretches for hundreds of miles across the horizon.

When the High Sierra is visible, the range so dominates the eastern horizon that it is easy to forget there are other mountains about the size of Diablo on both sides of the South Bay. Loma Prieta rises 3,791 feet over the Santa Clara Valley in the Santa Cruz Mountains to the west, and Mount Rose rises 3,817 feet from a continuation of the Diablo Range in southern Alameda County's Ohlone Regional Wilderness to the east of the Bay. Just outside this book's forty-mile radius from the perimeter of San Francisco, east of San Jose, Copernicus Peak rises slightly higher than Mount Diablo, at 4,373 feet. Surprisingly clear infrared photographs of Half Dome in Yosemite have been made through the astronomical telescope atop nearby 4,209-foot Mount Hamilton.

Though the Bay Area's heights attract visitors with their breathtaking views, the lowlands, sculpted by moving waters into diverse forms, have a special appeal of their own. The Delta area, for example, is the result of the great San Joaquin and Sacramento Rivers coursing down from the High Sierra and depositing sands and soils from far away. The powerful tides that rush through the Golden Gate into the Bay and back again originate in the great Pacific Ocean. Yet these waterborne forces are all too easily taken for granted. In many urban parts of the Bay Area, great efforts have been made to negate their effects with dams, levees, landfills, breakwaters, and bridges.

It is no coincidence that many of the most eloquent descriptions of journeys in the wilds of the Bay Area have come from the fresh eyes and pens of travelers rather than from residents. John Muir's poetic description of seeing "the Range of Light" from the wildflower-carpeted Coast Ranges above the Bay recounts a novel experience he had just days after arriving in California in 1868. Later, as a Bay Area resident, he fell into the trap of familiarity, and his writings never again reflected the sense of wonder he expressed in his first days here. We owe him a great debt—not so much for what he did or wrote concerning the Bay Area but more for the parks and preserves he worked so hard to create elsewhere in America, which provided a model for later generations to use here. It is this, combined with the wilderness consciousness he engendered through his writings, that enables Bay Area residents and visitors today to experience a wildness not unlike what Muir pursued and cherished in other parts of the American West. European cities have their manicured parks and gardens, but they have nothing whatsoever to match San Francisco's unique integration of metropolis and natural world.

I can think of no better example of how the modern Bay Area's lands and waters can influence the human spirit in an urban setting than the words of resident writer Harold Gilliam. In a booklet published by the Golden Gate National Park Association, he describes the broader meaning of the preservation of the wild Marin Headlands, rising just across the Bay from San Francisco:

> The ocean, which shaped these headlands, was the first geological feature on Earth and the source of the life that eventually spread across the continents. The marine creatures swimming offshore here represent our own "ancestors". . . .
>
> Life slowly emerged from the waters to the land—first the sea plants that could grow in brackish water and evolved to survive on the shores, then amphibious animals that developed into land dwellers. . . . Plant and animal life spread from the lagoons and ponds and streams to the riparian zones along the shores, the meadows, and the hillsides, developing over the eons into the many forms we encounter there today. Back in the ocean are seals and sea lions and whales—mammals that evolved on land and returned to the sea.
>
> Perhaps as residents of the cities around the Bay, we are metaphorically undergoing a parallel return of our own—in a faster time frame. Our species first lived in the wilds, then became urban dwellers and are now returning as visitors to the natural scenes from which we came. As we begin to spend more time in nature and to understand its work-ings, we are perhaps "evolving" into creatures who will adapt our ways of living and working to the needs and processes of the natural environment, the Earth itself. In this sense, the close encounter of the urban with the natural . . . can offer a view of the future as well as the past.

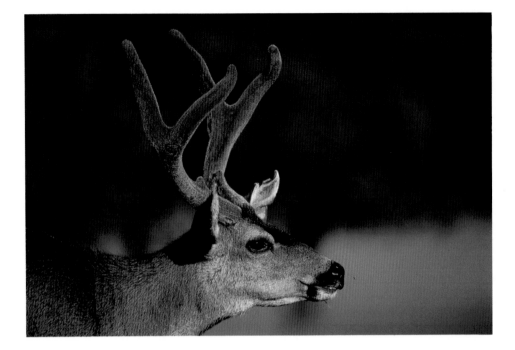

*A lone egret (**right**) struts through the shallow waters of Rodeo Lagoon in the GGNRA. The exceptionally crimson twilight sky color is due to suspended particulate matter from the 1991 eruption of Mount Pinatubo a few weeks earlier. A black-tailed buck (**above**) in fall velvet raises his head from grazing open grasslands on Mount Tamalpais.*

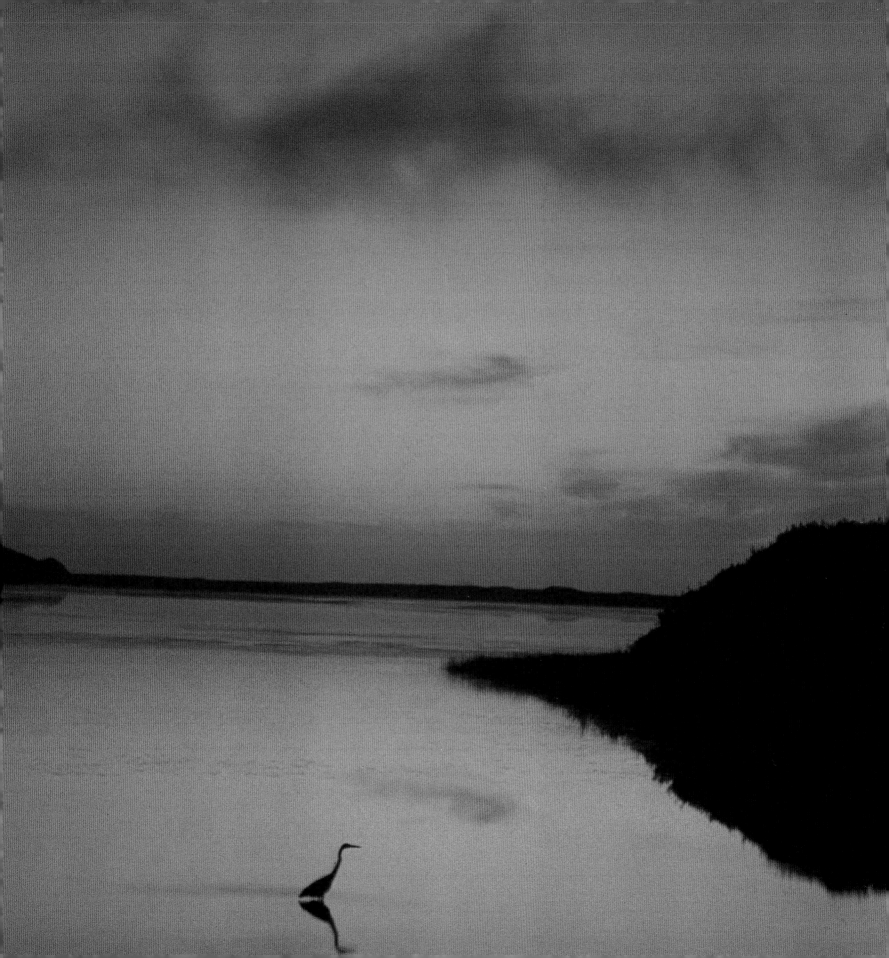

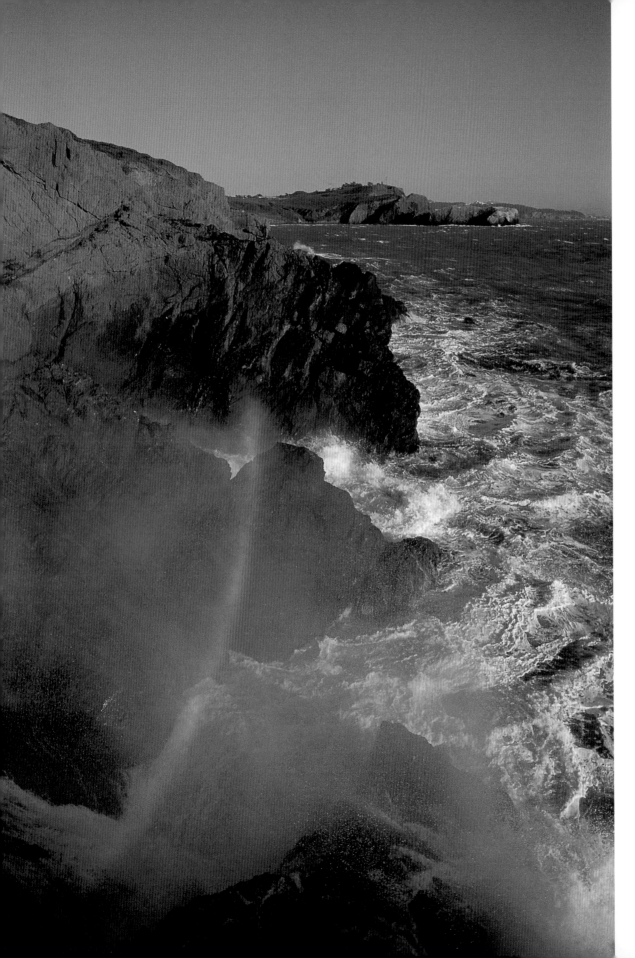

*Breaking surf creates a rainbow (**left**) over the sea cliffs of the Marin Headlands in the GGNRA. Farther north along the coast at Mickey's Beach, a rock climber (**right**) scales an incredibly overhanging sea cliff by a direct route aptly named Endless Bummer.*

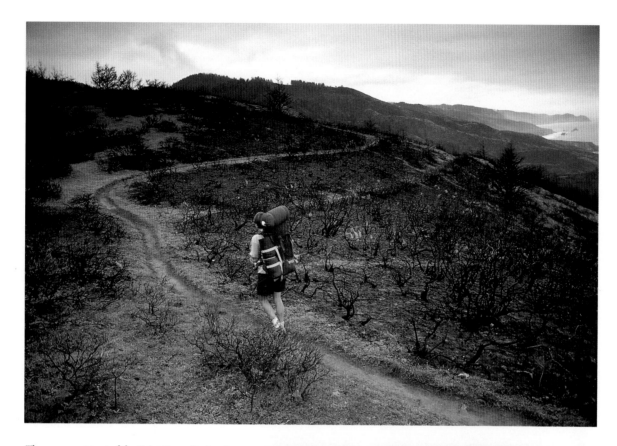

The narrowest part of the Point Reyes Peninsula, near its northern tip (**left**), is shown in this aerial view across Tomales Bay in the rift zone of the San Andreas Fault. Though the mainland on the opposite side appears close, it is 310 miles distant to geologists, who have found rocks matching the peninsula that far down the fault, in southern California. At Point Reyes during the 1906 earthquake, the fault shifted twenty-one feet. In the hills above Drakes Bay (**above**), a backpacker on the Woodward Valley Trail walks through winter greenery sprouting beside charred shrubs soon after the disastrous 1995 Point Reyes fire. Needles of frost (**right**) coat the leaves of a rare plant, Sidalcea calycosa, popularly called Point Reyes checkerbloom.

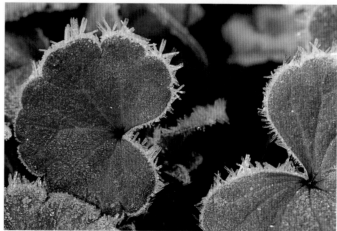

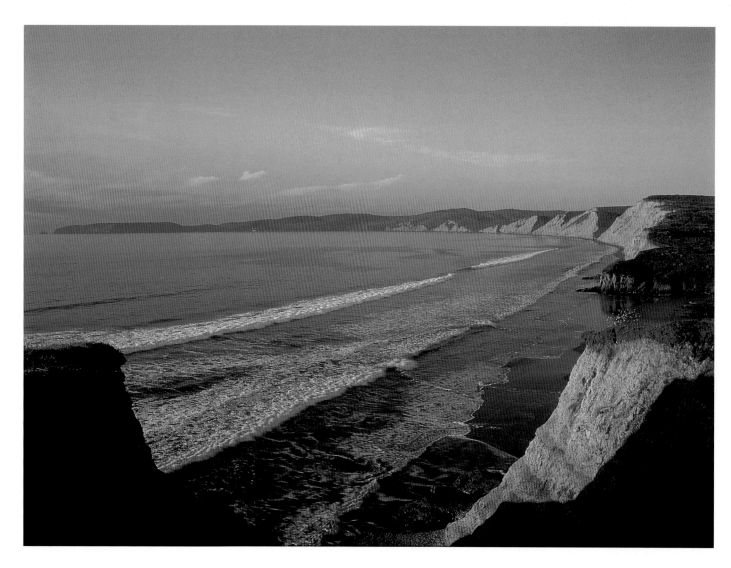

*A dip in a fog bank over the Pacific Ocean (**left**) reveals the last moment of sunset above a wind-flagged Monterey pine on Mount Tamalpais. Belying the west-facing trend of the Pacific coast, Drakes Beach (**above**), at Point Reyes National Seashore, catches the first light of sunrise where the shores of Drakes Bay arc around to face southeast before rounding the distant tip of Point Reyes.*

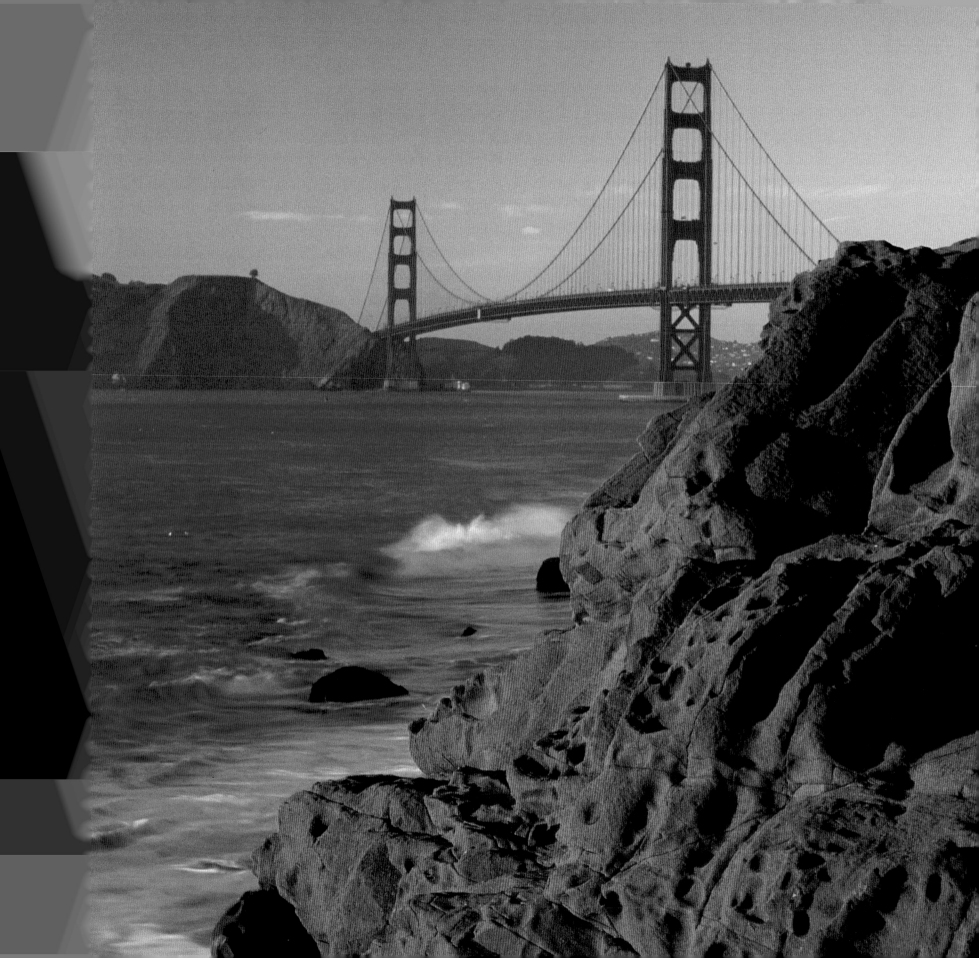

P E N I N S U L A   &   S O U T H   B A Y

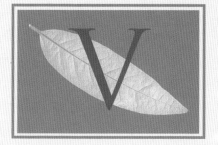

iewed at night from afar, the glowing tip of the Peninsula, moated on three sides by salt water, looks like a city of dreams. Borders as sharp as medieval walls hold back suburban sprawl. Golden Gate Park and the Presidio of San Francisco stand out here as stripes of darkness. Rugged highlands on the city's fourth side stem the urban tide with natural preserves. Beyond fifty square miles of the San Francisco Watershed in the valley of the San Andreas Fault, county parks, national park lands, and dozens of recently created regional open space preserves extend south through San Mateo and Santa Clara Counties.

Highway 1 traces a winding path along the western edge of the Peninsula between the ocean and a rural landscape with development held in check by the California Coastal Commission. Beyond Half Moon Bay and a series of state beaches, Año Nuevo State Reserve hosts as many as 2,000 elephant seals during breeding season. The old-growth redwood forest of nearby Big Basin became the first state park in 1902 after local grassroots action.

The Farallon Islands, twenty-five miles out to sea, harbor the nation's largest breeding colony of seabirds outside Alaska. The San Francisco Bay National Wildlife Refuge, on the inland side of the Peninsula, protects large areas of wetlands and endangered wildlife.

Protection in the Santa Clara Valley began in 1872 with state designation of Alum Rock as a recreational park. Newer county parks and open space preserves in the Diablo Range and the Santa Cruz Mountains complete the full spectrum of Bay Area natural environments.

The Golden Gate from Baker Beach, GGNRA

Looking like a celestial city floating in the clouds, downtown San Francisco lies partly veiled in twilight fog in this extreme telephoto view from the Berkeley Hills. San Francisco writer Harold Gilliam describes how the advance of summer fog over the Bay "brings word of the elemental forces with which city-dwellers too often lose touch— the turning of the earth, the flowing of the ocean waters, the rising of the giant winds."

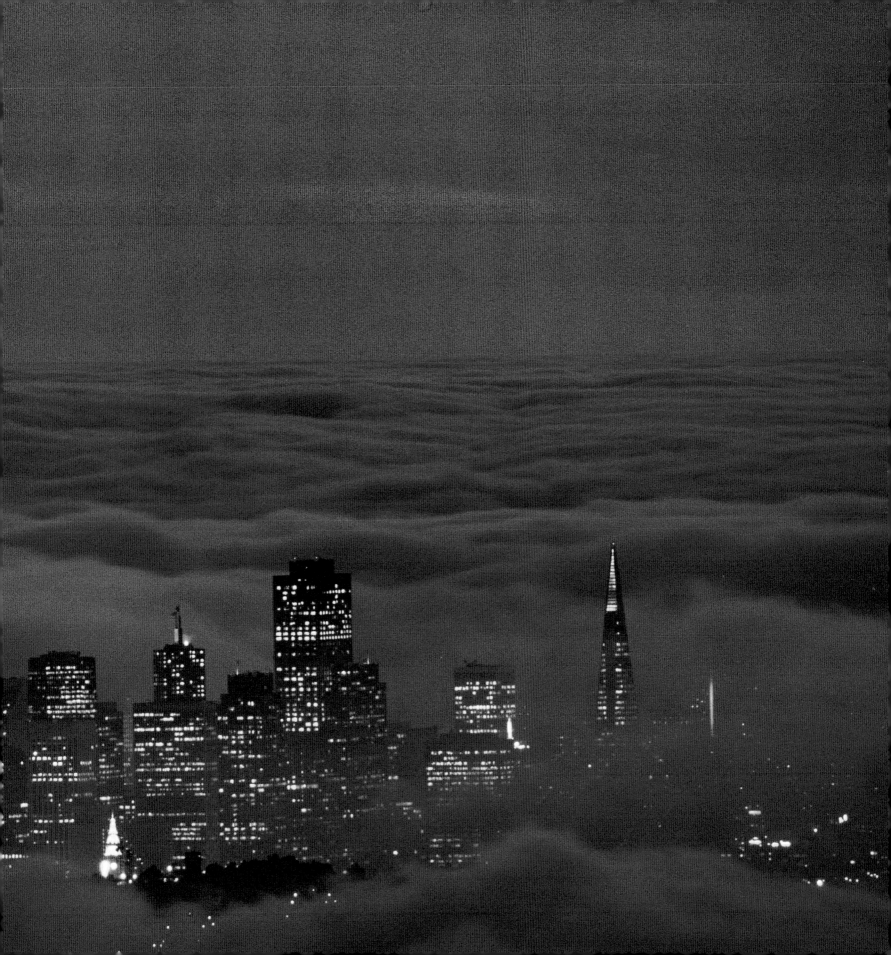

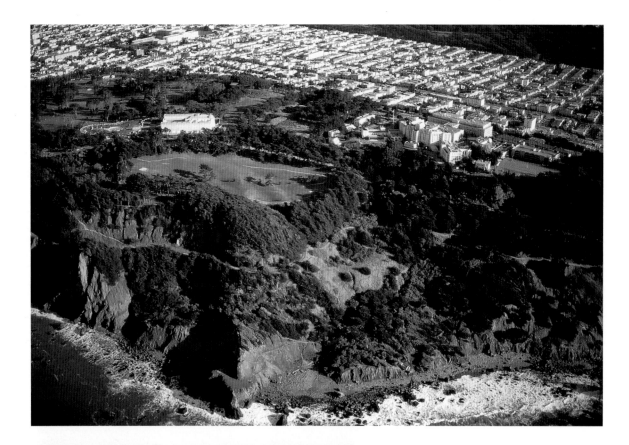

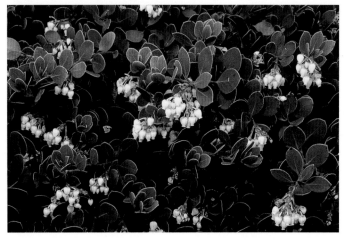

*From the air, a portion of the 1,480 acres of the Presidio of San Francisco (**above**) stands out as the city's most natural and spectacular chunk of open space. After more than two centuries of military control by Spain, Mexico, and finally the U.S. government, these partly wild lands at the southern end of the Golden Gate Bridge are now administered by the National Park Service as part of the GGNRA. Native wildflowers (**right**) abound in spring on the floor of a cypress forest. A Russian naturalist who combed the Presidio grounds in 1816 named thirty-three new species. Today, only a single highly endangered Presidio manzanita (**left**) survives in the wild, though it has grown a few nearby clones.*

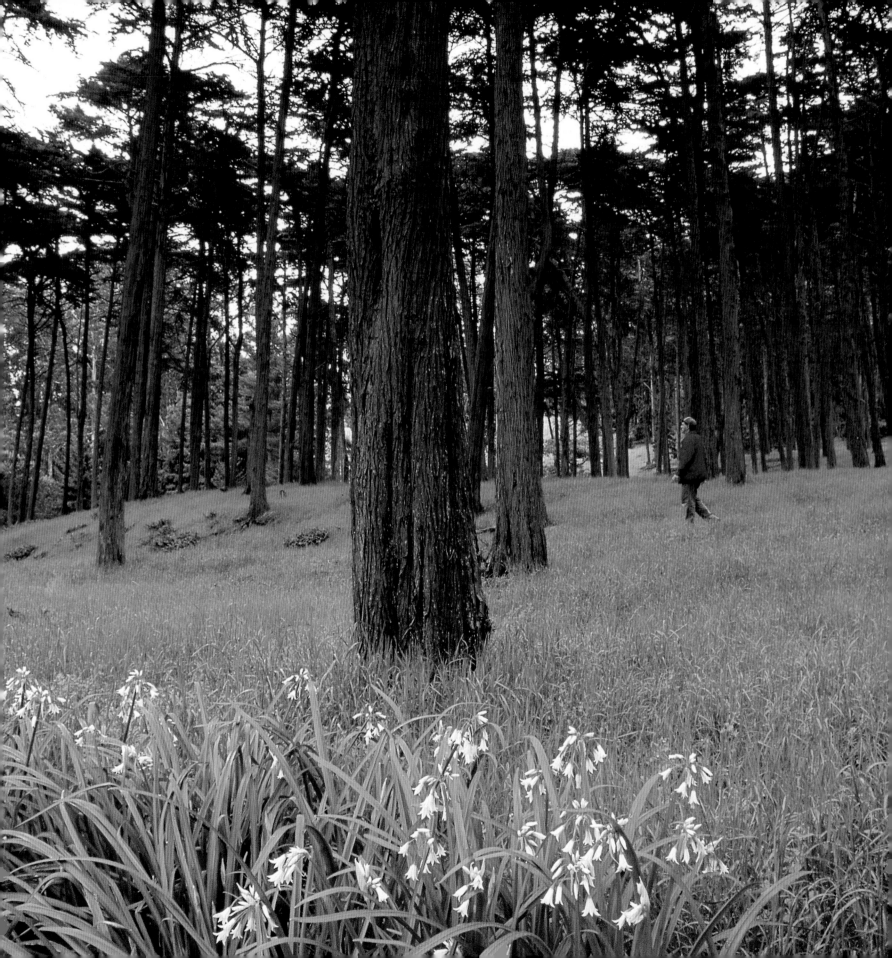

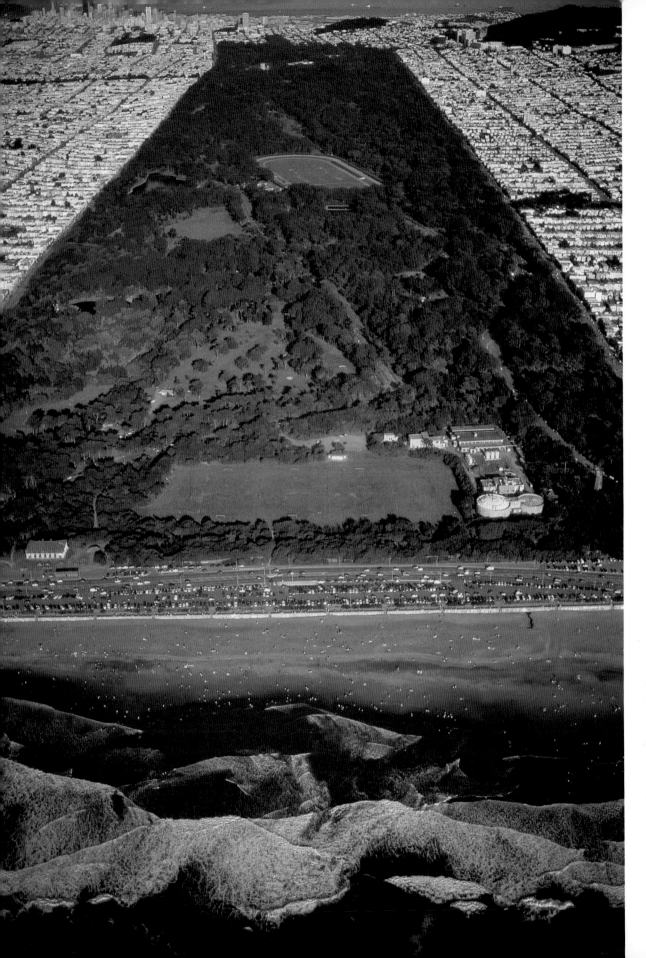

The classic greenbelt of Golden Gate Park (**left**) stretches from Ocean Beach well across San Francisco toward the Bay, but it is not a true natural preserve. The unique appearance of these 1,017 urban acres of open space is due to their having been designed, landscaped, and planted to create a city woodland and cultural park on top of reclaimed sand dunes. Another aerial view (**right, below**) shows the park as one of many greenbelts of open space visible from over San Francisco, including the Presidio, the Marin Headlands, and Angel Island State Park. Pier 39, near Fisherman's Wharf, is the best place in the Bay Area to get a close look at California sea lions (**right, above**), which bask daily around the structure.

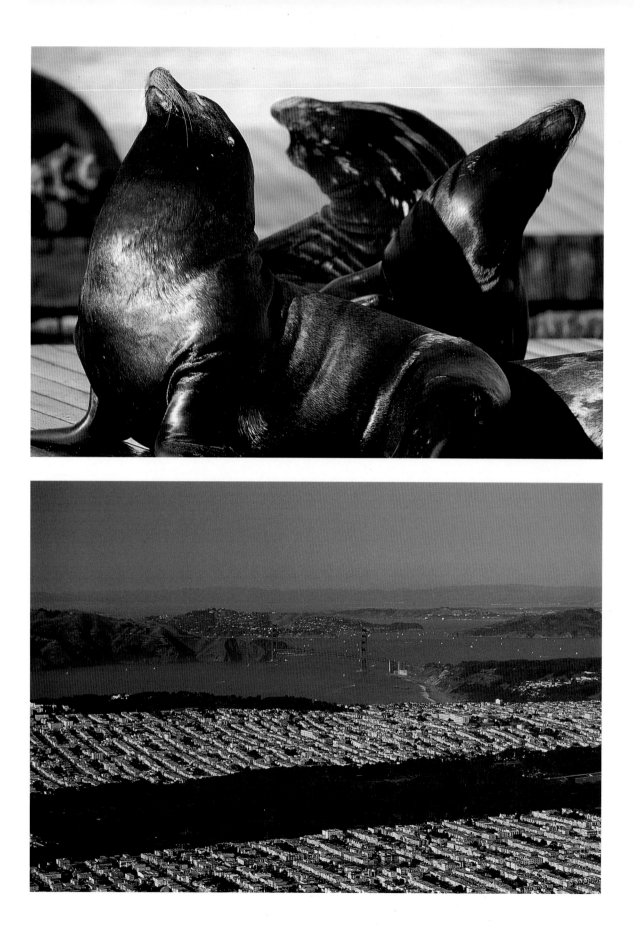

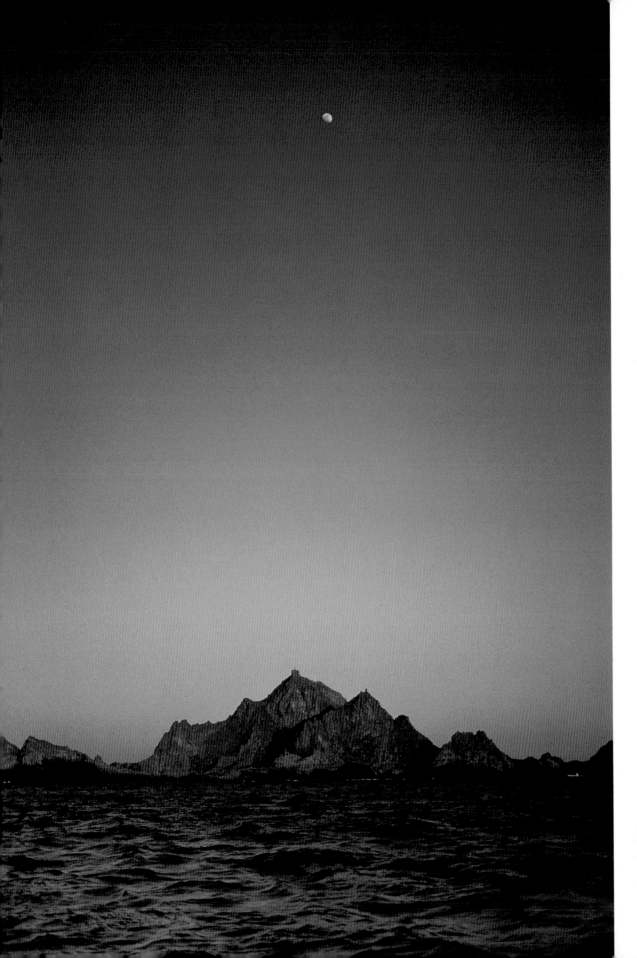

*The Farallon Islands (**left**), twenty-seven miles out to sea from the Golden Gate, are at the heart of the Gulf of the Farallones National Marine Sanctuary, which protects 948 square nautical miles of the Pacific Ocean as well as coastal bays, estuaries, and lagoons from Bolinas to Bodega Bay.*

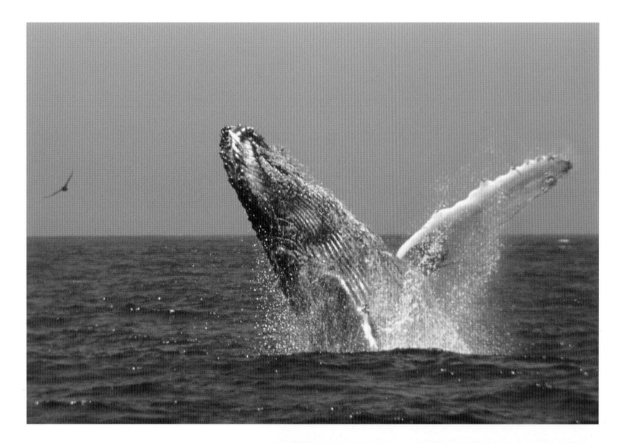

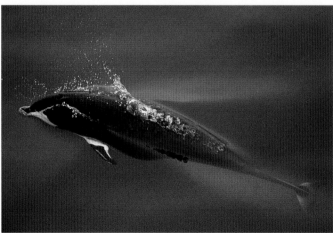

Northern right whale dolphins (right) are among the twenty-three species of marine mammal found in the sanctuary. Both humpback (above) and gray whales are commonly seen during the winter months, either at a distance from the coast or more closely on whale-watching day cruises from the mainland. The islands are closed to visitation except for research and official business under a complex fabric of governmental controls. The waters of the sanctuary are managed by the National Oceanic and Atmospheric Administration. The land of the islands constitutes the Farallon National Wildlife Refuge of the U.S. Fish and Wildlife Service, monitored under contract by the Point Reyes Bird Observatory but legally within the city limits of San Francisco.

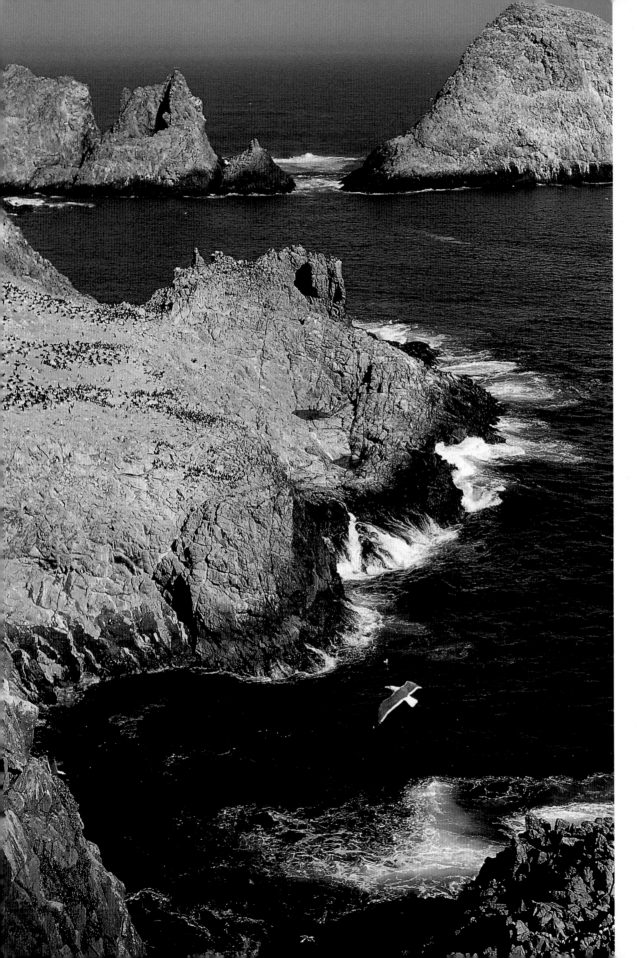

*A western gull (**left**) soars over a cove on Southeast Farallon Island beside tens of thousands of nesting birds. The Farallon group of seven islands houses the largest seabird breeding colony in the contiguous forty-eight states. Seen from the air (**right**), the granite rock spires rising like an apparition from the shimmering ocean give no hint that they were once connected to the southern Sierra Nevada. Sixty million years of movements of the San Andreas Fault shifted them more than 300 miles apart.*

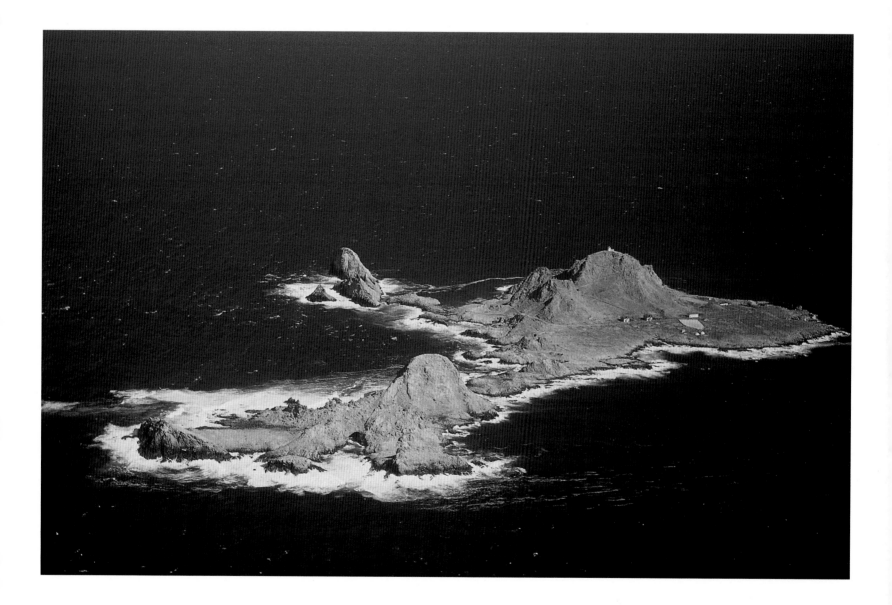

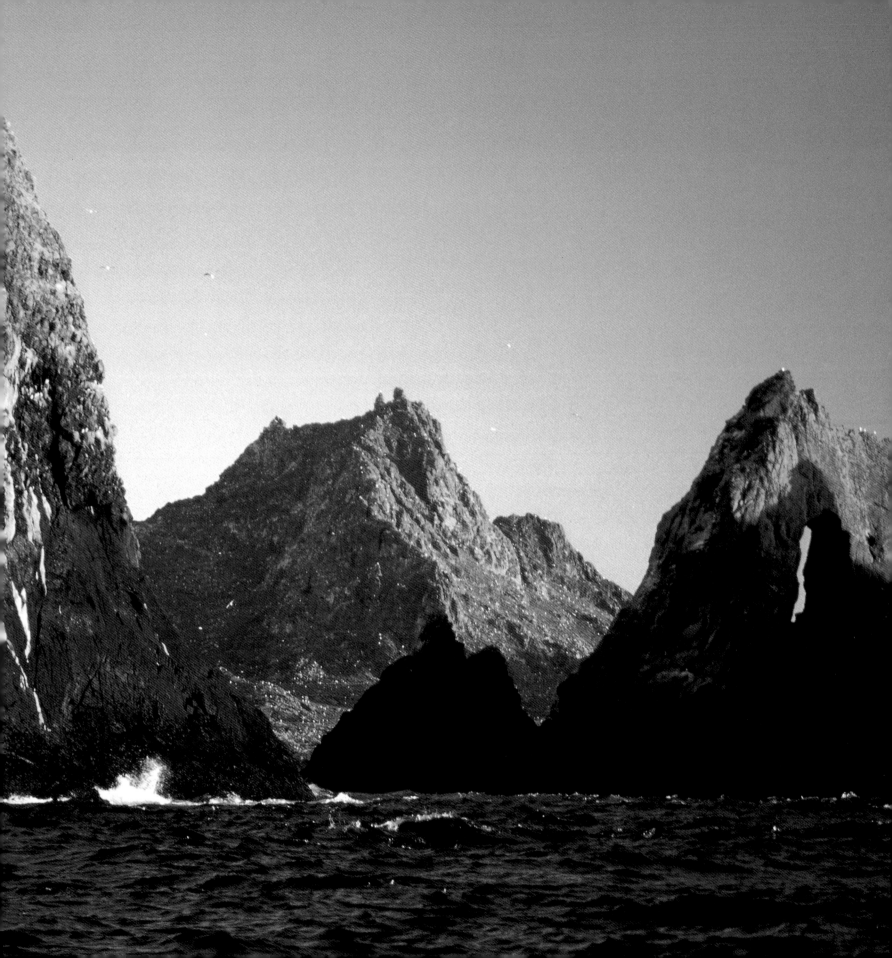

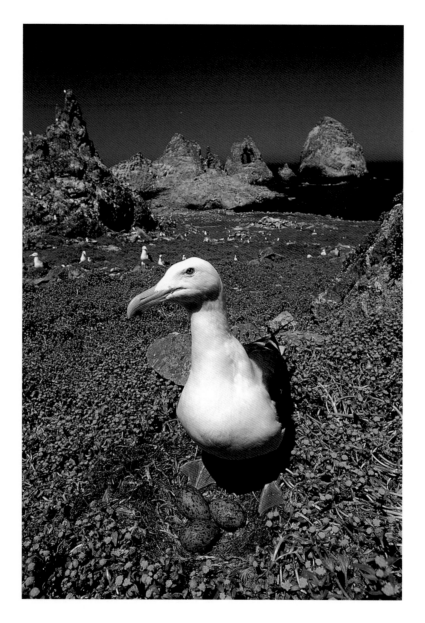

*The rugged Farallon Islands rise abruptly out of the sea (**left**) in this view from a departing boat at sunset. Behind a western gull (**above**) sitting on its nest on Southeast Farallon Island, the same offshore rocks are seen from the opposite direction. The lush ground cover is known as Farallon weed, an annual herb of the sunflower family that covers marine terraces with vivid yellow blossoms every spring. The plant is endemic to the Farallones, a few other small islands, and patches of ground at Point Reyes where seabirds from these islands have deposited both seed and fertilizer.*

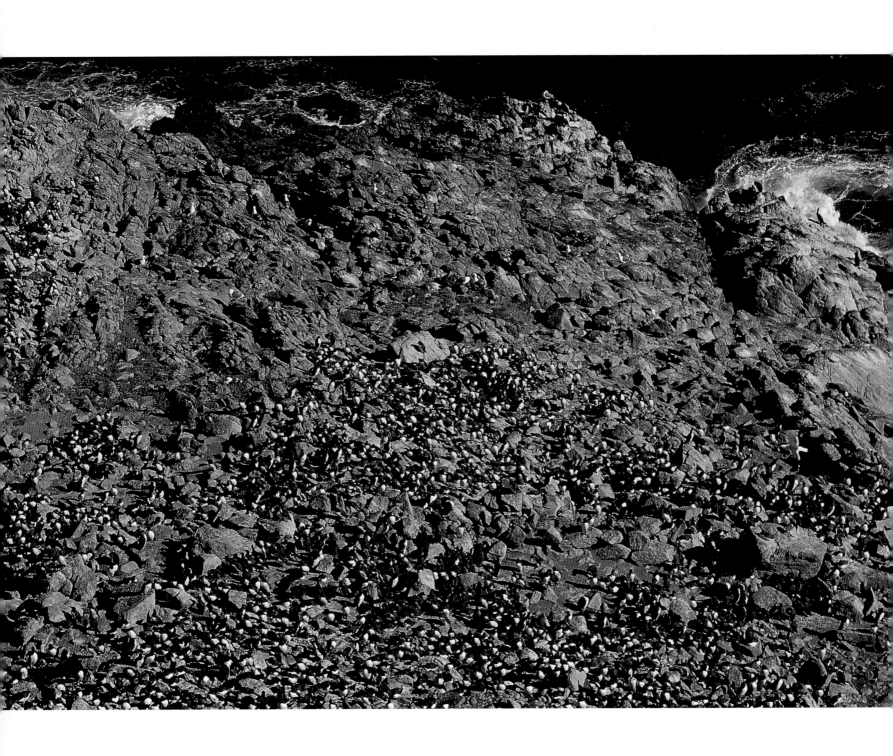

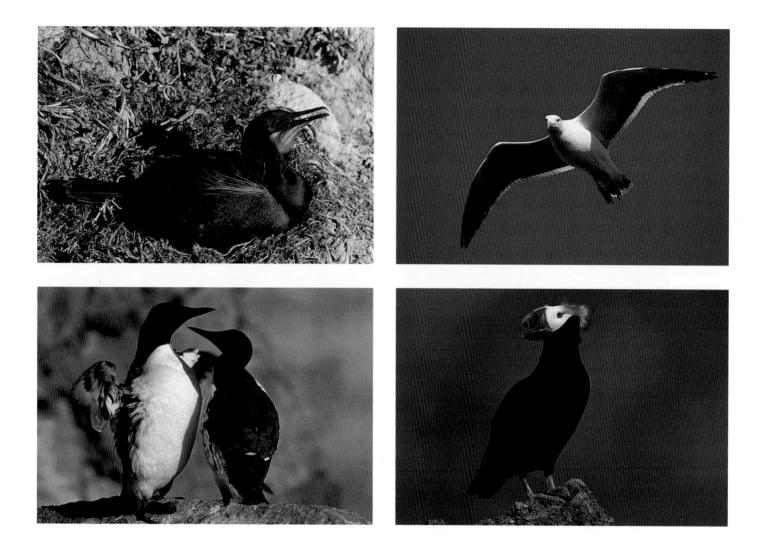

Thousands of common murres (**left**) *nest on the sea cliffs of the Farallon Islands, where more than 370 bird species have been recorded. Among the most significant nesting species of the islands' 250,000 annual visitors are* (**above, clockwise from top left**) *Brandt's cormorants, western gulls, tufted puffins, and common murres.*

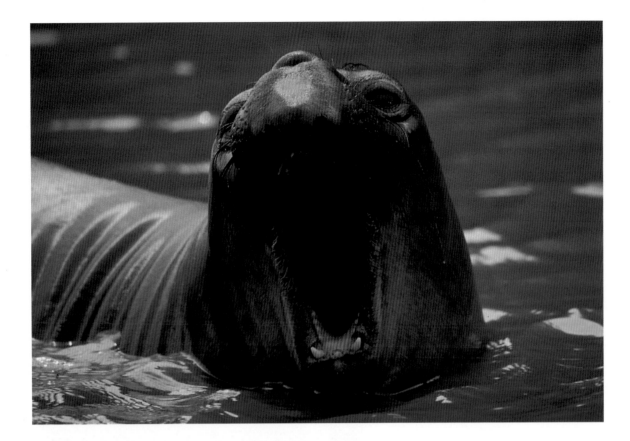

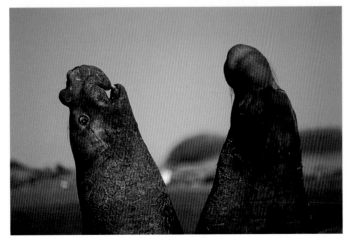

Elephant seals up to sixteen feet long and weighing two and a half tons strut ashore each winter to fight, molt, mate, and give birth at Año Nuevo State Reserve. A young bull (**above**) is a handsome fellow—for an elephant seal—but older bulls (**left**) have grotesquely extended proboscises and many scars. From hundreds of thousands, the population of northern elephant seals dropped below a hundred before the turn of the century. After protection, the first returnees came to Año Nuevo in 1955, the first pup was born in 1975, and today more than 2,000 animals show up each year. The 4,000-acre state reserve includes miles of shoreline, seen behind a sea stack (**right**) crowned with gulls and cormorants in this dawn view from Pigeon Point.

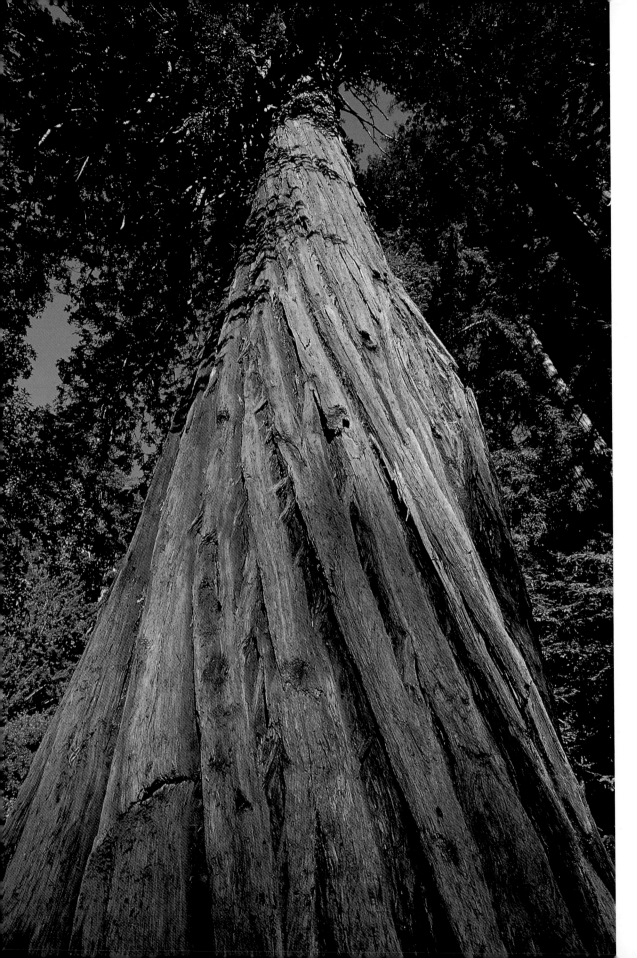

The redwood groves (left) of Big Basin Redwoods State Park in the Santa Cruz Mountains are among the world's finest—by default. More than 95 percent of the world's old-growth redwoods have now been cut. A photographer named Andrew Hill formed the Sempervirens Club, which acquired the forest as the first state park

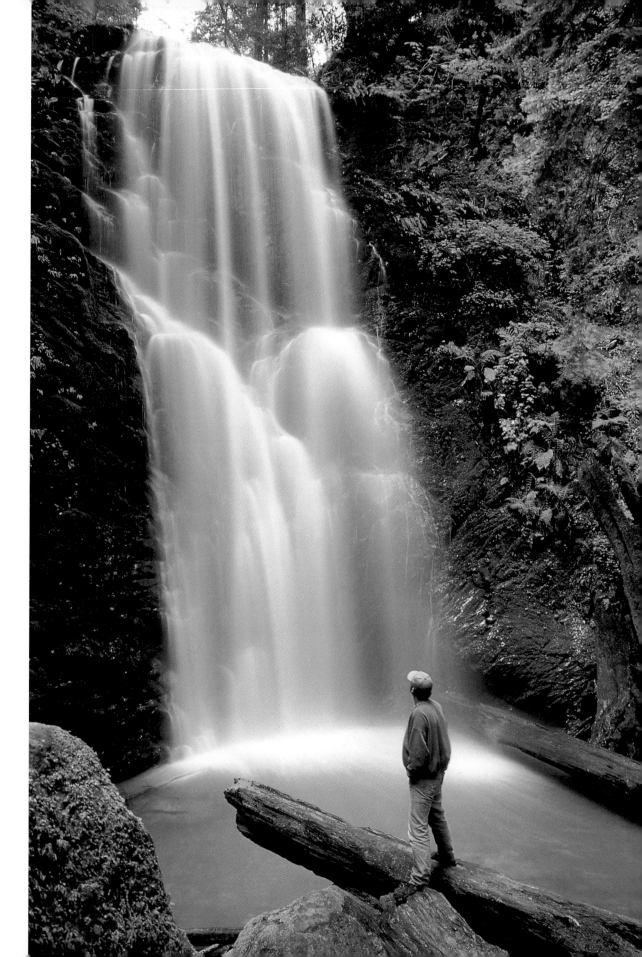

in 1902, after a landowner prevented him from taking photographs of the trees. Hill considered them "among the natural wonders of the world" that "should be saved for posterity." The 18,000-acre park also includes the remote and powerful Berry Creek Falls (**right**), *seen here at high water after a winter storm.*

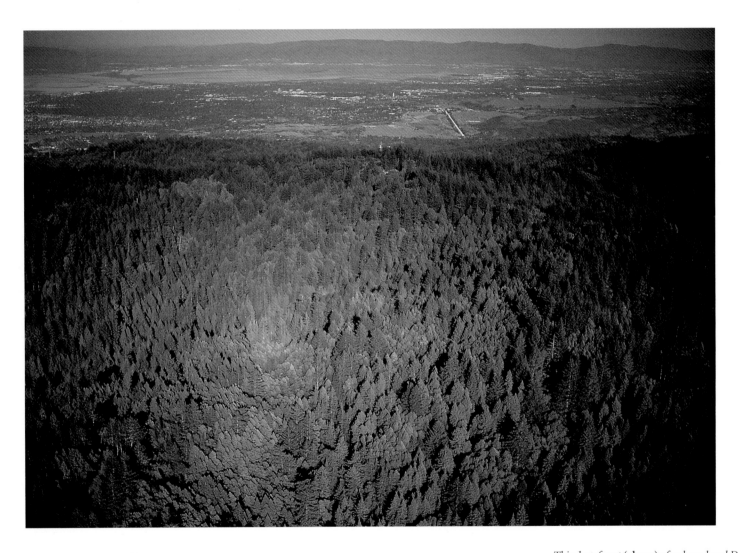

*This deep forest (**above**) of redwood and Douglas fir on the western slope of the Santa Cruz Mountains sits high above the South Bay and the mile-long Stanford University linear accelerator, visible in the distance. It was acquired as the El Corte de Madera Creek Open Space Preserve by the Midpeninsula Regional Open Space District in 1985. Since 1972, the district has created twenty-two other preserves, including the Duveneck Windmill Pasture Area (**right**), on the slopes of Black Mountain. Here, the intense green of a lone bay tree seems to glow against a shadowed forest beneath a stormy evening sky.*

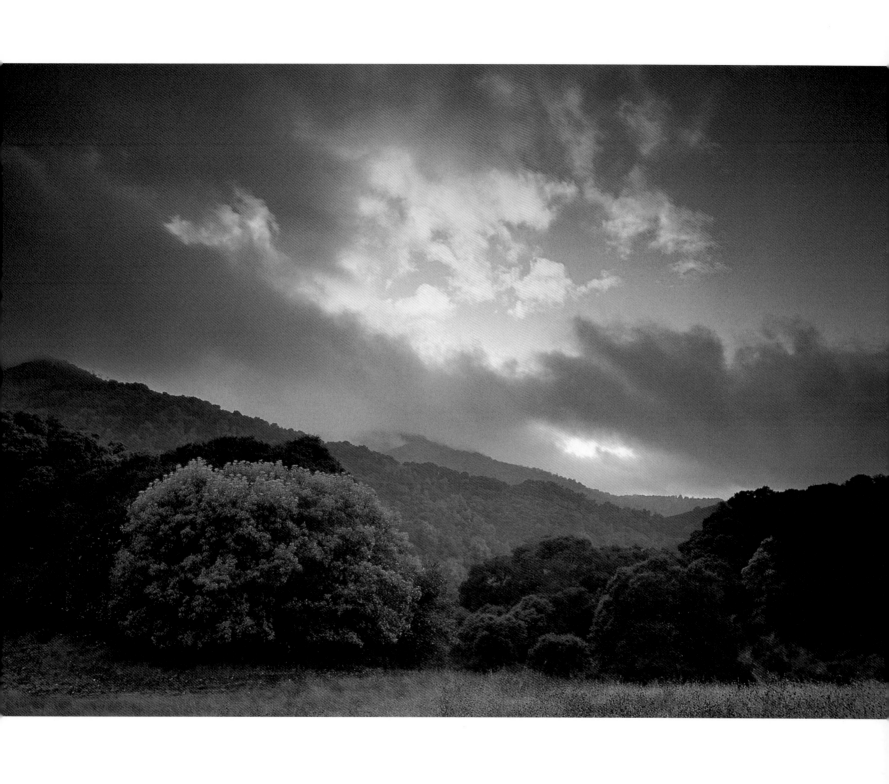

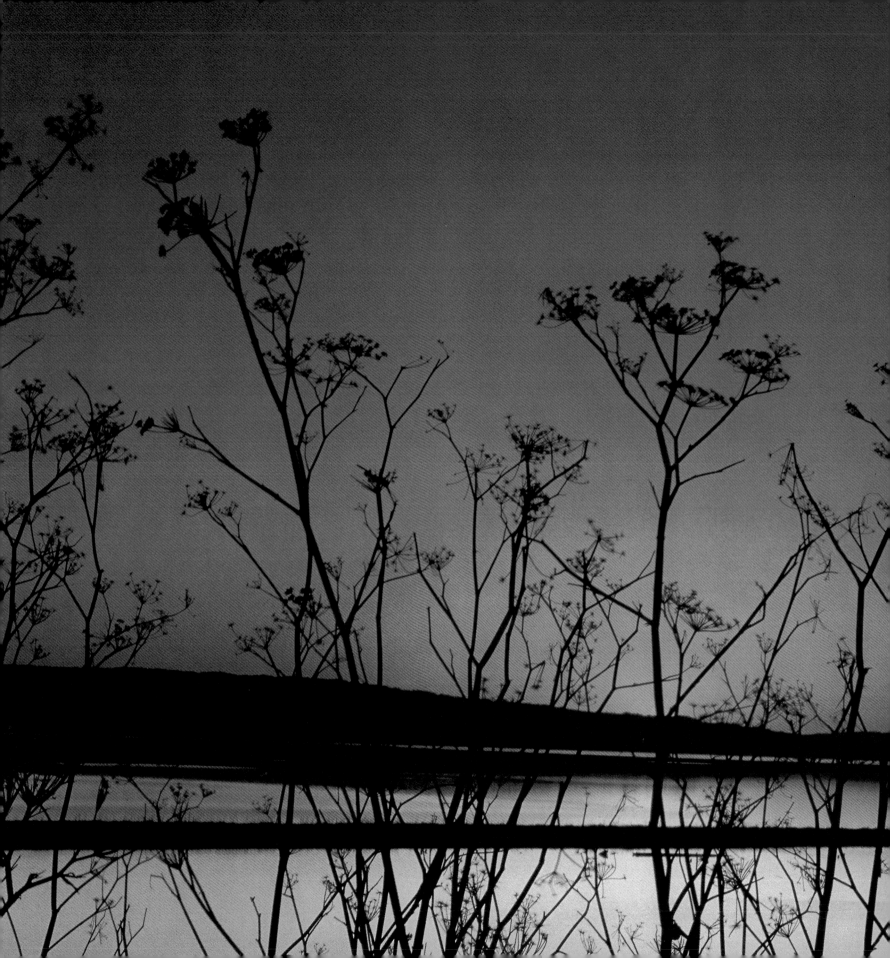

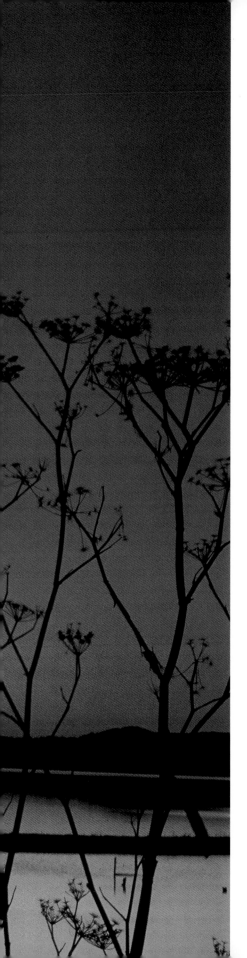

Living Visionaries

These two concluding chapters focus on the motivations of some of the Bay Area's most successful environmental activists. Much of the information in them comes from a series of personal interviews. My aim in conducting these interviews was to move beyond the usual chronologies of political victories to gain deeper insight into what emotional experiences empowered these individuals to take action. Their diverse responses not only help explain why the Bay Area has a higher degree of environmental protection than any other large metropolitan area in America but also suggest some things that must be done to maintain and further that position.

I wanted to keep the number of people interviewed small and intimate, yet I also felt the need to reflect views from several different regions, agencies, and advocacy groups. Thus I narrowed down my list to a few individuals who have spearheaded protection efforts for the National Park Service, the Sierra Club, the Save San Francisco Bay Association, Save Mount Diablo, People for a Golden Gate National Recreation Area, the Midpeninsula Regional Open Space District, and the East Bay Regional Park District.

My fascination with the relationship between preserved areas and those who have gone out of their way to save them dates back to childhood. Over the course of hundreds of visits to wildlands on seven continents, I have yet to find any place saved strictly by the vote of a democratic majority or the benevolence of a government. Passionate individuals have always played a leading role.

I did my first interview with an inspired conservationist at age thirteen, for my junior high school civics class. The year was 1953, and I was writing a term paper about a proposal to build a dam on a tributary of the Colorado River within Dinosaur National Monument. Politics held little interest for me, but this issue caught my fancy because I felt a deep personal connection to the land and to the people who were most opposed to altering it.

I had visited Dinosaur with my family the previous summer and walked the edge of that wild river with my father as he told me that it might be no more. The very idea challenged some of my closely held assumptions about the world in which I lived. I also felt triggered in a more general sense. I had spent much of my young life trying to sort out which things I could count on as enduring entities. I had already decided to study rocks, rather than plants or animals, because they seemed as immutable as the mountains, the oceans, or the sky. I saw a stark contrast between the impermanence of the man-made cities that were creeping up the East Bay hills all around our family home and the timeless High Sierra wilderness we visited for several weeks each year on Sierra Club outings. I thought that lands administered by the National Park Service were supposed to be kept forever inviolate. I had also placed the giant rock form and wild river junction we saw in Dinosaur into the mental

Seen across the South Bay at sunset, the northern Santa Cruz Mountains of the Peninsula dominate the skyline through a curtain of fennel in Coyote Hills Regional Park, on the East Bay shoreline.

compartment marked "enduring" until I received the rude shock of learning that the primeval scene was soon to be flooded.

After we returned home, my father told me that a man on my Berkeley newspaper route had just testified before Congress to stop the dam. In doing so, David Brower, the Sierra Club's executive director, was leading our small California outing club into its first political commitment on a major environmental issue outside its home state. A former mountain climber with many first ascents to his credit, Brower was boldly stepping into uncharted terrain that would eventually transform the organization into a global force for preservation. Dinosaur was saved, and in future decades Brower would be described as the archdruid of conservation and would receive two separate nominations for the Nobel Peace Prize.

Though Brower has been called "the most effective conservation activist in the world today" by the *New York Times* and continues to live in that same house in the Berkeley Hills on my old newspaper route, I decided that his profile doesn't fit this chapter. Instead, I asked him to write a foreword for this book recounting some of his boyhood experiences in Bay Area wildlands and how they shaped his later life. Brower, like John Muir before him, appreciated the wild areas around his home yet directed most of his conservation efforts farther afield. As Brower recalls, "It was far more fun to look across the state from the High Sierra to Mount Diablo than to look at Diablo from the Berkeley Hills."

The scenario of preservation in the Bay Area is clearly different from that in more remote parts of the world. Efforts to protect rugged environments usually begin with individuals who have an unusually strong spirit of adventure. The connection is so predictable that a common argument against legal protection is that an intrepid minority is trying to lock up public lands for its own use. Climbers, for example, have always been extremely visible in the environmental movement. In their later years, John Muir, David Brower, and Sir Edmund Hillary all refocused their considerable energies to create parks around peaks they had ascended and in wild valleys through which they had trekked. In the equally unexplored realm beneath the sea, Jacques Cousteau fought for protection of the oceans after he had intimately viewed them from within, thanks to his invention of the Aqua-Lung.

At first glance, the protection of more than two hundred natural areas around the Bay doesn't fit this pattern. Nor does the Bay Area's geography. Because the region lacks world-class mountain faces or ocean depths, there aren't many aging adventurers running around trying to preserve the sites of their most memorable achievements. To underscore this point, remember that two of the greatest conservationists in history—David Brower and John Muir—lived in the Bay Area yet had little to do with local preservation efforts. Both were adventurers in their youth who spent their later years living near the Bay and doing conservation work for regions far afield.

In contrast, the individuals most involved with creating Bay Area open space were not well known before they began their personal crusades. By focusing the majority of their efforts on grassroots acquisitions of private lands for the public good, their organizations appeal to a far broader political spectrum than do wilderness advocacy groups working toward restrictive political designations of existing public lands.

The passions that have moved these urban activists are just as firmly rooted in deeply felt natural experiences as are those of the great adventurers. If anything, simple emotional responses to beauty and solitude are more relevant to the general public. What the pattern of Bay Area preservation proves is that it doesn't take a world-class adventurer or a high-level politician to make a difference. One citizen powered by passion tempered with common sense can overcome the complacency of millions.

I have to number myself among those complacent millions who grew up around San Francisco Bay, unconcerned about its cumulative degradation. During my childhood, I locked it away in my mind as an enduring entity, something that would always be there, looking much the same.

Catherine Spaulding Kerr, on the other hand, not only avoided this mistake but took decisive action about it. As a young child growing up in Los Angeles during World War I, she spent countless summer afternoons on the beach at Santa Monica. The beauty of open water imprinted on her soul without her having much of an active physical involvement with it beyond an occasional swim. Similarly, she experienced the natural world out her back door at a time when Wilshire Boulevard was a country road running through broad areas of open space between small towns now subsumed by Los Angeles. When she went camping in the Sierra on family vacations, she avoided rugged hiking and climbing. By all accounts she was a most unlikely candidate to boldly spearhead the founding of the Save San Francisco Bay Association nearly half a century later.

"Why do people like hiking up steep trails and mountains?" she asked me in the living room of her East Bay home, perched atop a cliff high above the Bay. "You always have to look down at your feet and can't appreciate the beauty of the scenery. When you get to be eighty-five, like me, views of open space are just as important as when you're young. You realize how the very old and the very young are cut off from these views much of the time unless someone drives them to a place where they can see. You shouldn't have to get into a motor vehicle to see the Bay, but in most cases it's obscured even then by a wall of buildings, an opaque fence, or a bridge guardrail.

"I came up to the Bay Area to go to Stanford. Later, I was working in Los Angeles when one of my best friends from college contracted tuberculosis. She lived her last years in a Vallejo hospital, and I took a job in San Francisco in order to be closer to her. Every weekend I went back and forth across the Bay on a ferryboat. After being on the water and seeing it up close so often, I fell in love with the Bay and its natural beauty.

"After I got married, while my husband was a graduate student at Berkeley, we used to drive around looking at hilltops on which to someday build a dream house overlooking the Bay. We moved away for some years, but when we returned we built the first of two houses here in El Cerrito with a view of the Bay. After my husband became president of the University of California, I would often pick up important visitors at the airport and drive them back over the Bay Bridge to our home. They always commented on the Bay's beauty. But from our living room windows we began to see garbage fills in Albany and Berkeley encroaching into the open waters. My husband and I watched bulldozers level the trees around Point Isabel and fill in the little harbor there. In 1960, when I first saw that Army Corps of Engineers map showing the Bay as a river in the year 2020, I was already deeply concerned. Berkeley was developing a waterfront master plan that would fill 2,000 more acres of the Bay—virtually creating a second Berkeley rising out of the Bay."

Over tea at Berkeley's Town and Gown Club, Kerr had mentioned her worries to Sylvia McLaughlin, who replied that she would rather work on saving the Bay than on anything else she could think of. Another woman at the tea commented, "They say if you have three people, you can change the world." Kerr said jokingly to McLaughlin, "When I find a third person, I'll call you."

McLaughlin had developed broad organizational skills while working with civic and university groups, but she had no conservation background. Like Kerr, she had grown up in a more arid place than the Bay Area and had become attracted to the region's beauty only after moving here as an adult. Coming from Denver, where her father had managed city and mountain parks, she was naturally more active in the outdoors. In her spare time, she burned off some of her abundant energy by hiking and skiing. She was especially concerned with what the Bay meant to the people who lived around it and how much everyone had to lose.

Kerr enlisted a third faculty wife, Esther Gulick, who also had grown up in an arid place before moving to the Bay Area. Her family had a cattle ranch in the Central Valley, and they often came to San Francisco to visit relatives. After Gulick came to Berkeley to attend the university, she began to notice that something was happening to the Bay. Beyond watching the Bay slowly shrinking due to filling in of its shorelines, "smelling it when I went near the edge made me realize that something I loved and had grown up thinking was always going to be there maybe wasn't going to be. That was what really got me concerned." Among Gulick's special talents was a penchant for detailed management of administrative and financial tasks, which would prove invaluable in the very near future.

As described in chapter two, the threesome soon invited thirteen carefully selected conservationists and concerned citizens to a meeting at Gulick's Berkeley home overlooking the Bay. Kerr recalls how they felt in a terrible bind that night. Having decided that they were not conservationists, they were hoping to rely on others who had the expertise to deal with such issues. Yet one by one, representatives of the Audubon Society, Citizens for Regional Recreation and Parks, the East Bay Regional Park District, the Save-the-Redwoods League, and the Sierra Club expressed both their heartfelt concern and their inability to devote time or money to an issue outside their core missions of preserving birds, parks, trees, or wilderness. Finally, David Brower got up and said, "If nobody here can take on the job, somebody should start a new organization." He suggested that everyone present hand over their Bay Area mailing lists.

The odds against three faculty wives saving San Francisco Bay in 1961 were no greater than the odds of winning the California state lottery today. In those days, "ecology" was a term heard less often than "entomology." Environmental impact reports did not exist. The Wilderness Act had not been passed. Earth Day was almost a decade in the future. More than two hundred square miles of the Bay had been filled, and only 5 of 276 miles of shoreline were available for public access. Much of the water and shore access was controlled by powerful developers, politicians, port authorities, airports, railroads, and absentee landlords.

The three women, considered politically naive by some conservationists present that first evening, promptly stuffed 700 envelopes, sent them to Berkeley names on their mailing lists, and immediately got back more than 600 memberships in the newborn Save San Francisco Bay Association. When I asked Catherine Kerr and Sylvia McLaughlin how they managed to get such an unheard-of 90 percent direct-mail response, Kerr smiled and said, "We had a policy: never charge more than a dollar for membership. It's still that price today."

McLaughlin added, "I'd watched how city council members would listen politely when people spoke representing only themselves but would lean forward in their seats the moment they heard someone else say he or she represented a group of thus-and-so-many members. We cared less about the money than about representing a large number of people who cared, people who were willing to go to meetings or write to their legislators and governor. We ended up with more than 20,000 members—all volunteers."

Kerr recalled how their first newsletter announced that the Bay was for beauty and recreation. "We didn't learn about ecology until later." She then persuaded the area's most popular morning radio personality, Don Sherwood, to mention threats to the Bay that commuters could personally witness. He would say over and over again, "Don't drink your morning coffee until you've written to the governor and the legislature and told them how much you love the Bay."

Kerr also expressed a basic mistrust of do-gooders. "I don't like people who do things for other people. If you don't feel like you're doing it for yourself, it's not worth anything."

Ansel Adams, already revered as the greatest nature photographer of his generation, joined the advisory board and wrote strongly worded letters to politicians urging them to work to preserve the Bay's visual appearance. William Penn Mott became president of the association in 1963, spearheading its efforts to form

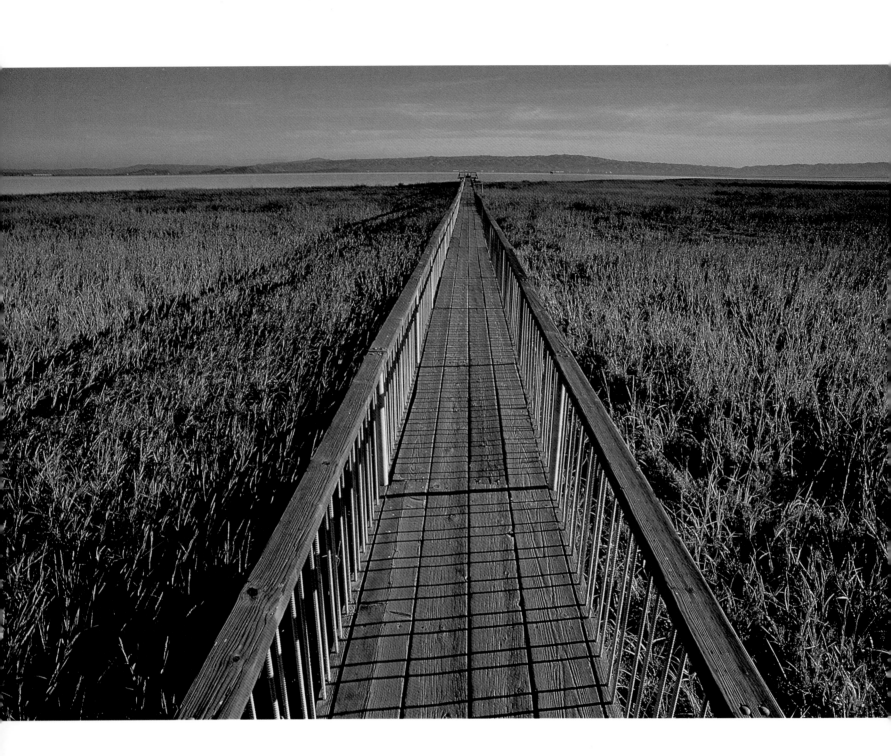

154

a state commission to stop the filling of the Bay and regulate both waters and shoreline. Mott was on his way up through an illustrious career in park management. A year earlier he had moved on from the city parks of Oakland to become general manager of the East Bay Regional Park District. He would eventually direct the California State Park System and, finally, the National Park Service. The faculty wives, however, were already working behind the scenes, at a level beyond his access.

Kerr's husband, Clark, had become president of the University of California System and a member of its board of regents, of which McLaughlin's husband, Don, was chairman. California's governor, Pat Brown, and lieutenant governor, Glenn Anderson, always attended the board's monthly meetings. The women took part in the dinners that followed. "We would be very careful to position ourselves next to one or the other to talk about the Bay, to the point that it became a joke," Kerr recalls.

After the women learned that the lieutenant governor was also legally designated as chairman of the State Lands Commission, they tried to determine from Anderson the specific location of the 50 percent of the Bay owned by the state, but he was unable to give them precise answers for quite some time, until he had researched the matter. When Kerr cornered him at the regents' dinners, he would say, "Now, Kay, I'll devote half our conversation to the Bay, but that's all."

A first bill in the state legislature to control filling of the Bay was defeated, but as grassroots action spread to every layer of the state's social, political, and media spectrums, unprecedented victories came in rapid succession. Berkeley halted its Bay development plans. The state legislature established a temporary San Francisco Bay Conservation and Development Commission in 1965 and voted it a permanent regional agency in 1969, signed into law by Governor Ronald Reagan with the comment "This bill will save the Bay," in one of his rare actions on behalf of the environment. The very next year, the campaign to save the Bay was singled out at the United Nations Conference on the Human Environment in Stockholm as an international model of citizens working together to control the powerful forces shaping their future surroundings.

When I asked Kerr and McLaughlin more than twenty-five years later if they were happy with the way the commission has worked out, Kerr said, "The history of the Bay Commission is unique. It saved the Bay because it's the only public commission, as far as I know, that represents every aspect of the community. Usually some elected body, like the state government, has a veto power, but there isn't any here. The commission involves public organizations like ours; the political entities of the Bay Area's nine counties and the cities, which each send a representative; the state, which sends two, appointed by the governor; plus the State Lands Commission and the federal government. They all have to cooperate, so the public interest is really served."

McLaughlin added: "We tried to get the commission a 1,000-foot shoreline jurisdiction, but the

A boardwalk across the preserved wetlands of the Palo Alto Baylands is conspicuously empty on a weekday winter morning while the salt marshes below teem with migratory shorebirds.

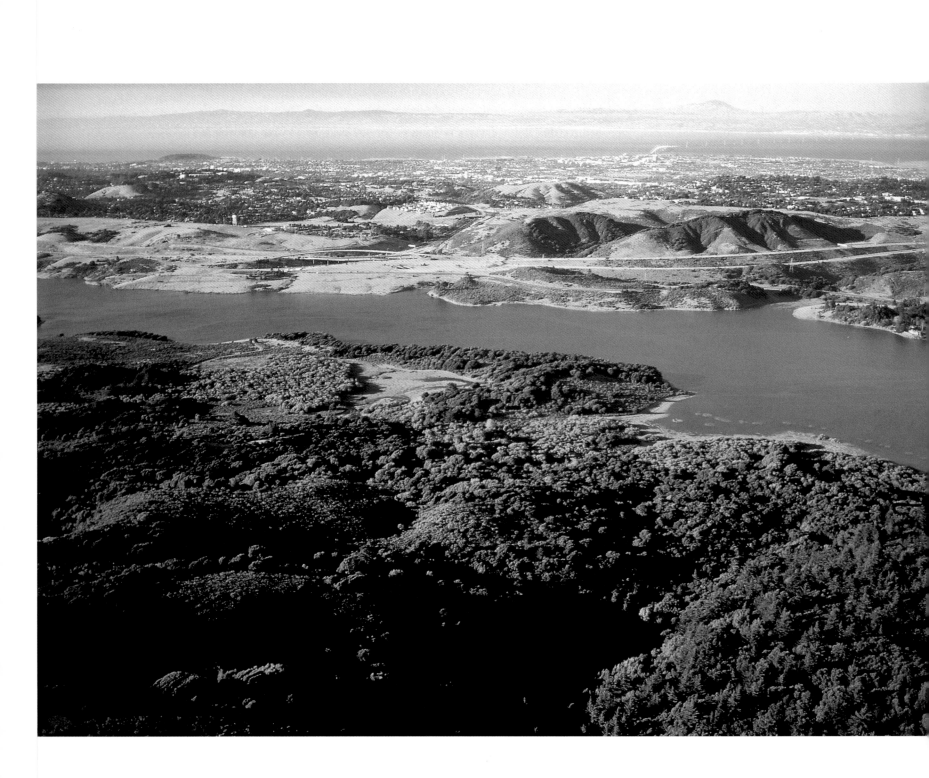

He rented me a gray wool tank suit, a towel, and a locker for fifty cents, and we went swimming. Afterward, we had to climb back up 1,600 feet! That almost ended a beautiful friendship. I didn't make it in to work the next day. After that first date, though, everything else on Tam seemed pretty easy."

"By the start of the sixties," Ed said, moving on with his narrative, "we had a vision of parklands extending from Tomales Bay to the Golden Gate across the entire Pacific coastline of Marin County. At about the same time, the federal government began declaring certain military lands as surplus. Other branches of the government, such as the National Park Service, had the right of first refusal. I began working with a group called The Headlands Incorporated to turn these lands into parks, but when the military parcels began to become available in Marin County, we couldn't get the National Park Service interested.

"Almost every park I've pushed for has at first met with objections from the National Park Service. They didn't want the added administrative and financial burdens. The manager of a duck club on the Point Reyes Peninsula told me that the federal government had never put up a dollar for a national park and wasn't going to do it now—yet the unique legislation that created Point Reyes National Seashore in 1962 did authorize $14 million to buy out ranchers. That was increased to $58 million within a few years."

Peggy interjected, "We had worse problems with inholdings in the Golden Gate National Recreation Area. Gulf Oil owned the whole Gerbode Valley, next to Tennessee Valley. In 1964 they revealed a plan in partnership with a developer to build Marincello, a city of 30,000 with luxury hotels and high-rises."

Ed continued, "We prevailed on the owners not to build there until the developer died, in 1969, and we found a benefactor—Martha Alexander Gerbode—to buy the entire valley for a million dollars and put it under the control of The Nature Conservancy until legislation could be passed.

"In January 1971, we formed People for Golden Gate National Recreation Area with Amy Meyer, and that April I went to Washington with a plan outlining 34,000 acres for inclusion. The two California senators and one local congressman thought we were asking for an awful lot, but they went along with it. Another local congressman, our San Francisco representative, Phil Burton, was a strong conservationist who later chaired the House Subcommittee on National Parks and Insular Affairs. He looked at me and asked, 'Is this what you want?'

"When I admitted that it wasn't, he said, 'Get the hell out of here and come back to me when you have what you want.'

"I told him I didn't think all of it was politically feasible. There would be too many acres of ranch land in the Olema Valley to buy. Burton countered, 'Don't tell *me* what's politically feasible. Tell me what you want and I'll get it through Congress.'

The vast San Francisco Watershed lands surrounding Crystal Springs Reservoirs are well preserved but almost entirely closed to the public. The lakes fill the depressed rift zone of the San Andreas Fault with water piped from Hetch Hetchy Reservoir in Yosemite National Park on its way to end users in the city.

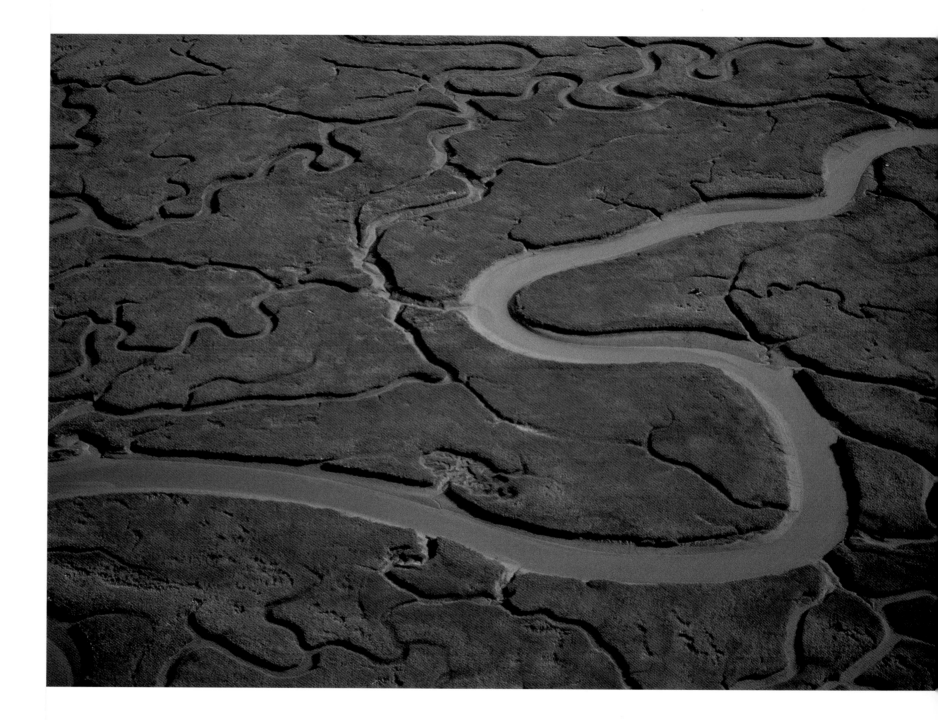

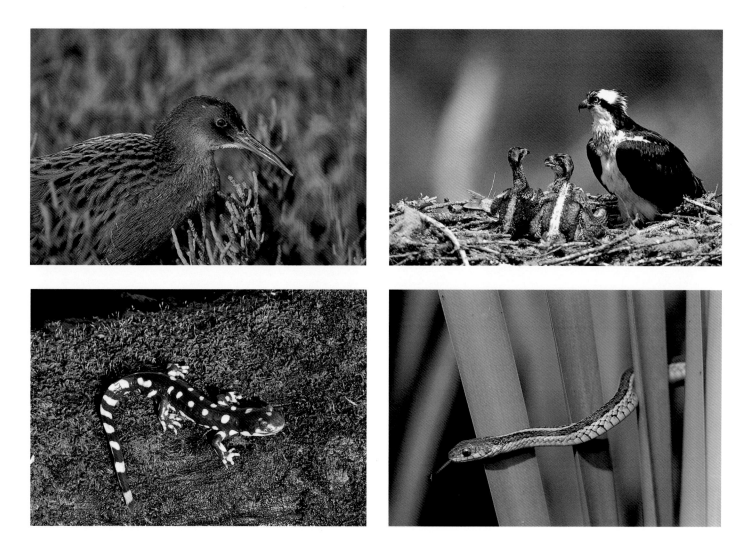

By the 1950s, only 15 percent of the Bay's wetlands remained. Today, the wetlands of Bair Island (**left**), *partly in the San Francisco Bay National Wildlife Refuge, support some rare and endangered species. The endangered California clapper rail* (**above, top left**) *has begun to recover from a 1992 population of fewer than 300 birds around the Bay. The osprey* (**above, top right**) *is recovering from a population crash caused by* DDT-thinned eggshells. Although this nest is in Marin County, ospreys are now seen in the South Bay year-round. DDT may also be implicated in the rapid decline of Bay Area amphibians such as the California tiger salamander (**above, lower left**), *a species of special concern for future listing. The endangered San Francisco garter snake* (**above, lower right**), *native only to the Peninsula, is now confined to a few marshy areas.*

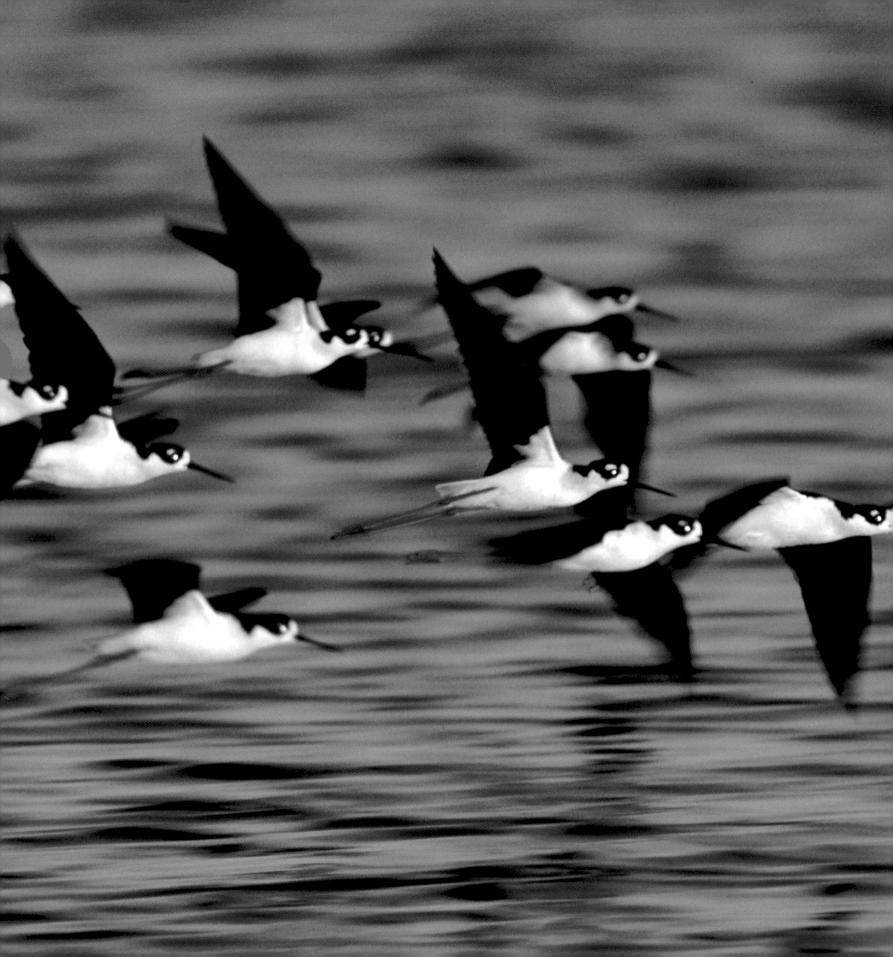

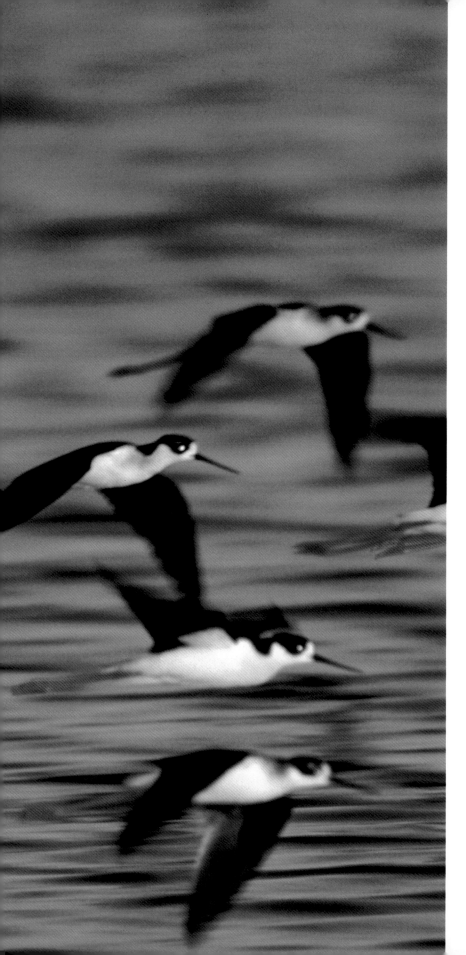

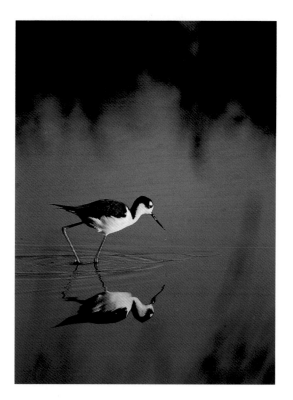

A flock of black-necked stilts (**left**) flies just above the waters of the San Francisco Bay National Wildlife Refuge. A wandering single bird (**above**) is reflected in the tidal waters of the Palo Alto Baylands Nature Preserve at dawn. On both sides of the South Bay (**following pages**), mountains of the Coast Ranges rise to around 4,000 feet. This aerial view at dawn south of San Jose shows the high receding ridges of the Diablo Range above the Santa Clara Valley shrouded in fog to the left.

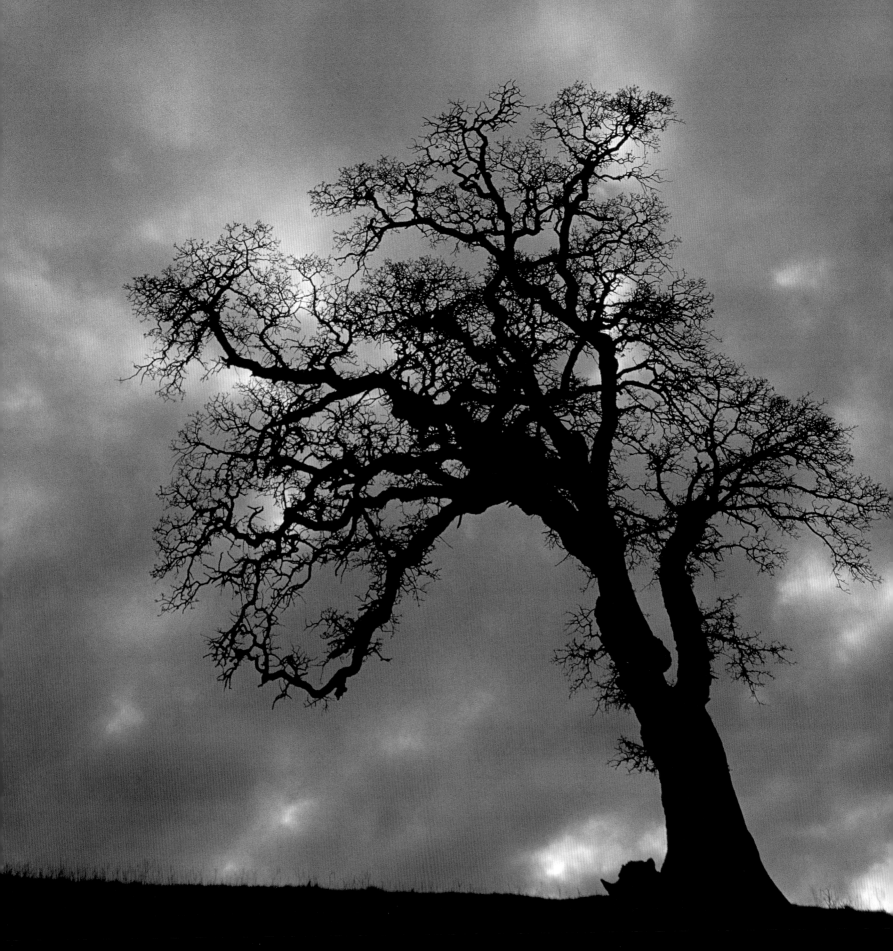

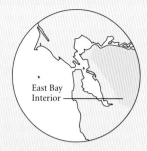

East Bay
Interior

E A S T   B A Y   I N T E R I O R

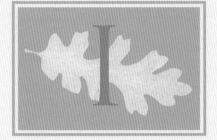

I n both physical and political climate, the valley bottom beyond the crest of the East Bay hills divides the warmer and drier rural (but increasingly suburban) East Bay interior from the cooler and wetter hills that bound the urban belt beside the Bay. Oak woodland and open grassland rolling endlessly over hill and dale give preserved areas of the interior an unparalleled continuity of wildness. In southern Alameda County, the Ohlone Wilderness Trail runs twenty-eight miles through four regional parks and preserves. Pleasanton Ridge Regional Park, just south of Dublin, also protects miles of wild hills.

Before World War II, the pastoral ranches and watershed lands of this region were de facto greenbelts extending from tiny valley towns over the crests of countless ridges. Ironically, the suburban sprawl that began to devour them soon overcame the rural bias of Contra Costa County that kept the East Bay Regional Park District out until an initiative was passed in 1964, three decades after Alameda County voters had created the district.

Without coastline or bay shore, this least varied part of the Bay Area was the last to secure public preserves, with the exception of one square mile set aside as the original Mount Diablo State Park in 1931. Today, Briones Regional Park, Las Trampas Regional Wilderness, and a greatly enlarged Mount Diablo State Park are interconnected by long trail systems with Morgan Territory Regional Preserve to the east and the Berkeley Hills to the west. Select public trails have also been opened on watershed of the East Bay Municipal Utility District that was previously closed to public access.

Lone oak above Marsh Creek, east of Mount Diablo

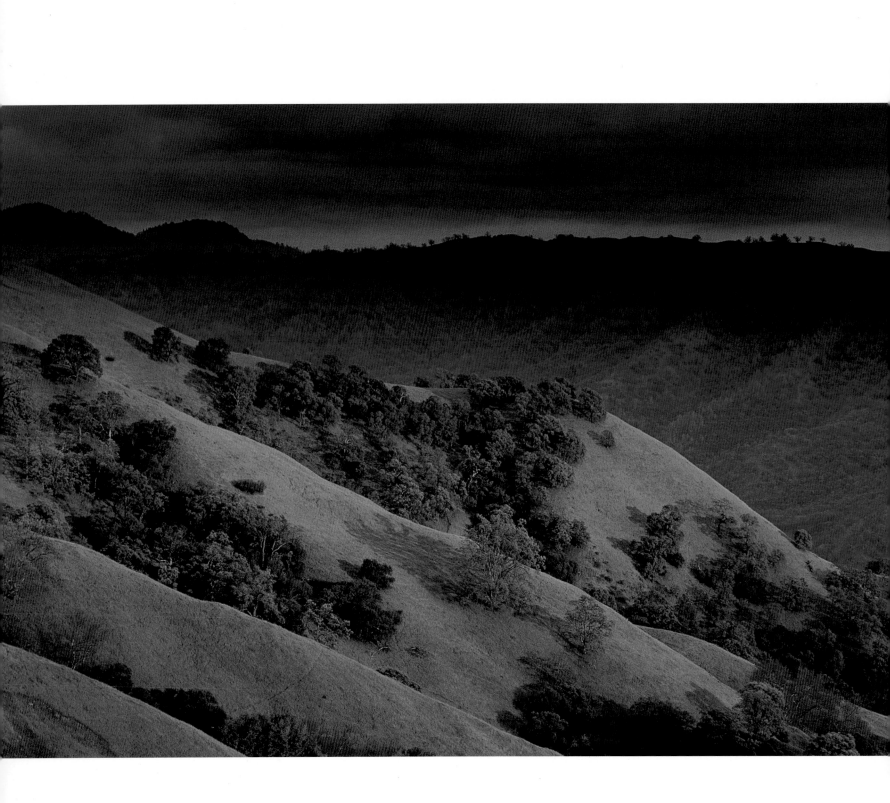

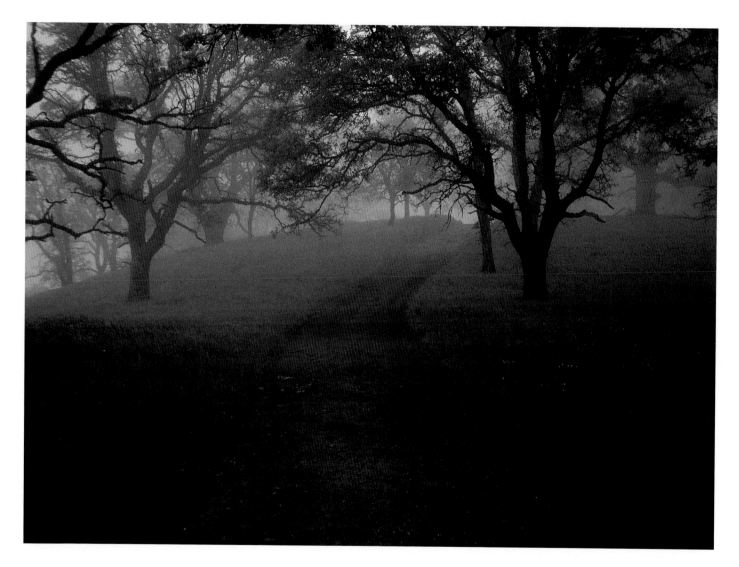

*The Ohlone Wilderness Trail (**above**) traverses twenty-eight miles of open grassland and oak woodland through the backcountry of four regional parks in southern Alameda County. This most wild and remote of Bay Area trails crosses only a single road as it follows a roller-coaster route up peaks and down canyons (**left**), as seen here on a spring evening in Sunol Regional Wilderness. The route begins on the outskirts of Fremont in Mission Peak Regional Preserve, traverses the Sunol and Ohlone Regional Wildernesses, and ends in Del Valle Regional Park, near Livermore.*

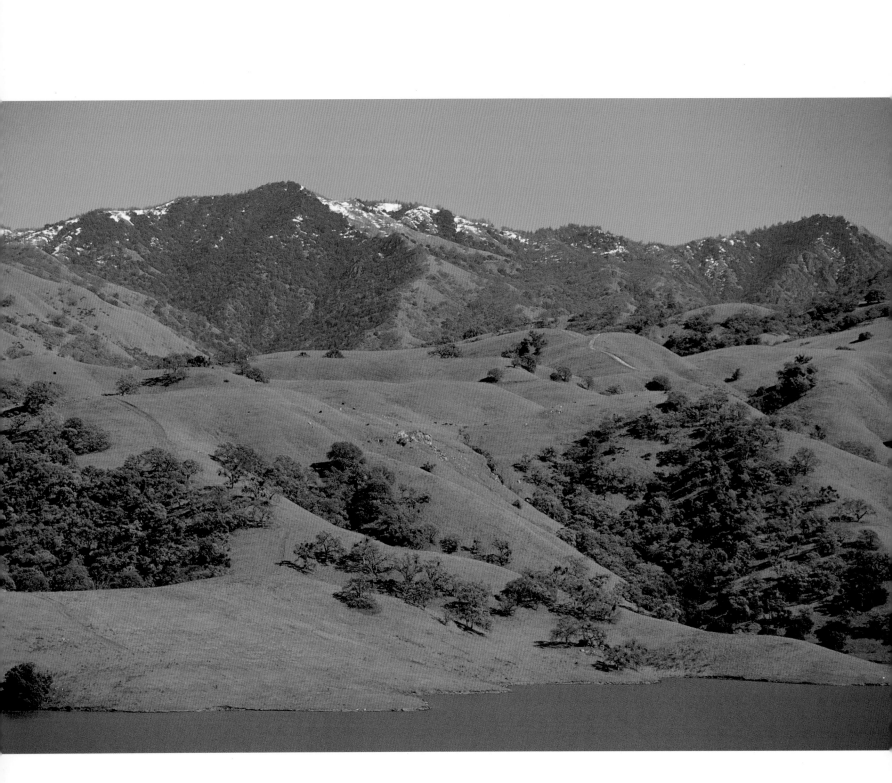

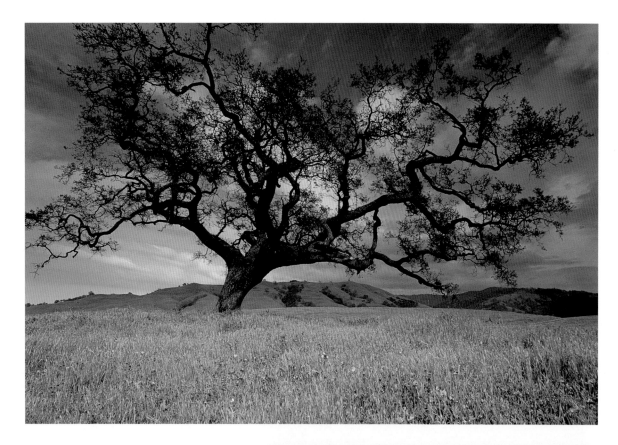

Winter snow caps the highest peaks of the Sunol and Ohlone Regional Wildernesses (**left**), seen from Calaveras Reservoir in Santa Clara County. Most hikers of the 28-mile Ohlone Wilderness Trail spend a night or two camping out, although runners have done the annual 50-kilometer Ohlone Wilderness ultramarathon, a slightly longer course, in less than four hours. Spring is the best time to visit the highlands, when streams are flowing and wildflowers (**above**) carpet the black oak and grassland savannah, which reaches as high as 3,817 feet—within 32 feet of the height of Mount Diablo, on the opposite side of the Livermore Valley. Lower down in a secluded Ohlone pond (**right**), a western pond turtle and a wood duck chance to meet on a tiny island.

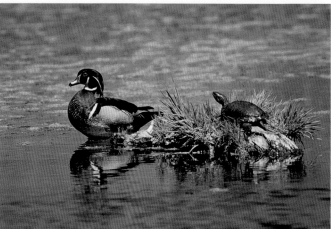

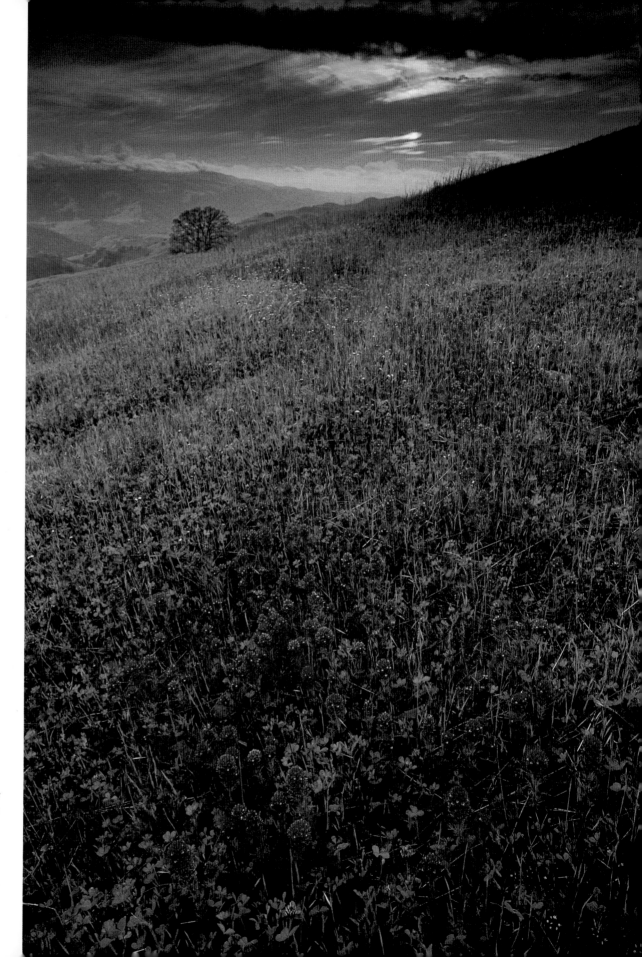

Beneath a spring sunset in the heart of the Ohlone Regional Wilderness (right), a profusion of purple owl's clover carpets an open meadow near Telles Rock. The oak-lined upper ridges of Ohlone (left) usually stay above the fog layer that often moves in from the Bay on clear evenings during spring and summer.

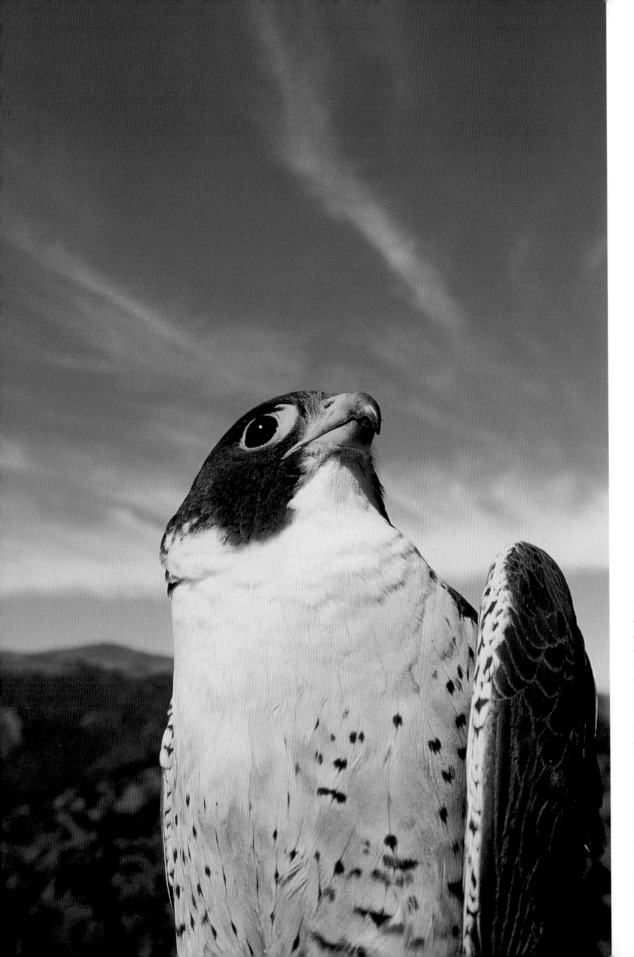

The peregrine falcon (**left**) has been variously described as the fiercest, fastest, most efficient, and best-designed of all birds. Unlike most endangered species, the peregrine suffered an abrupt population crash rather than a gradual slide toward oblivion. After World War II, DDT-induced eggshell thinning caused massive reproductive failure that wiped out the entire Bay Area population and all but two known pairs in the state by 1970. When biologists trapped this healthy male near the Ohlone Wilderness to check its blood for toxins in 1995, its band number matched that of a captive-bred chick (**right, below**) photographed in 1990 as it was being "cross-fostered" into a prairie falcon nest in a cave high on a Mount Diablo cliff similar to those of Castle Rock (**right, above**), where falcons have also nested. After fledging, it flew off and eventually joined the state's recovering peregrine population of 120 breeding pairs.

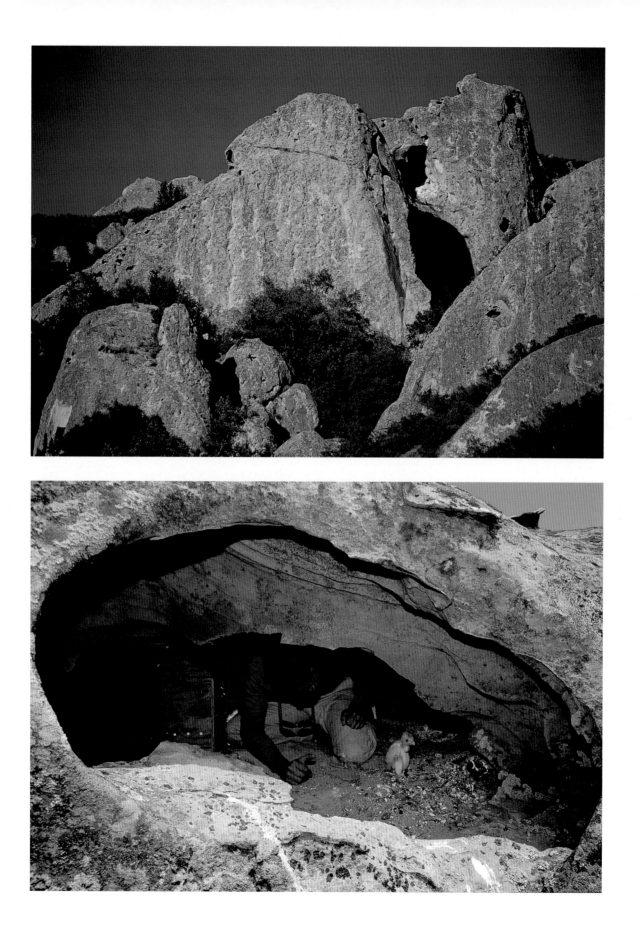

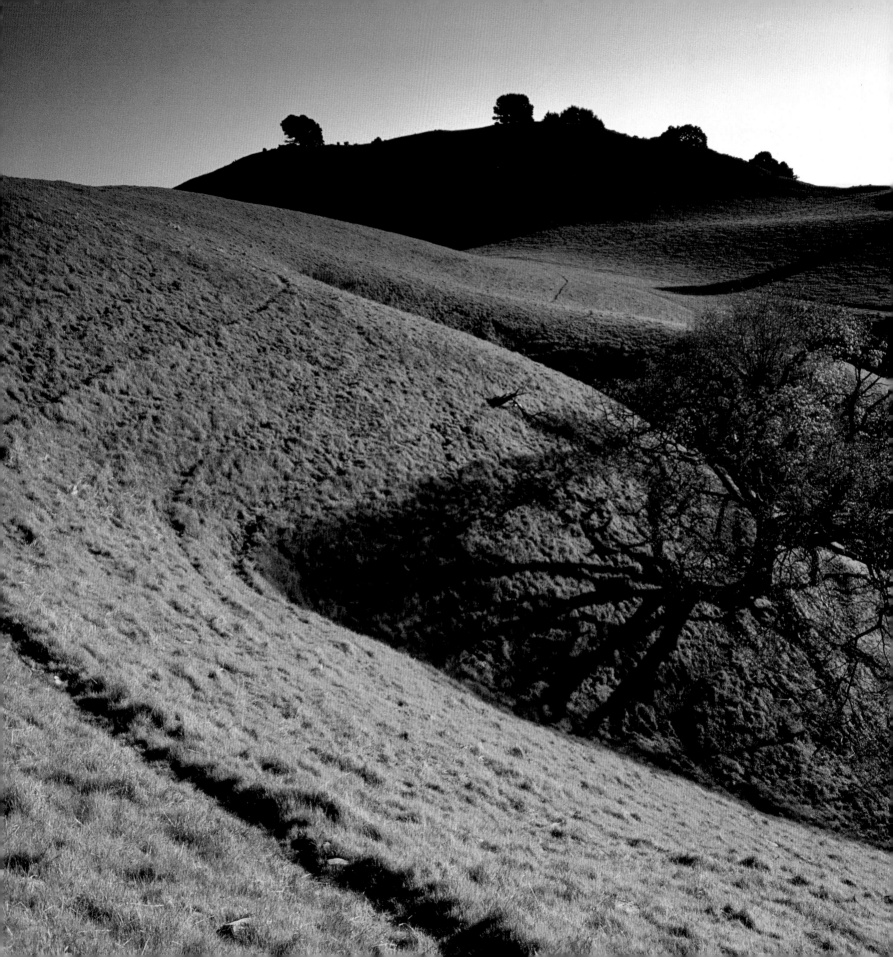

The Roots of Passion

The San Francisco Peninsula of the thirties was poised at the brink of transition. Only a few small towns dotted the two-lane road between a San Jose a twentieth of its present size and the city of San Francisco, at the Peninsula's very tip. Palo Alto, Atherton, Woodside, Belmont, Hillsborough, Burlingame, and Millbrae were often referred to as garden spots rather than cities or towns, places where the natural landscape was sprinkled with tasteful and spacious homes. Between them were vast old estates below forested hills that extended to the skyline of the northern Santa Cruz Mountains, up to three thousand feet above the Bay.

A nineteenth-century banker named William Ralston anticipated modern Peninsula commuters when he set up teams of fresh horses along the way to pull his buggy at breakneck speed between San Francisco and the eighty-room mansion he called Belmont. Ralston's pace probably exceeded that of a Mercedes-Benz caught in the present "commute from hell" along Highway 101 through a continuous urban swath where Belmont is now a city of 25,000 people. It also led inexorably toward his suicide. Believing that completion of the transcontinental railroad would foster rapid Bay Area growth, Ralston overinvested in real estate and building materials for a boom that would wait a century. His Bank of California failed.

Farther to the south was a large farm owned by a former Sacramento shopkeeper who had made a fortune investing in what became the Southern Pacific Railroad, complete with a right-of-way that included millions of acres of prime California lands. Former California governor Leland Stanford built a plush San Francisco mansion but also had a farm on several thousand acres above the Palo Alto railway station, where he began a tradition of inviting the best and the brightest of his generation to perform eclectic tasks. Eadweard Muybridge came in 1872 to make a legendary set of photographs to settle Stanford's $25,000 bet with a friend that all four of a horse's feet are in the air at once at some point during a gallop. Frederick Law Olmsted, the great landscape architect and park designer, was hired to create a university campus on the farm in memory of Stanford's only child, Leland Jr., who died at age sixteen.

Another wealthy financier of the period, Darius Mills, built an ostentatious mansion called Millbrae on an estate that included creeks flowing down from the mountains to the Bay. From a huge master bedroom finished in ebony and mother-of-pearl, Mills had a grand view of the pristine Bay over a pastoral landscape that has now disappeared beneath the cities of Burlingame and Millbrae. Mills Field Municipal Airport, built on the edge of the Bay in 1927, later evolved into San Francisco International Airport atop five thousand acres of fill.

When Palo Alto music teacher Nonette Hanko was growing up in Burlingame during the thirties, she "needed a place to go and just be alone, just listen, and hear nothing." Having studied piano since age three and imagining a career as a concert pianist, Hanko was particularly sensitive to unwanted sounds. "We lived a couple

Springtime on Rocky Ridge, Las Trampas
Regional Wilderness

of blocks from the Mills Estate, where there were wild creeks and trees hundreds of years old. I could go out and pretend I was in Africa there," she recalled during our interview. "My mom didn't want me to go there alone, but she always knew when I had. I never figured out how until I grew up and realized the pungency of the wild onions I always ate there in the spring.

"Wanting to be a concert pianist meant practicing two, three, four hours a day, plus doing all my school-work. I was always so busy, but there are times when life just gets to you and you really have to find a place that's quiet and alone. The Mills Estate was where I used to go. I'd hear an owl, and that would revive me.

"The huge estate went all the way up to the crest of the hills, but after World War II it began to be covered over with Peninsula Hospital and apartment buildings. Would you believe it? They actually covered over the creeks and put them in culverts under the houses. You can't even tell they were ever there."

Hanko's words rang true and echoed my own childhood experience, but few kids make an effort to discover the natural world on their own. As we sat in Hanko's living room, which could have served as a fifties movie set except for the recent titles of some of her many books, I wanted to know why that owl's cry had meant so much to her when she could so effortlessly produce beautiful sounds from the piano beside her. I was interested in how she had helped found the Midpeninsula Regional Open Space District, but as she spoke, unfolding the story in greater complexity than is related here, I kept wanting to know more about what had made her care so much. Why did this shy, creative person step so far beyond her childhood goal of being a concert musician? Why—and how—did someone who looks like everyone's smiling grandmother make such a singular effort to stand up against the formidable pressures of development in what was then a Bay Area backwater of environmental awareness? Only after I had pursued the question in a number of ways did the rest of her story emerge.

"Having access to nature is something I always kind of took for granted. My parents took me on camping trips in the Sierra beside the Stanislaus River every summer from the time I was less than a year old. When I grew up and moved here to Palo Alto, I found myself in a city where they had filled in all the creeks with cement. When my kids went looking for tadpoles, they didn't have any of the natural places to explore that I remember so well. It made me so sad to see kids and tadpoles on slimy concrete instead of in a real creek, where they belong. And as expressways and freeways were built up all around us, the noise became frightful to my trained ears. I needed a place to listen to the silence, and I started driving up Page Mill Road to find one. At first, I went miles up into the hills without seeing a single spot that didn't have barbed wire or 'No Trespassing' signs all around.

"I know this is going to sound kind of corny, but one day I found a place where I could get under a fence and into a walnut orchard. I sat down under one of the trees and began to pray. I guess I was about twenty-two then, and I was praying that I would find something meaningful to do with my life. That's an age when you're really looking for something. Even though I had a young child and my family was very important to me, I felt a calling to do something more. I was teaching piano in my home, and that was interesting, but I felt as if there must be some sort of destiny for people that they have to discover for themselves. I can't explain it any better than that. I felt as if there was something to come, and I needed to get in touch with it.

"Years later, that spot where I sat down and prayed was included in one of our first acquisitions for the Midpeninsula Regional Open Space District. Those walnut trees, which have since died but are still standing, are now in Los Trancos Open Space Preserve. Now anybody can go there and sit. It just thrills me to go up there where it used to be all private property and 'No Trespassing' signs and see our district signs inviting people in to have a natural experience. They have a chance to recapture some of the ties to the land that the Indians once had. It's very, very rewarding.

"I didn't know it at the time, but a closer 'quiet spot' that I'd discovered in a valley of spreading oak trees belonged to Stanford University. Stanford hadn't taken very good care of its fences, though, and it's probably the university's fault that some people fell in love with places like mine in the shadow of Coyote Hill where signs weren't posted properly. Being involved with procuring an open space agreement from Stanford University is something I've always thought of as my crowning glory: Stanford had a reputation for never allowing any of its lands to be designated as public open space. But the way it all came about isn't as simple as you might assume.

"Before I found out that my favorite place to go to recharge my batteries was on Stanford land and was about to be developed as an industrial park, I'd already helped found a group called the Palo Alto Civic League. We became concerned about development interests influencing the city council after the husband of one of my friends was forced into a recall election because he was one of a group of 'bickerers' who wouldn't agree to uncontrolled growth. After I started attending council meetings, I realized that nine square miles of foothills were in the jurisdiction of the city of Palo Alto, all undeveloped but in private ownership. The general manager of the city had no concept of open space. As far as he was concerned, the foothills were destined to be developed.

"Over a period of three years, I began networking with my friends in the League of Women Voters, the American Association of University Women, and the Committee for Green Foothills. When the *Palo Alto Times* began reporting prodevelopment discussions by the Palo Alto Planning Commission that I knew had not occurred, I called the editor and said, 'I'd like to come in and talk to you about this.' He turned out to be glad to see me because he'd heard rumors about problems with that particular reporter, who was eventually fired. The planning commissioners also appreciated that I took action because I was protecting their interests too. With the reporter gone, they were able to arrive at a consensus that every one of them, even the ones appointed through the influence of business interests, was willing to do something about protecting the foothills. I got the support needed for them to commission a study of the city's options regarding its remaining open space. But when the Palo Alto Foothills Design Study came in, it was all about development. I was so timid back then that when I rose to speak before the council, tears were coming down my face. I got up the courage to ask, 'What happened to the cost-benefit study that was supposed to tell us whether it's financially practical to develop the foothills?'

"The consultants finally brought in figures showing that a substantial subsidy would be required, which would actually cost the city and its citizens out of their pockets. Their final report suggested the option of some kind of open space district, like the East Bay Regional Park District, to save the hills all the way from San Carlos in San Mateo County down to the highest point south, in Santa Clara County."

"Did they actually refer to the East Bay Regional Park District as a possible model?" I interrupted. "What year was the study done?"

"Yes, they did, and it was 1969. One night, I cried myself to sleep because of a *Palo Alto Times* editorial that I was sure was aimed at me. It criticized local conservationists fighting rear-guard actions against ongoing development and said something like 'Why don't they get off their duffs, put their money where their mouth is, and form an open space district?'

"I'd previously had an argument with another *Palo Alto Times* writer over whether it was the city council's duty to do something toward preserving open space. My point was: what do citizen groups know about forming new public agencies? I was serving on the Coyote Hill lawsuit negotiating team for the Committee for Green Foothills. We were suing Stanford University, the city of Palo Alto, and two council members for conflict of interest and creation of an illegal lot. Stanford had begun bulldozing roads on Coyote Hill for a new development, without proper notification of the city, on a holiday weekend. When I went to the city council on Monday, they were either unable or unwilling to do anything about it. One member worked for Stanford and another was with a company hired to work on the lots. The lawsuit was a pretty big deal for several years, but we eventually reached an agreement, in 1972, by which Stanford would grant some long-term easements for public open space.

"But that's getting ahead of the story of what happened after that editorial came out in the paper. I took it personally and felt bad about it overnight, but when I woke up in the morning, I turned it around and thought, 'Gosh, what we really have is an editorial in support of what we want.' So I got my son Val's permission to postpone his eighteenth birthday party and held a brainstorming meeting at my house of about a dozen people I'd been networking with. Two attorneys at the meeting immediately checked out the state law that had allowed the counties to create the East Bay Regional Park District. Though it dated back to the early thirties and could be applied anywhere in California, the law hadn't been used anywhere except in the East Bay, where they didn't have county parks with playgrounds and other recreational facilities at the time. We already had county parks in both Santa Clara and San Mateo Counties, but nothing would prevent us from using the same law to create regional open space preserves if the voters would go for it.

"We did a survey and arrived at results that amazed us. Volunteers, mainly from the League of Women Voters and the Committee for Green Foothills, got 79 percent 'yes' answers as to whether a person would be willing to pay for local open space by adding an additional tax that we estimated by giving a yearly cost per average household."

"Sounds great," I commented, "but wasn't that highly favorable response only from Santa Clara County?"

"No. San Mateo County residents were highly supportive, except in one town. I have to laugh when I recall one of our survey ladies reporting back from there: 'I can't tell you where they stand on open space, but I can tell you that two out of three men are drunk on Saturday night.' Our problem was with the county supervisors, who were clearly prodevelopment in 1970 and refused to put us on the ballot. Many of our supporters thought our initiative was dead. We were saved when northern Santa Clara County voters formed the Midpeninsula Regional Open Space District in 1972 by a wide margin. Four years later, southern San Mateo County voted to join us, in a citizen initiative that did not require approval by the county supervisors, finally creating the two-county district we'd originally intended.

"It's hard to believe that twenty-four years have gone by and that I've had the privilege of serving a fourth term as board president. The district now has twenty-three open space preserves with 41,000 acres, and so many people appreciate what we've done. Ours were California's first regional open space preserves—as opposed to parks for recreation—and they've become models for other communities, both in the Bay Area and around the nation. Our best supporters have been people from other areas who saw places dear to them become irrevocably changed before they moved here. After they've lost their special places elsewhere, they don't want to watch it happen again here.

"Even Stanford is showing pride in its open space lands now. When university officials brought Queen Elizabeth down for a luncheon some years ago, they didn't bring her in the direct way, from the side toward the Bay, where all the development is. They drove her down from the top of the hills, through the open space. I think that's a good sign and reason enough for Stanford to create some permanent open space, instead of the twenty-five- and forty-nine-year easements, which are soon to elapse. In the meantime, I'm talking to members of the city Planning Commission who are discussing the creation of an urban service limit line that I'm hoping will exclude those areas from any further development.

"In Santa Clara County, we've formed a new open space district in the south county. It completes a ring of agencies circling San Francisco Bay that are implementing two greenbelts—one around the Bay front, the other on the ridges that overlook the Bay and the Pacific Ocean. Another of my hopes for the future is that our electorate will agree to expand our boundaries to the ocean before it's too late. When I look out from the ridge crest along Skyline Boulevard, I think it's still possible to preserve lands all the way to the San Mateo coast."

When I left Nonette Hanko's home, I decided to drive back to the East Bay the long way. As I headed west on the Page Mill Expressway beside Coyote Hill, on Stanford University lands still graced by spreading oak trees, I felt a new appreciation for how so much of the wildness of the hills before me had been preserved so recently through the efforts of a woman who has never forgotten what it meant to play in her "Africa" as a

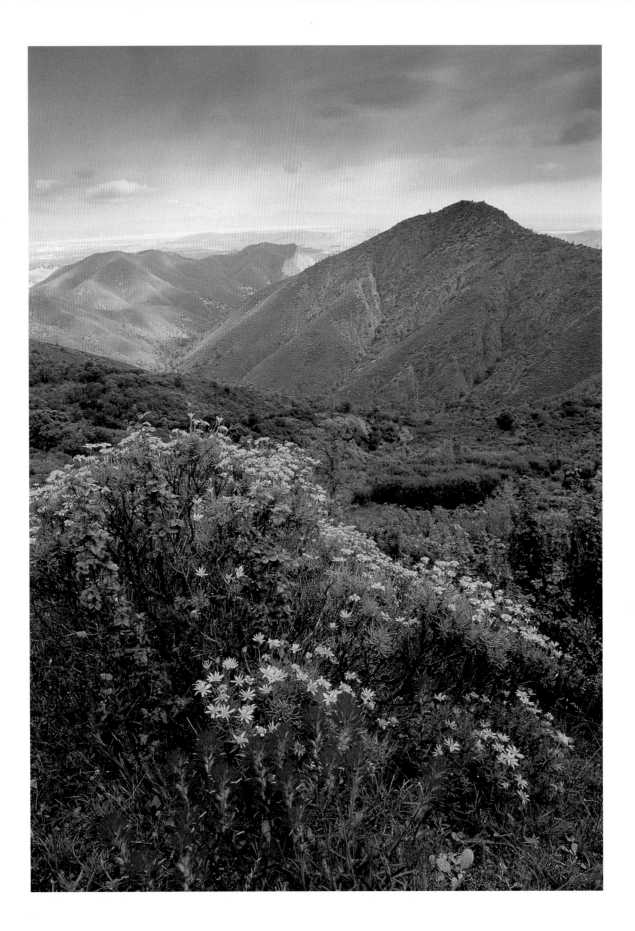

little girl so long ago. As the multilane expressway became Page Mill Road, reverting to its old, twisting, two-lane self, I passed the turnoff my parents used to take when they drove me to Hidden Villa summer camp in the early fifties. The Duveneck family, who managed the camp and owned the vast property, had later bequested part of it as an open space preserve and the rest as an environmental education center. I continued upward, past the old walnut trees on Los Trancos Open Space Preserve, before cresting out to a distant view across the Bay where the only interruption to the perfect blue sky was the noble outline of Mount Diablo.

A week before, I had spent a hot fall afternoon in Diablo's shadow with another champion of Bay Area open space. Dr. Mary Bowerman had also made a personal connection in the thirties with land she eventually worked to save, but unlike Nonette Hanko, she had not been a young child at play. In 1930 she was already a botany major at the University of California, working on her senior project on Mount Diablo.

Sixty-six years later, this delightful woman of eighty-eight drove her own car to meet me at an air-conditioned hotel over tea and a shared chocolate dessert. As we began talking about her role in the founding of Save Mount Diablo and the organization's continuing efforts to acquire more private lands to add to Mount Diablo State Park, I donned reading glasses to write down notes to supplement the words picked up by my tape recorder. My first entries were about Bowerman's conspicuous lack of glasses; hands that look like those of a woman half her age, with straight fingers and small joints; and similarly youthful mind. I observed how she walked slowly but confidently, like some of the older Sherpas and climbers I've known. The years seem to count differently for those who actively enjoy nature. One of my first questions was whether she had been hiking on the mountain lately.

"I still go out some, but rarely with groups. My old walking companions are now incapacitated, and I don't travel as fast as the younger people anymore.

"Back in the thirties, there weren't many trails. I started going up there every week about a year before the top became a state park, in 1931. There was a private toll road with a steep entrance fee, but when I went to the owner in Oakland and told him I was studying all the flowering plants and ferns and didn't want to pay each time, he graciously agreed. I was usually working on private property, even after the park was created. If I went to Sycamore Canyon, for example, I'd knock on a door, tell the occupants what I was doing, and ask their permission to proceed; they would always say yes. If there was no house or owner nearby, I would just go anyway."

"What was it about the mountain that was special for you?" I asked, hoping to glean an anecdote about an instant emotional connection with the land.

"I don't think I thought of Mount Diablo as being anything special, at least in the beginning. I was a student at Berkeley, and Professor Mason had suggested I do a study to identify all the plants up there, and that was all there was to it. I wasn't sufficiently knowledgeable to realize whether anything was special on Mount

Wildflowers in upper Mitchell Canyon, Mount Diablo State Park

187

Diablo because I'd been living in England and then Pasadena. My father would have sent me to Stanford, but I said no. He saved himself some money because my botany teacher at junior college in Pasadena said I must go to Berkeley."

"How did you come to choose botany?" I asked.

"That's a good question. My father had always wanted to be a physician, and he picked out the courses I should take at junior college, hoping to steer me in that direction. I was generally unhappy in my human physiology class, but I had seen this nice classroom with plants in it through an open door, so I switched to botany about two weeks after I registered. Though I had never taken a botany or biology course, my interest went back a long way. My kindergarten teacher had sent home a note remarking that I was especially interested in natural history. When I was fifteen, I thought I wanted to be a landscape gardener.

"The year after I graduated from the University of California, I began working under the world-famous botanist Willis Linn Jepson, who had been on leave. When he saw what a big project Mount Diablo had turned out to be, he approved my request to work toward a master's thesis on it. A year later I made my way into Jepson's inner sanctum in the Life Sciences Building at Berkeley, and when I announced that my thesis was now going to be a doctoral dissertation, he looked a little startled and fell silent."

"Your decision?" I asked, similarly surprised by her boldness.

"Yes. I had decided. I remember standing there while he discussed the pros and cons. After a while he said, 'All right.' I eventually listed more than 600 species of trees and flowering plants in a book, *The Flowering Plants and Ferns of Mount Diablo, California: Their Distribution and Association into Plant Communities,* which wasn't published until 1944. During my studies, I became more interested in ecology than in straight identification. I kept track of which plants were growing together because it was all so completely fresh to me. In the beginning, there was some advantage to being a complete ignoramus as far as this part of the world was concerned. People into botany who grew up here already knew things of that sort and weren't likely to question them.

"I soon realized that Mount Diablo is in a unique geographical location. It's part of the inner Coast Ranges yet is subject to coastal influence owing to the absence of high mountains to the west over the Bay. It's also a pivotal link between the differing vegetation units of the north and south Coast Ranges. The broad variations in temperature, rainfall, wind exposure, and altitude account for its wide variety of plant life.

"My botanist's reasons for urging preservation of the whole of Mount Diablo go well beyond its being a refuge for some endemic and rare species. Because there's so much variation between different parts of the mountain, we need preservation of the whole to understand the whole ecological picture."

Jepson's unconditional support of Bowerman's botanical work on Mount Diablo came as no surprise to me. My aunt, Marion Avery, an amateur naturalist born in 1896, knew both Jepson and Bowerman. My father,

Field of California poppies below Mitchell Canyon, Mount Diablo State Park

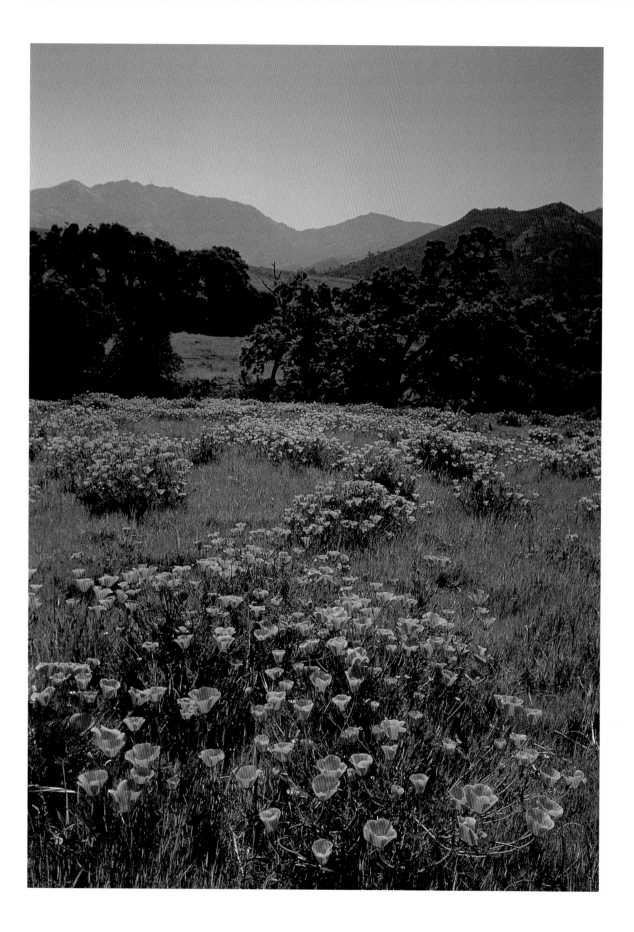

born in 1884, had read me Jepson's romantic plea to preserve East Bay open space for wildflowers from a booklet published in 1909 by the Women's Auxiliary of the First Unitarian Church of Berkeley, where both he and Jepson were members. Anticipating the land ethic to be expressed by Aldo Leopold three decades later, Jepson spoke of "the right of the flowers, children of the Sun, to possess the cañons, slopes, and fields" and how that right "of exceedingly ancient origin" was being infringed on by "our own house-building and pasture-inclosing people who left scarcely a common where the delicate first inhabitants might live." Jepson went on to predict: "Some time there will be here in Berkeley a wild-flower protection society, just as in older States, and those who have wide grounds will give the wild flowers a corner—all their own." Recalling this scenario, I asked Bowerman to tell me about her first direct involvement with protecting Mount Diablo.

"I joined the Sierra Club in 1942 and became involved with its Natural Science Section. After I moved out here to Lafayette, I joined a local Sierra Club conservation group. In 1971, a member named Art Bonwell came up to me and said, 'Don't you think we ought to do something about Mount Diablo?' He was referring to how moneys appropriated by the state to buy additional lands for Mount Diablo State Park had been diverted to buy Franks Tract in the Sacramento–San Joaquin Delta for a state recreation area."

I recalled the almost biblical parable of what had happened at Franks Tract, an outcome that some conservationists see as divine retribution for the misguided act of diverting California state park funding, set aside for the protection of Mount Diablo, to the purchase of an island for fishing and water sports. A few years later, a levee gave way and Franks Tract vanished under the waters of the Delta, where it remains as a wide spot in the river channel to this day, still officially a state recreation area.

Bowerman vividly remembers the result of suggesting that Art Bonwell, who was an electrical engineer at Dupont, organize a meeting of representatives of local groups. "On December 7, 1971, fifteen people came, and I stated my dream that the whole of Mount Diablo, including its foothills, should remain in open space. We formed Save Mount Diablo that night, elected a president, and set objectives to educate the public and acquire lands rather than to maintain the existing park or promote recreation.

"I served as vice president for resources until the end of 1995, and I'm still on the Land Acquisition Committee. The state park started out with an initial 1,463 acres at the top of the mountain in 1931. From 6,778 acres in 1971, we've brought it up to 18,393 acres in 1996.

"I'm most concerned about the habitat. Mount Diablo State Park has more of a mandate to preserve vegetation for the future than do the regional parks, which are more recreation oriented, but I'm afraid the mountain isn't going to stay as wild as I would like it to be, no matter how much more of it we acquire.

"My word—I'm talking like an old mother hen! Of course, I should have mentioned that we didn't do this alone. We encouraged the State Department of Parks and Recreation and the California legislature to add these parcels, about one third of which were obtained without cost to the state. Other public agencies have acquired open space lands around the mountain, but ten or fifteen thousand more acres are needed to preserve the core of the ecosystem. With the rapid population growth in Contra Costa County, we need to include all the lower slopes of the mountain soon, before they're developed and lost forever.

"Right now, our Land Acquisition Committee is Bob Doyle and me. Bob has been the backbone of our organization. He came to our first meeting back in 1971 as a high school student, and he was our president from 1978 to 1989. I believe he was first inspired by a local biology teacher, Jane Helrich, a friend of mine who became a member of our board. Perhaps Bob would have been involved with us anyway. You should ask him about that."

"As a matter of fact, he's on my short list to interview," I responded, "but mainly about his other land acquisitions while working for the East Bay Regional Park District. Before we conclude, is there anything else you'd like to add?"

"Yes. We need a fairy godfather who will give us twenty million dollars. There's no money coming in from the state at this time. What's left in private ownership on the mountain are mostly multimillion-dollar parcels that will probably be developed if we don't have the funds to buy them when they come on the market. We continue to be optimistic and believe that 'our mountain' can remain wild—and a joy to all of us."

I later learned that the place where Bowerman mentioned she used to botanize on private property, lower Sycamore Canyon, had just been added to the park after years of negotiations. Developers had purchased 300 acres there on which they proposed to build forty-four large homes. They persuaded Contra Costa County to approve a negative declaration, meaning that no environmental impact report was necessary, but the canyon does have some rare species, like the Mount Diablo sunflower, the Alameda whipsnake, and a pair of peregrine falcons nesting on its cliffs. Save Mount Diablo appealed, won, and convinced the developer to donate 252 acres to the park.

When I met with Bob Doyle at the spacious headquarters of the East Bay Regional Park District in the Oakland hills, his answers to my questions about his childhood passions seemed to perfectly anticipate his present career. Perhaps touching his personal destiny early in life had empowered him with the certitude that made his statements in response to my questions flow together without hesitation, like the movements of a dancer. There was no question in my mind that the EBRPD assistant general manager for advanced planning and acquisition is one and the same person as the little boy who witnessed pressures for development wreaking havoc on Contra Costa County open space.

"As I was growing up in Concord during the sixties," Doyle began, "Contra Costa County was going crazy with growth. Once Bay Area Rapid Transit trains and new freeways connected us to San Francisco, we had this tremendous surge of suburban growth. The orchards and fields of the central county, with their walnuts and mustard blossoms, were being rapidly plowed under all around my home. By the late sixties and early seventies, they were gone.

"Like a lemming driven into the sea, I was driven into the hills. My personal commitment to and deep affection for the hills and canyons came out of trying to get my head together by hiking through them as familiar orchards and open fields were disappearing all around. The beginning of the Earth Day movement, when I was still in high school, was a wild period of turmoil. I became kind of swept up by it. My science and biology teachers were deep into the ecology movement—saving the whales and the coast and getting involved with environmental legislation coming out of a groundswell of public concern.

"My conservation ethic, as well as many of the skills I've learned relating to advocacy and land issues, has come from my having been blessed with a series of phenomenal mentors. The best botanists in the East Bay happened to become my friends by accident, as it seemed to me then. Of course, I've always been interested in plants, and I developed an interest in botany apart from any conservation issues. With the support of my high school biology teacher, Martin Shea, I helped found a botanical society that raised money for Mount Diablo, recycling, and a whole bunch of ecological things. I also joined a youth group called SANE (Save America's Natural Environment) and became a volunteer teaching assistant for an activist elementary school teacher named Jane Helrich, who organized a field trip to Sacramento for youth representatives of all ages. They got to see firsthand how the legislative side of environmental protection worked and how their studies of the biological sciences directly related to the process. I got to speak to a legislative committee for parks and park funding. That was my first experience with advocacy and the start of my interest in environmental politics.

"Dr. Mary Bowerman joined us on that bus ride to Sacramento and voiced her own advocacy. She became a very dear friend before she cofounded Save Mount Diablo with Art Bonwell. I was the kid among this group of elder statespersons, witnessing a series of battles that mustered grassroots support for funding of parks and conservation efforts. Their successes at that time—not just locally but also statewide and in Washington—are a fantastic legacy that I feel so lucky to have been a part of at such a young age. The Bay Area was leading the nation in clean air and clean water initiatives, defeating major developments, and creating local land preserves. When we started Save Mount Diablo in 1971, I never thought we'd get nearly as far as we have.

"The hills I hiked in my youth, primarily around Mount Diablo, were mostly private property. I came from a position of appreciating what the finality of development would have meant to all those areas, which have since become Shell Ridge Open Space, Lime Ridge Open Space, Black Diamond Mines Regional Preserve, Las Trampas Regional Wilderness, Diablo Foothills Regional Park, Castle Rock Regional Park, and Morgan Territory Regional Preserve, plus additions to the existing Briones Regional Park and Mount Diablo State Park.

"What's frustrating in my profession today is how people seem to think that we go out and buy some property and, gee, it's a wonderful park now, isn't it? The public commitment and long-term struggle required to set aside land against overwhelming odds go unnoticed, as does the need to preserve more open space for our own future.

Intersecting ridges in the foothills of Mount Diablo near Morgan Territory Regional Preserve

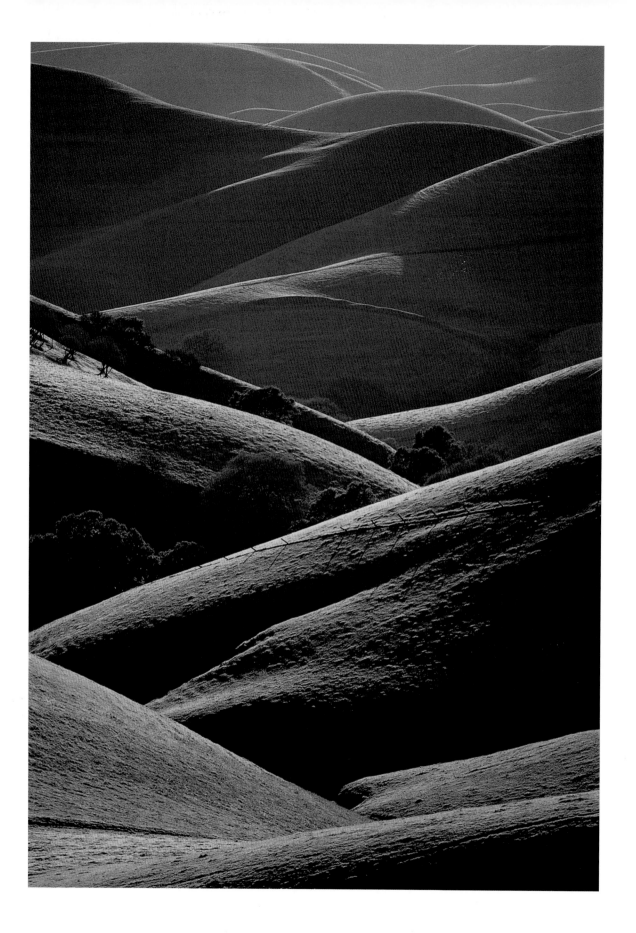

"Right after we started Save Mount Diablo, people would show up at our meetings and say: 'What are you talking about? What are you trying to save from what? You've already got a park up there. Nobody's ever going to build way up there,' or 'Why should I care what they do with it? I never go up on Mount Diablo.'

"I would reply: 'So when you're stuck in gridlock on the freeway, you don't ever look up there and appreciate the sunrise or the clouds?' And they would always say yes. They'd admit that there's a value to them that's intrinsic, whether or not it can be quantified in numbers or even words. And I'd ask if they really wanted to see the gridlock worsen, as it surely would with more development. Right at the time this was happening, Blackhawk and some other huge developments were being proposed on the lower slopes of the mountain."

"Can you give me an example of how your personal background has helped you in your present job with the EBRPD?" I asked.

"To begin with, I learned the importance of attention to detail from my fieldwork. Mary Bowerman was always, always questioning me: 'Are you sure? Explain exactly what you saw.' I watched her exercise that same precision in her land and financial dealings for Save Mount Diablo—taking the principles of natural science and applying them to the political world. In my dealings with the conservation movement, I used to find a lot of people in leadership roles who had the scientific training to be accurate and the level of commitment—the moral courage—to take a controversial position, be correct about it, and give it the long-term effort required for success. There are fewer people like that now. There's a vacuum of leadership in the conservation movement today. And, frankly, I see a problem with the next generation—the third generation of conservation students—in that too many of them tend to be emotional about issues without being accurate in their science or rational in their positions.

"An example of committing to a controversial strategy and seeing it through happened on Pleasanton Ridge, where we've created another major regional park. I'm sort of a strategic chess player, and a while ago I recommended to my board that we do something that might sound a little crazy. A developer had nearly completed controversial plans for 2,600 units and a golf course on part of Pleasanton Ridge. I found out that if we acted fast, we could buy a middle piece of the property, at what would have been the fourteenth hole. The board said to go for it, and the end result was that it stopped the whole development in its tracks. The developer couldn't find a way around not having our small parcel. We've now acquired the entire area for the park."

"That's great," I acknowledged, never having heard the story before, despite being a member of the board of the American Land Conservancy, which had purchased 656 acres of Pleasanton Ridge to convey into park land. "But how do you see Pleasanton Ridge fitting into your long-term plans? Is it just a random area within your boundaries where opportunity knocked, or did you have a firm strategy?"

"My basic vision isn't rocket science. It takes a long-term view to repeat the EBRPD's original vision of parks all along the ridge tops, as was done in the Berkeley Hills, both in the southern end of our district and out in Contra Costa County. Pleasanton Ridge fits into the southern vision, and we've now sewed together a thirty-mile strip of parks, from Morgan Territory through Mount Diablo State Park all the way to the city limits of Walnut Creek, that fulfills part of my Contra Costa dream.

"I was one of the founding members of the Bay Area Ridge Trail Council, which, as you know, began as Bill Mott's vision when he was the EBRPD's general manager in the sixties. He was another of my older mentors, along with Hulet Hornbeck, who was my immediate predecessor in charge of land acquisitions. I began thinking that however great it is to create the Ridge Trail, let's buy broader corridors along those ridges and make them into scenic corridors. A trail along a twenty-foot fenced strip between a bunch of subdivisions is not much fun for us or of much value as a wildlife corridor.

"The way I see it, trails really aren't development. If we don't have an active use program, an educational program, an interpretive program, the public isn't going to support us. A huge amount of our success is our regional trail system. It's got about an 80 percent public rating for such questions as 'Are you aware of it? Do you use it? Do you think it's important?' So it's not just that we have some special natural areas set aside in the East Bay. What's unique is our trail system that links the community directly to these parks. In many places you can leave your backyard, go down the street, get on a regional trail, and be in one of our parks in fifteen minutes or less.

"I'm frustrated when people don't see the need for recreation and for having these parks open. We are not buying these lands just to set aside habitat. There has to be money to keep these places protected, maintain them, make them safe for the people, and expand them into continuous strips of open space. In good economic times or bad, open space and conservation and recreation are just as important as transportation and other infrastructure that we fund continuously without question.

"When I got this job in 1986, I was frankly told that we would be going out of the land business. The passing of Measure AA in 1988 by the necessary two-thirds majority basically changed the world for the district. The two hundred twenty-five million dollar Regional Open Space, Wildlife, Shoreline, and Park Bond Act is still funding all our acquisitions. It also places high priority on shoreline acquisitions and restoration, what I call 'recapturing the Bay.'

"Though we probably now have 75 percent of the key scenic natural areas in parks or public ownership, it's not time to sit back and be complacent. Do you settle for having half the ridge top? Or do you *complete* that vision, like the dream Mary Bowerman had for Mount Diablo?

"The original water districts didn't seek to buy scenic areas. They bought bowls to put their water in. That's where we got our first lands, when it became known that the water company was about to sell off large parcels to developers. Remember that the EBRPD was created in the heart of the Great Depression, yet people voted to tax themselves to protect the East Bay hills. The situation isn't as different now as you might think. Our 1996 master plan states that the persistent climate of economic uncertainty is one of the key challenges that will shape the EBRPD of the twenty-first century.

"One change for the worse is that today's Republican party is the party of conservativeness and not of conservation. It used to be both. We had a long history of Republican support for park funding. We need to make it ever more clear to the people we're electing that the natural beauty and integrity of the environment we live in is a key element to the economic success of this increasingly urban area. It's always been a joke to me that when you open the real estate page of an East Bay paper, the ads for every new development or old subdivision talk about access to a recreational trail or a park or views of Mount Diablo. It equates directly to what people do in their limited free time to have a life outside work.

"And there's lots of work to do. Here, take along this copy of our new master plan."

Back at home, with Tilden Regional Park spread outside my library window, I turned to the first page of the master plan and read the following vision statement, quoted from a 1930 report: "The need is a vital one. . . . The charm of the region as a place in which to live will depend largely upon natural conditions that are destined to disappear unless properly protected for the public in general."

The concluding section, "Our Shared Future," declares the master plan to be "a rededication of the East Bay Regional Park District to the vision of its founders . . . and an acknowledgment of the continued commitment of the citizens, elected officials, and staff whose dedicated efforts have expanded the District from the first four parks established in 1934 to the present system of 56 regional parks and nearly 30 regional trails."

That quotation from the 1930 report, written by the Olmsted brothers and Ansel Hall, came out of prototypical interagency environmental cooperation. Hall, chief naturalist at Yosemite National Park and later a Berkeley Hills resident, was loaned by the National Park Service to assist the sons of Frederick Law Olmsted in preparing a commissioned report assessing the need to preserve recreational open space in the East Bay; the University of California was also involved in direct assistance and loan of personnel. The three were chosen because they had drafted a similar survey for the infant California State Park System. The Olmsted-Hall report looked beyond the team's charge to examine the lands of the East Bay and envisioned a ring of parks circling the Bay, recognizing the need to make a fair part of the Bay's shoreline accessible to the public and to keep it safe from filling of wetlands for development.

As I look out my library window at the parklands where my dog is now nudging me to take him on a trail run, I realize I would have moved away from the Bay Area long ago were it not for the efforts of the few who have saved so much for so many. Like the places they have fought to preserve, these visionaries are a diverse lot, seemingly separate yet interconnected by collaborative bonds that are usually overlooked.

The fine balance of open space and urban access that exists all around the Bay Area is clearly beyond the mandate or ability of any single city, county, regional, state, or national agency to control; it has come about only because key individuals cared enough to give cooperative support to groups outside their own. It is my hope that this book will help this practice become as enduring as the lands themselves.

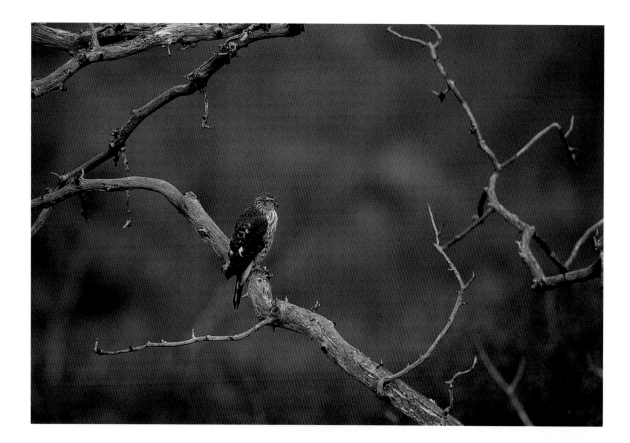

A sharp-shinned hawk (**above**) perches on a manzanita branch on Mount Diablo, the Bay Area's most dominant mountain (**right**). *In this hawk's-eye view through an extreme telephoto lens from the Golden Gate National Recreation Area in Marin County, the peak's noble outline crowns a series of wild ridges on both sides of the Bay that form ideal habitat for this relatively common but secretive bird, which usually stays within the forest canopy. Not far from this viewpoint is a site known as Hawk Hill, where observers routinely count more than 2,000 sharp-shins passing overhead during the annual fall raptor migration. The birds are sometimes confused with falcons because of their small size, continual alternation of multiple wing beats with long glides, and frequent dives from above on larger raptors.*

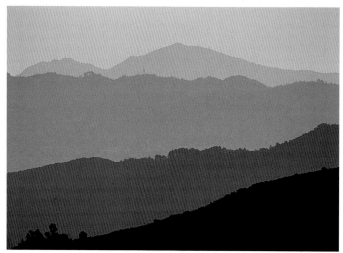

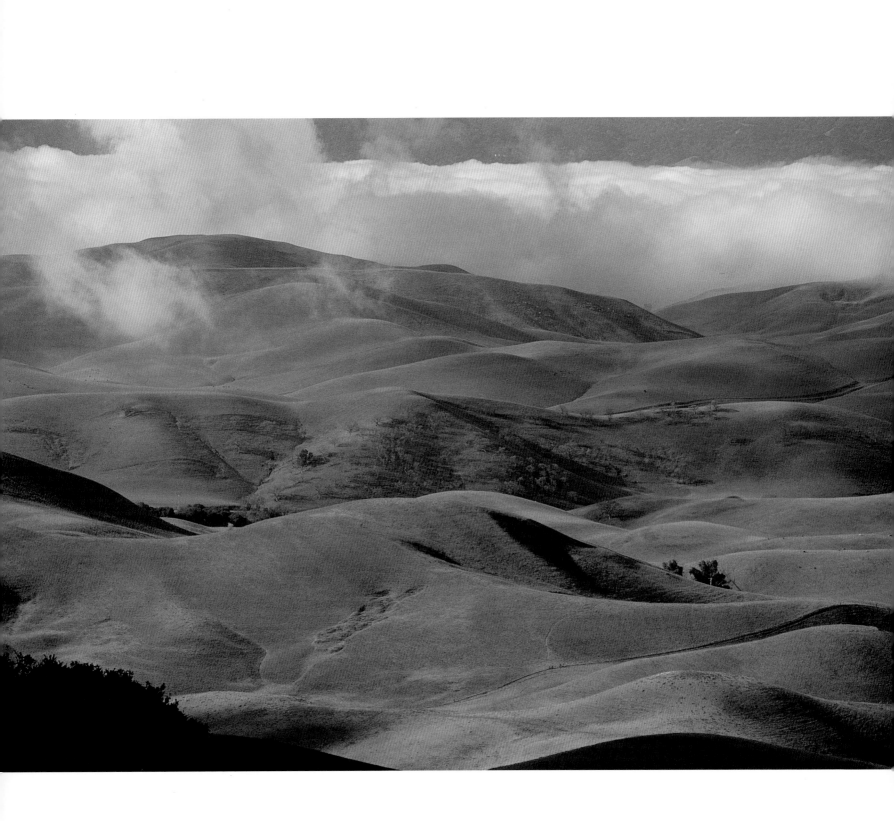

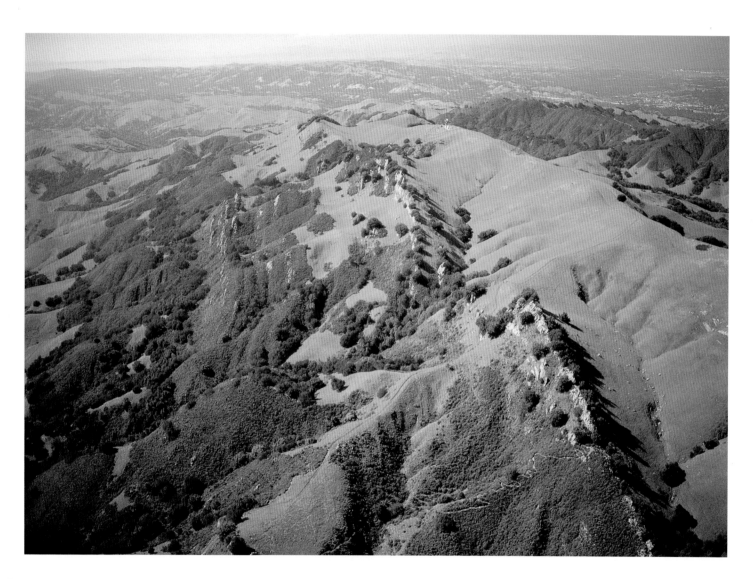

*Viewed from the air, Rocky Ridge in Las Trampas Regional Wilderness (**above**) resembles the spine of some ancient creature. On closer inspection, the wind-eroded sediments contain small marine fossils, now thrust 2,000 feet above the sea in wildly tilted sandstone. Preserved open space continues on the left side of the ridge into the EBMUD Upper San Leandro Watershed. The sensuous rolling hills (**left**) below Mount Diablo west of Morgan Territory Road form an important part of the Bay Area greenbelt, though they have no legal protection or public access. Other agricultural acreage below the mountain has recently sprouted luxury tract homes.*

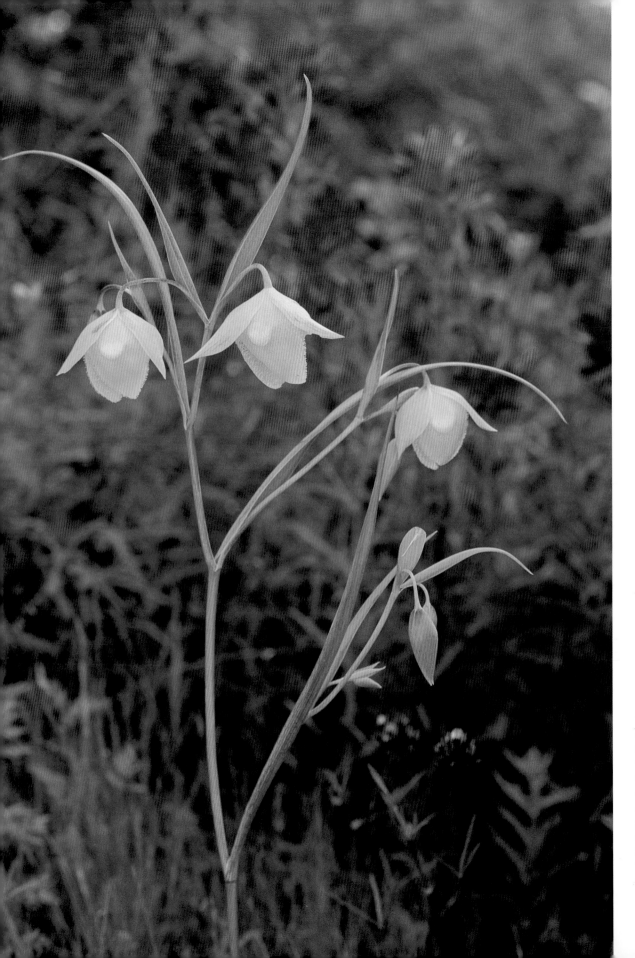

The Mount Diablo fairy lantern (**left**), a rare lemon-yellow globe tulip, is native only to the slopes of the mountain and surrounding foothills, where it blooms in spring with other vivid flowers, such as purple owl's clover. Aptly named shooting stars (**right**) begin to bloom on the mountain as early as February. They are a different species from a similar one that blooms in midsummer in the High Sierra. Mule's ears (**far right**) are named for their broad, erect leaves, but for a few weeks during the spring bloom, they display their relationship to the sunflower family.

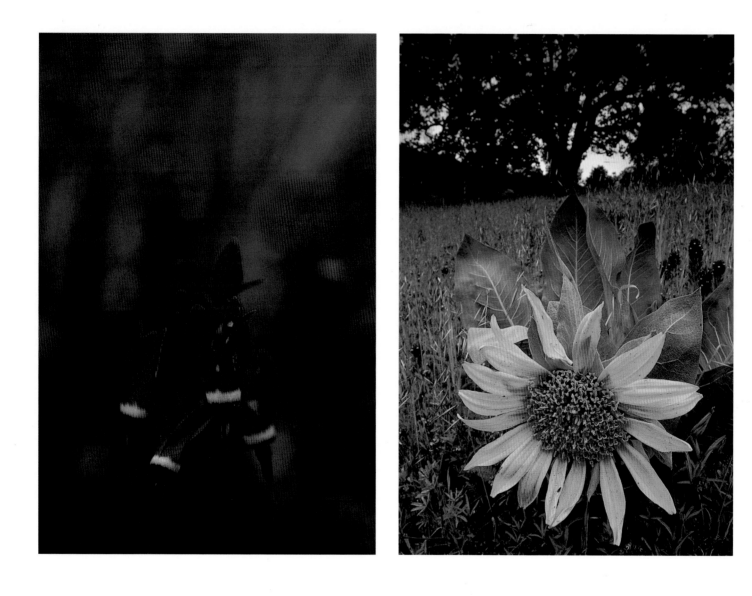

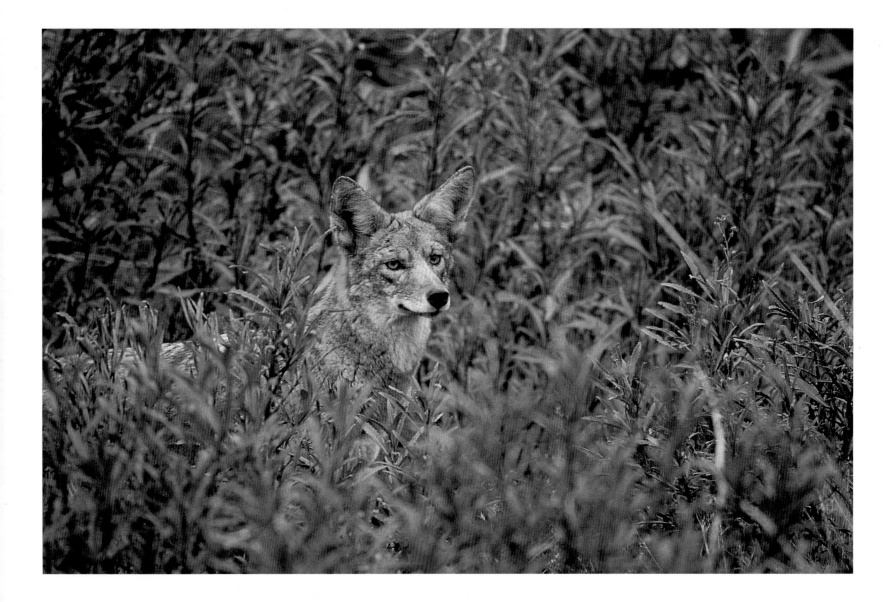

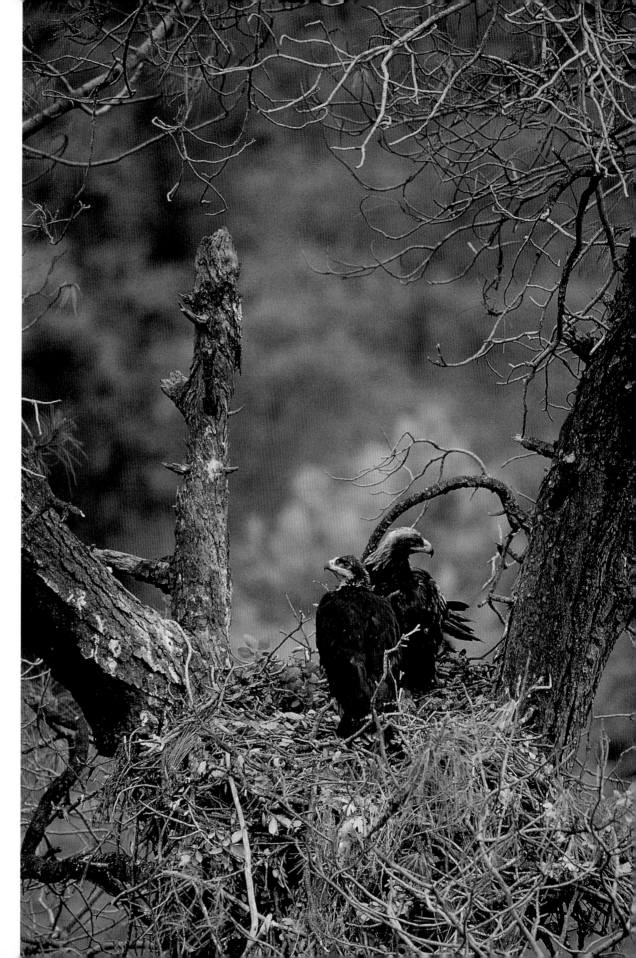

*A coyote (**left**) stares out of deep brush in Mitchell Canyon on Mount Diablo, lured by a predator call imitating the sound of a wounded rabbit. Higher up in the fork of a tree (**right**), a five-foot-wide nest used every year for decades in Pine Canyon provides a literal bird's-eye view for this adult golden eagle and fledgling.*

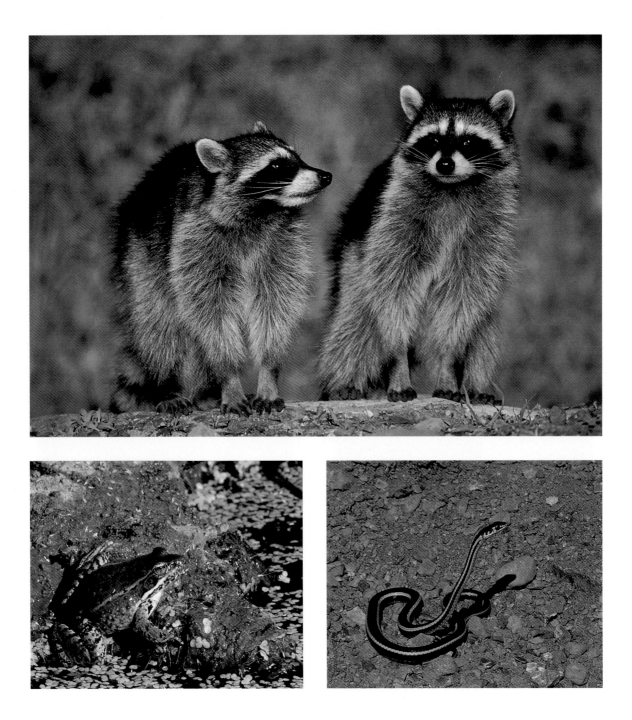

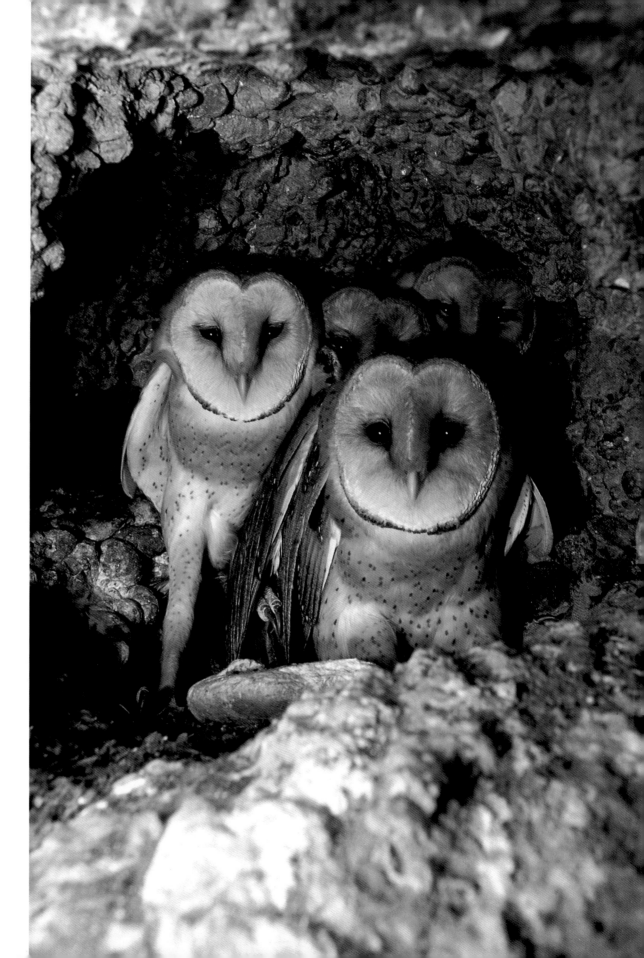

*Ubiquitous barn owls (**right**) roost in a cave on an eastern spur of Mount Diablo near Morgan Territory Regional Park. A raccoon couple out before sunset for some early evening pillaging of a Mount Diablo picnic area (**left, above**), stops long enough to pose for a picture. The extremely fast Alameda whipsnake (**left, lower right**) lives in only a few hilly grasslands of the East Bay, such as this spot on Mount Diablo. In 1991, the threatened species stopped a reservoir project on EBMUD lands. The California red-legged frog (**left, lower left**), pictured here in Morgan Territory Regional Preserve, is probably Mark Twain's "celebrated jumping frog of Calaveras County." Its most recent publication credits are as a newly listed threatened species.*

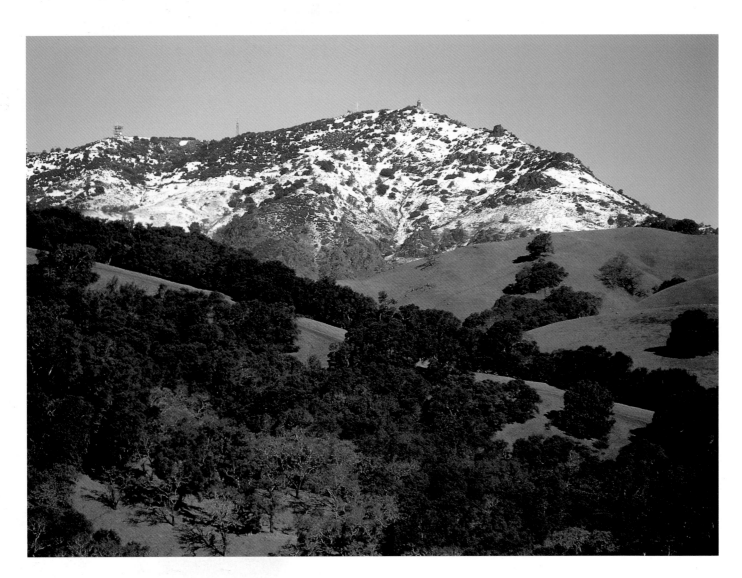

*Mount Diablo briefly takes on an alpine look (**above**) with a snowcap that lasts no more than a few days, even in an exceptional winter. The view from near the summit (**right**) above Juniper Camp on a snowy morning shows the protected wildlands of the mountain reaching all the way to the valley floor, where the towns of Walnut Creek and Lafayette can be seen in the distance. Being on Mount Diablo would feel very different had homes been allowed to climb its slopes up to the edge of the far smaller original 1931 state park, confined to the summit area.*

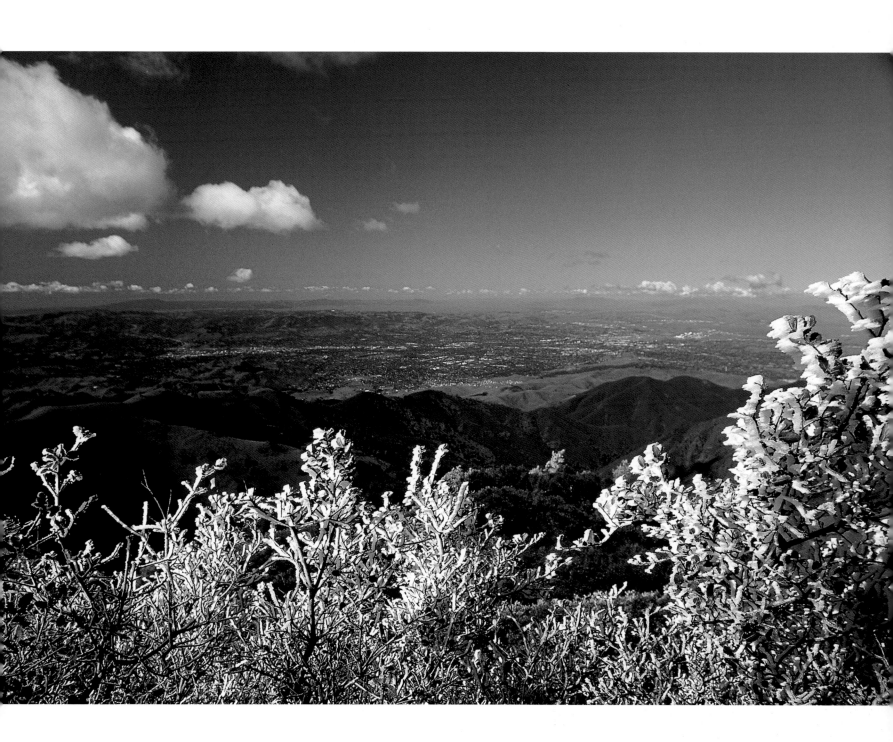

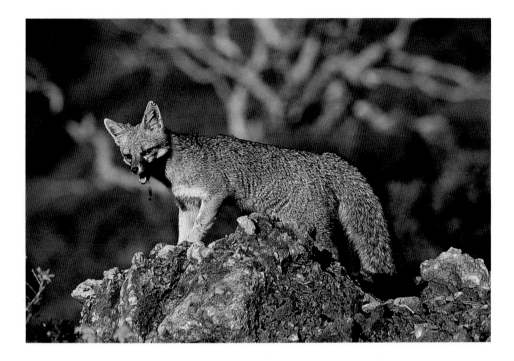

*Rising far above a veil of winter fog that obscures the ever more populous valleys of the East Bay Interior, Mount Diablo (**right**) typifies the essential wildness so important for the survival of the native gray fox (**above**) and the remaining sanity of that introduced species* Homo sapiens, *which has a nasty habit of imprisoning itself in urban enclosures even when the doors are wide open.*

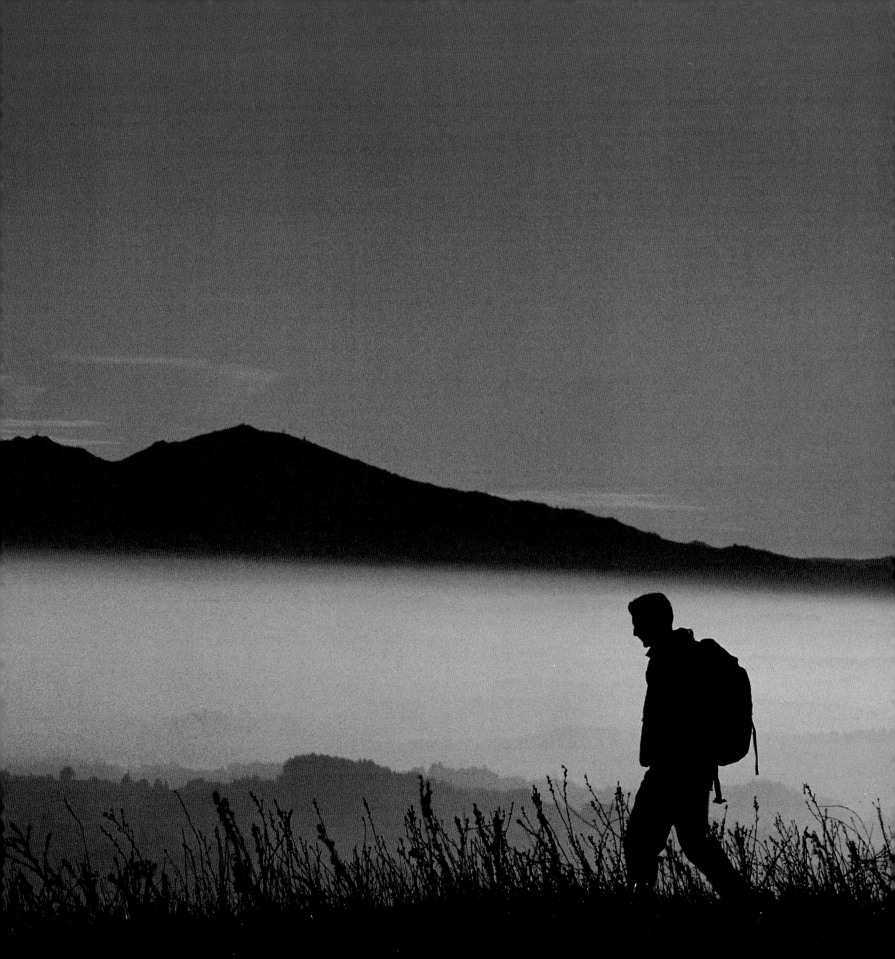

PHOTOGRAPHIC NOTES

San Francisco at dawn from Mount Tamalpais, Marin County; 1996 cover

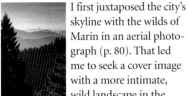

I first juxtaposed the city's skyline with the wilds of Marin in an aerial photograph (p. 80). That led me to seek a cover image with a more intimate, wild landscape in the foreground. I found the perfect site high up on Mount Tamalpais within the state park, but to show detail in the bright golden haze and the green of the dark forest, I had to utilize five stops of graduated neutral-density filters.
(Rowell—Nikon F5, 80–200mm f2.8 lens, Fuji Velvia)

Male bobcat with deer, Point Reyes Peninsula; 1989 p. 1

After I discovered a fresh deer carcass, I set up my portable blind, hoping to photograph a scavenging eagle. I read a book, waited 14 hours, and just before giving up tried some predator calling, imitating the sound of a wounded rabbit. At sunset, a bobcat appeared in warm, golden light.
(Sewell—Nikon F3, 150–500mm f5.6 lens, Fuji 100)

Twilight fog over San Francisco Bay from the Berkeley Hills; 1991 pp. 2–3

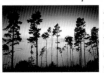

As a fog bank hit the hills and began to creep over them at sunset, I made this image looking through a pine forest on University of California open space lands above Strawberry Canyon. An hour earlier, a workshop student had voiced disappointment about the lack of scenic grandeur at this location. Another student, who shot a different personal vision of this same moment, won a trip to the Caribbean in a *National Geographic* photo contest.
(Rowell—Nikon F4, 35mm f2 lens, Fuji Velvia)

Coast redwoods in fog, Redwood Regional Park, Oakland hills; 1995 pp. 4–5

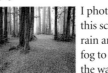

I photographed this scene in light rain and heavy fog to enhance the warm colors of the forest floor and add a sense of atmospheric perspective. My camera was within a stone's throw of a plaque where two great redwoods once grew. The trees were used as landmarks to guide ships through treacherous rocks near Alcatraz Island, 16 miles away.
(Rowell—Nikon F4, 20mm f4 lens, Fuji Velvia)

Aerial view of Mount Diablo over Las Trampas Regional Wilderness and East Bay Municipal Utility District lands; 1995 pp. 6–7

At dawn on a spring morning, my wife, Barbara, flew her Cessna 206 around Mount Diablo while I photographed through the open window. We made several passes to get just the right foreground of ridges at the proper elevation so the mountain would fill the skyline.
(Rowell—Nikon F4, 35mm f1.4 lens, Fuji Velvia)

Sunset at Pescadero State Beach, San Mateo coast; 1995 pp. 8–9

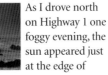

As I drove north on Highway 1 one foggy evening, the sun appeared just at the edge of the mist behind giant winter storm waves crashing over the rocks. I ran to the water's edge with my camera on a tripod and shot dozens of frames before I caught the serendipity of this moment, with a wave up high and the sun almost down.
(Rowell—Nikon F4, 80–200mm f2.8 lens, Fuji Velvia)

Tule Elk at sunset, Point Reyes National Seashore; 1995 pp. 10–11

Just off the road to Tomales Point, I spotted a herd of elk on the crest of a coastal bluff and waited for the sun to set behind a bank of storm clouds.
(Rowell—Nikon F4, 80–200mm f2.8 lens, Fuji Velvia)

Golden Gate Bridge at sunset, San Francisco Presidio; 1996 pp. 12–13

I discovered this unusual angle after scouting for a horizontal view of the Golden Gate Bridge. I composed a photograph featuring wildflowers and waited for sunset.
(Sewell—Nikon N90, 24–50mm f3.3 lens, Fuji Velvia)

David Brower in Tilden Regional Park; 1996 p. 16

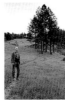

When I was commissioned by Powerfood to produce an "advertorial" for *Outside* magazine celebrating Brower's active outdoor life as well as his lifetime efforts in global conservation, I asked the 84-year-old Berkeleyan to pose for me in the soft light of a winter morning. Over the years, I had met Brower countless times on Tilden trails.
(Rowell—Nikon F4, 35mm f2 lens, Fuji Velvia)

Hiker on Vollmer Peak, Berkeley Hills; 1994 p. 21

A hiker in Tilden Regional Park had stopped on a misty winter morning to look out over the wild ridges and valleys of EBMUD lands and Briones Regional Park. This spot is just off the Sea View Trail section of the Bay Area Ridge Trail.
(Rowell—Nikon N70, 80–200mm f2.8 lens, Fuji Velvia)

Burrowing owl near the Berkeley Marina; 1993 p. 24

I am always looking for opportunities to show how animals adapt to urban expansion. When I found this burrowing owl, I positioned myself near the ground to show the bird with the city of Berkeley and the University of California in the background.
(Sewell—Nikon N90, 200–400mm f4 lens, Fuji Velvia)

Bobcat and San Francisco, Marin Headlands, GGNRA; 1995 p. 24

From a ridge, I spotted this bobcat roaming a hillside in the Marin Headlands. I quickly climbed down and composed a scene to show the animal with the San Francisco skyline in the background.
(Sewell—Nikon N90, 80–200mm f2.8 lens, Fuji Velvia)

Ohlone Indian bedrock mortars, San Francisco Bay National Wildlife Refuge; 1996 p. 27

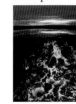

While searching the refuge for an interesting landscape, I was excited to discover these ancient Ohlone mortars and decided to use them as a foreground against a striking sunset.
(Sewell—Nikon N90, 24–50mm f3.3 lens, SB-25 flash, Fuji Velvia)

Monterey pine and rising fog at sunset, Mount Tamalpais; 1996 p. 28

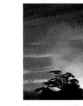

On a dismal, foggy afternoon in October, I made a fast decision to take a photo workshop group high up on Mount Tamalpais instead of to a scheduled location on the coast. The mountain was also in deep fog, but it began to clear a few minutes before sunset. As pink wisps of mist began rising into the blue sky, I positioned myself beneath a wind-flagged pine and waited for the two chaotic forms to coalesce.
(Rowell—Nikon F5, 35–70mm f2.8 lens, Fuji Velvia)

Claremont Canyon Regional Preserve above the fog at dawn, Berkeley Hills; 1995 p. 30

I had hoped to catch the fog pouring over the east side of the hills at dawn from a viewpoint on Grizzly Peak Boulevard, but the level of the typical morning blanket wasn't quite high enough. Instead, I turned around and saw the crimson first light singling out the top of Claremont Canyon Regional Preserve as an island in the mist.
(Rowell—Nikon F4, 80–200mm f2.8 lens, Fuji Velvia)

California poppy (*Eschscholzia californica*) silhouetted at sunset, Vollmer Peak, Berkeley Hills; 1995 p. 32

I was searching for a perfect specimen of the California state flower to photograph in sunset light when this one begged to be silhouetted against the blue and gold of the evening sky. The flower was so close to the ground that I had to lay my tripod on its side to make this tight close-up.
(Rowell—Nikon F4, 55mm f2.8 lens, Fuji Velvia)

Runner at dawn on Vollmer Peak, Berkeley Hills; 1995 pp. 32–33

With a lightweight camera set on a tiny tripod near ground level, I profiled my running companion, Brian Maxwell, beneath a Monterey pine on the Sea View Trail. I previsualized the image to symbolize my strong memories of cresting the Berkeley Hills at sunrise beside this same prominent tree on many previous runs.
(Rowell—Canon Rebel X, 20–35mm f3.5 lens, Fuji Velvia)

Fall view over San Pablo Reservoir from Inspiration Point, Berkeley Hills; 1986 p. 34

I made this photo looking out over EBMUD lands at dawn because I was attracted to the receding ridges and the feeling of open space. The open grasslands are the result of cattle grazing since the disastrous 1923 Berkeley fire, which swept up the slopes in the foreground on a hot fall day, driven by easterly winds.
(Rowell—Nikon F3, 75–150mm f3.5 lens, Fuji Pro 50)

Spring view over San Pablo Reservoir from Inspiration Point, Berkeley Hills; 1996 p. 35

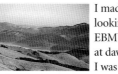

I framed this view to match the preceding photograph, made ten years earlier when the hills were brown. Beyond the vivid difference in color and morning mist is an enduring sameness, with no major human intrusions. I remember the scene looking the same when I was a Tilden Junior Ranger in 1950.
(Rowell—Nikon F4, 80–200mm f2.8 lens, Fuji Velvia)

December grass in pine forest, Quarry Trail, Berkeley Hills; 1994 p. 36

After the early rains, the first grasses to sprout in the fog-drenched soil beneath the forests of Tilden Regional Park are an especially vivid green. To get a unique perspective including the trail and as much of the forest floor as possible, I climbed a tree and propped my tripod in its limbs.
(Rowell—Nikon N90s, 20mm f4 lens, Fuji Velvia)

Forest floor beneath bay tree, Berkeley Hills; 1991 p. 37

On a fall day when the hills were brown, I found these multicolored bay leaves set in fresh green grass. Bay Area fog drip can accentuate normal precipitation up to seven times, creating a virtual rain-forest microclimate in deep shade. I spotted this scene beside a section of the East Bay Skyline National Recreation Trail on EBMUD lands just south of Tilden Regional Park.
(Rowell—Nikon N90, 55mm f2.8 lens, Fuji Velvia)

Starry false Solomon's seal (*Smilacina stellata*), Berkeley Hills; 1994 p. 37

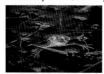

I found this beautiful plant growing in the deep shade of Huckleberry Botanic Regional Preserve and used a macro lens to capture its fine detail.
(Rowell—Nikon F4, 55mm f2.8 lens, Fuji Velvia)

Bullfrog in pond, Strawberry Canyon, Berkeley Hills; 1992 p. 38

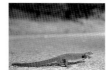

I noticed this bullfrog from a distance and crept up quietly on my hands and knees so as not to frighten it. The frog tolerated my presence while I moved in slow motion to make this image with a telephoto lens.
(Sewell—Nikon F3, 200–400mm f4 lens, Fuji Velvia)

California newt crawling across South Park Drive, Berkeley Hills; 1995 p. 38

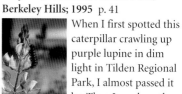

This 1.6-mile road through Tilden Regional Park is closed from November to April to keep migrating California newts from being squashed. The species is rapidly declining but is not yet listed as endangered. This newt was crossing the asphalt very slowly on a cold winter morning.
(Rowell—Nikon F4, 105mm f4 lens, SB-26 flash, Fuji Velvia)

Wildcat Creek in flood, Wildcat Gorge, Berkeley Hills; 1994 p. 39

Below Lake Anza in Tilden Regional Park, Wildcat Gorge takes on the appearance of an Amazonian rain forest during major winter storms. With the water, mosses, and ferns at their height, I set up my camera near the ground in a drizzle to catch the flow of water and the detail of the forest floor. A wide-angle lens and a two-second shutter speed rendered the water silky white.
(Rowell—Nikon N90s, 20mm f4 lens, Fuji Velvia)

Silver lupine (*Lupinus albifrons*) at sunset, Berkeley Hills; 1996 p. 40

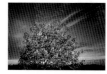

I selected this lupine plant hours in advance to photograph at sunset on the ridge crest above the Sea View Trail in Tilden Regional Park. I composed the setting sun as a diffraction star breaking through its branches and used fill flash to light the plant against an underexposed sky.
(Rowell—Nikon F4, 20mm f4 lens, SB-26 flash, Fuji Velvia)

Caterpillar on silver lupine (*Lupinus albifrons*) at sunset, Vollmer Peak, Berkeley Hills; 1995 p. 41

When I first spotted this caterpillar crawling up purple lupine in dim light in Tilden Regional Park, I almost passed it by. Then I saw how the orange sunset echoed the hue of a California poppy and set up a flash mounted in a portable soft box to add natural-looking foreground light.
(Rowell—Nikon F4, 55mm f2.8 lens, SB-25 flash, Fuji Velvia)

Monarch butterfly cluster, Ardenwood Regional Preserve; 1995 p. 41

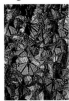

Wintering monarchs, one of my favorite subjects, attract thousands of visitors each year along the California coast. They're difficult to photograph, usually clustering a minimum of 15–20 feet above the ground in the center of a wooded grove with limited natural lighting. *(Sewell—Nikon N90, 800mm f5.6 lens, Metz flash, Fuji Velvia)*

Nesting great horned owl with chick, Lafayette; 1989 p. 42

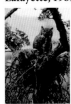

When this mother owl was away from the nest, I quickly climbed high up a nearby tree and set up my camera in a portable tree blind of my own design. After she returned, she remained completely unaware of me while I made this photograph. *(Sewell—Nikon F3, 200–400mm f4 lens, Fujichrome 100)*

Trillium (*Trillium chloropetalum*) and sword ferns, Redwood Regional Park; 1995 p. 42

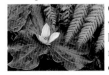

On a foggy day with even, soft light, I used a macro lens at f22 on a tripod to sharply render the contrasting pattern of the ferns and the trillium in bloom. *(Rowell—Nikon F4, 55mm f2.8 lens, Fuji Velvia)*

Foggy morning on the French Trail, Redwood Regional Park; 1995 p. 43

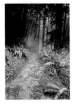

As close as it is to a city, this trail in Redwood Regional Park has an amazingly wild and remote character. I chose this particular spot to represent the overall feeling of hiking the never straight and always narrow path that rolls up and down through miles of ferns and redwood groves. *(Rowell—Nikon F4, 20mm f4 lens, Fuji Velvia)*

Dawn over San Francisco Bay from the Berkeley Hills; 1991 p. 44

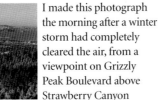

I made this photograph the morning after a winter storm had completely cleared the air, from a viewpoint on Grizzly Peak Boulevard above Strawberry Canyon on University of California open space lands. Berkeley and Emeryville can be seen in the foreground; San Francisco Bay Bridge is visible in the distance. *(Rowell—Nikon 8008s, 85mm f2 lens, Fuji Velvia)*

Spring dawn over San Pablo and Briones Reservoirs from the crest of the Berkeley Hills; 1995 p. 45

Several times a week, I run a Tilden Regional Park trail beside this view into EBMUD lands. On a windless spring morning when the lupine was in full bloom, I carried a camera and tripod to make this image at first light. Afterward, I ditched my pack in the bushes and continued my run unencumbered in the morning sun along the crest of the ridge, retrieving my gear on the way home. *(Rowell—Nikon F4, 24mm f2.8 lens, Fuji Velvia)*

Aerial view of Redwood Regional Park and San Francisco Bay; 1996 p. 46

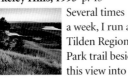

On a clear morning after a storm, I photographed from the open window of my wife, Barbara's, Cessna 206 as she flew along the back of the East Bay hills. We made several passes while I hand-held a three-stop graduated filter to hold back the exposure on the city, on top of a polarizer to richen the greens. *(Rowell—Nikon F4, 24mm f2.8 lens, Fuji Velvia)*

Sunbeams in morning fog, Berkeley Hills; 1996 p. 47

While returning from a morning run, I caught these crepuscular rays of sunlight breaking through a pine forest at the edge of a fog bank on University of California open space lands above Strawberry Canyon. *(Rowell—Olympus XA, 35mm f2.8 lens, Ektachrome 100S)*

Moonset over San Francisco Bay from the Berkeley Hills; 1995 p. 48

The hardest thing about photographing the full moon setting at dawn through the limbs of this dead tree was avoiding morning traffic, with my tripod set up on the asphalt of Grizzly Peak Boulevard. A telephoto lens pulls in Mount Tamalpais on the opposite side of the Bay, under a pink-and-blue twilight wedge descending through the sky to touch the earth at the moment of dawn. *(Rowell—Nikon F4, 80–200mm f2.8 lens, Fuji Velvia)*

Foggy dawn in the Berkeley Hills; 1996 p. 49

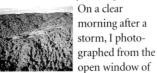

From a turnout on Grizzly Peak Boulevard at the edge of Claremont Canyon Regional Preserve, I carefully framed this view of a eucalyptus forest shrouded in fog below the pink glow of the predawn sky. It's possible to climb above the typical fog layer over the Bay on about half of the mornings. *(Rowell—Nikon F5, 80–200mm f2.8 lens, Fuji Velvia)*

Stormy dawn on the Sea View Trail, Berkeley Hills; 1996 pp. 50–51

As I hiked along this section of the Bay Area Ridge Trail through Tilden Regional Park, the morning sun broke through the dark storm clouds for a brief minute or two. I used a polarizing filter to help saturate the green of the first winter grasses against the brown of the remaining fall foliage. *(Rowell—Nikon N90s, 85mm f2 lens, Fuji Velvia)*

Moonrise over volcanic tuff outcrop, Sibley Volcanic Regional Preserve, Berkeley Hills; 1995 p. 56

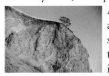

As I was running along a trail at sunset, I noticed the moon seemingly following the crest of the vivid red volcanic ridge above me. I found a spot where I could line up the moon with a descending curve of the ridge and brace my tiny point-and-shoot camera on a rock. *(Rowell—Olympus XA, 35mm f2.8 lens, Fuji Velvia)*

Dawn view from Vollmer Peak, Tilden Regional Park, Berkeley Hills; 1994 p. 56

First light colors the winter mist vivid orange in this compressed telephoto view that pulls in the distant ridges of the Ohlone Regional Wilderness, 40 miles to the south. *(Rowell—Nikon N70, 80–200mm f2.8 lens, Fuji Velvia)*

Spring wildflowers in the Berkeley Hills, Tilden Regional Park; 1984 p. 60

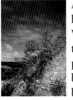

As I was hiking beneath heavy clouds on the Sea View Trail, the sun broke through to spotlight a patch of Indian paintbrush and pink checkerbloom. I climbed a rock outcrop ten feet above the trail to position the flowers against San Pablo Reservoir on EBMUD lands in the distance. *(Rowell—Nikon F3, 24mm f2.8 lens, Kodachrome 64)*

Red columbine (*Aquilegia formosa*) **beside the Grizzly Peak Trail, Tilden Regional Park; 1996** p. 61

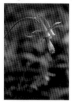

In June, long after most wildflower blossoms were gone, I came across these striking flowers in a marshy area inches from a north-facing trail that had just been weeded by a crew. They had stopped their handiwork for a short section so as not to disturb the blooms. I returned the next day with a tripod and macro lens. (*Rowell—Nikon F4, 55mm f2.8 lens, Fuji Velvia*)

Douglas iris (*Iris douglasiana*) **in Tilden Regional Park; 1995** p. 61

I found this spectacular flower at the height of its bloom near Lake Anza and photographed it with a macro lens and a translucent diffuser disc to soften the light. (*Rowell—Nikon F4, 55mm f2.8 lens, Fuji Velvia*)

Western leatherwood (*Dirca occidentalis*), **Huckleberry Botanic Regional Preserve; 1995** p. 61

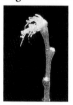

This rare flowering shrub is listed by the California Native Plant Society for future designation as an endangered species. When I moved in close to photograph the best bloom with my macro lens and a flash mounted in a soft box, I was shocked to discover that two adjoining stalks had recently been cut. (*Rowell—Nikon F4, 55mm f2.8 lens, SB-26 flash, Fuji Velvia*)

Caterpillar on Indian paintbrush (*Castilleja wightii*), **Tilden Regional Park; 1996** p. 61

When I spotted the caterpillar on this blossom, I immediately moved in tight with a macro lens and a flash mounted in a soft box. A lens aperture of f22 holds the fine hairs on the bracts in focus. (*Rowell—Nikon F4, 55mm f2.8 lens, SB-26 flash, Fuji Velvia*)

Sunset from Aquatic Park beside San Francisco Bay, Berkeley; 1996 pp. 62–63

I was amazed at how wild this city park appears under a crescent moon at sunset from a trail beside the lagoon, even though Interstate 80 is just behind the trees. (*Rowell—Nikon F5, 35mm f2 lens, Fuji Velvia*)

Egrets roosting in cypress tree, Aquatic Park, Berkeley; 1995 p. 64

During the winter months, egrets spend their nights roosting in a tree beside this urban lagoon. I used a long telephoto with a Projectaflash fresnel lens to light the birds a few minutes after sunset, when most of them had flown to their perches. (*Rowell—Nikon F4, 300mm f2.8 lens, SB-26 flash, Fuji Velvia*)

Brown pelican, Aquatic Park, Berkeley; 1996 p. 65

In the last moments of sunset, I panned this pelican at 1/30 second with a long telephoto lens on a tripod as it skimmed the water. Once highly endangered from eggshell thinning caused by DDT, the birds have become quite numerous again—25 years after a national ban on the pesticide. (*Rowell—Nikon F5, 600mm f5.6 lens, Ektachrome 100S*)

Sunset from Briones Regional Park over the Benicia–Martinez Bridge and the Delta; 1995 pp. 66–67

I climbed a ridge in this park behind Lafayette to photograph an evening vista down Alhambra Valley, where John Muir once took his children on long afternoon walks, and across the Carquinez Strait and Suisun Bay. I used a graduated neutral-density filter to hold detail in both the lower shadows and the upper highlights. (*Rowell—Nikon FM10, 75–150mm f3.5 lens, Fuji Velvia*)

Antioch Dunes evening primrose (*Oenothera deltoides* ssp. *howelli*), **Antioch Dunes; 1995** p. 67

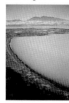

This highly endangered plant is known from only seven occurrences on sand dunes above the south side of Suisun Bay. The prime site is closed to the public. To capture the flowers at the time when they were open, late on a warm afternoon, I used a translucent diffuser disc to soften the direct sunlight. (*Rowell—Nikon F4, 55mm f2.8 lens, Fuji Velvia*)

The Coastal Trail along Bolinas Ridge, Mount Tamalpais; 1996 p. 68

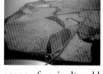

High above the ocean in a steep ravine on a fall afternoon, I set up a telephoto lens on a tripod to catch a hiker on this spectacular section of the Bay Area Ridge Trail in Mount Tamalpais State Park. (*Rowell—Nikon F5, 80–200mm f2.8 lens, Fuji Velvia*)

Mount Diablo over Grizzly Bay at the edge of Grizzly Island, Solano County; 1996 p. 70

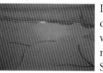

On an environmental flight over the Delta, my wife, Barbara, circled her Cessna 206 as I hung out the open window to line up Mount Diablo with the long arc of Grizzly Bay. (*Rowell—Nikon F5, 35mm f1.4 lens, Fuji Velvia*)

Canada geese wintering at Grizzly Island Wildlife Area; 1996 p. 71

These geese appeared nervous at the approach of my truck. I kept some distance, remained in my vehicle, and set up a window-mount tripod for my 800mm lens to capture the flock on the ground. (*Sewell—Nikon N90, 800mm f5.6 lens, Fuji Velvia*)

Fishermen near Grizzly Island Wildlife Area; 1996 p. 72

After photographing wildlife until sunset, I drove around the refuge looking for a last-minute landscape when I saw two fishermen silhouetted against the vibrantly colored reflection of the evening sky. (*Sewell—Nikon N90, 80–200mm f2.8 lens, Fuji Velvia*)

Aerial view of the Sacramento–San Joaquin Delta; 1996 p. 73

While on an environmental flight over the Delta with my wife, Barbara, I made this wide-angle view of wetlands extending northward for miles toward agricultural lands in the distance. (*Rowell—Nikon F4, 35mm f1.4 lens, Fuji Velvia*)

Aerial view of Tubbs Island, San Pablo Bay; 1996 p. 73

On the flight mentioned in the previous note, I singled out this richly colored scene of agricultural lands surrounding Highway 37 near Sears Point. The wetlands on the bay shore are part of the San Pablo Bay National Wildlife Refuge. (*Rowell—Nikon F4, 85mm f2 lens, Fuji Velvia*)

Aerial view of Sonoma Baylands Tidal Marsh Restoration Area, San Pablo Bay; 1996 p. 74

I took this image on a flight my wife, Barbara, made for the Save San Francisco Bay Association with its executive director, Barry Nelson. A few days earlier, he had been on the ground for the ceremony when Bay waters were released through a channel to complete a major three-year wetlands restoration of sunken land behind old levees. (*Rowell—Nikon F4, 85mm f2 lens, Fuji Velvia*)

Endangered salt marsh harvest mouse, San Francisco Bay National Wildlife Refuge; 1995 p. 75

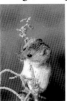

This mouse was trapped for a population study related to the decommissioning of the Mare Island naval shipyard. Two people kept the fast-moving animal from getting away while I made this photograph.
(Sewell—Nikon N90, 80–200mm f2.8 lens, Fuji Velvia)

Snowy egret eating salt marsh harvest mouse, San Francisco Bay National Wildlife Refuge; 1995 p. 75

I was photographing shorebirds at high tide when I saw an egret eating this rare mouse. I'd witnessed this before but hadn't been prepared to photograph it. This time, my exposure was preset for the birds with an extreme telephoto lens.
(Sewell—Nikon N90, 800mm f5.6 lens, Fuji Velvia)

Aerial view of Angel Island in fog, San Francisco Bay; 1995 p. 76

On a foggy morning over the Bay, forested Angel Island looks relatively pristine in this distant aerial view, despite a century of U.S. Army utilization. The island is now a state park, accessible only by boat.
(Rowell—Nikon N90s, 35mm f1.4 lens, Fuji Velvia)

Spring view of San Francisco and Alcatraz Island from Angel Island State Park; 1996 pp. 76–77

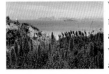

While hiking with my family, I came across these vibrant flowers—an introduced species called pride of Madiera—and envisioned them as a colorful foreground for a photograph of San Francisco and Alcatraz Island. I returned a few days later and waited for the fog to lift.
(Sewell—Nikon N90, 24–50mm f3.3 lens, Fuji Velvia)

Golden Gate Bridge at dusk from Marin Headlands, GGNRA; 1996 p. 78

I climbed down a steep deer trail a half dozen times hoping my predator calls might lure a bobcat onto a ridge so I could juxtapose it with the Golden Gate Bridge. On this visit, the native lupine and Indian paintbrush created an even more striking foreground than I'd visualized. I used a graduated neutral-density filter to allow the light on the land and sky to match what I saw.
(Sewell—Nikon N90, 24–50mm f3.3 lens, Fuji Velvia)

California quail, Marin Headlands, GGNRA; 1991 p. 79

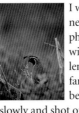

I was sitting in shrubbery near the water's edge to photograph shorebirds with my long telephoto lens when I heard the familiar call of a quail behind me. I turned slowly and shot one frame of the unsuspecting bird before it flushed.
(Rowell—Nikon F4, 500mm f4 lens, Fuji Velvia)

Aerial view of San Francisco and the Golden Gate Bridge from over Mount Tamalpais, Marin County; 1995 p. 80

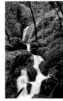

As my wife, Barbara, flew her Cessna 206 around Mount Tamalpais above the state park and the GGNRA, I noticed the way the city seemed to hang ethereally above the distant ridges. She circled ever lower until I was able to capture this perspective.
(Rowell—Nikon F4, 85mm f2 lens, Fuji Velvia)

Endangered mission blue butterfly, Marin Headlands, GGNRA; 1996 p. 81

These rare butterflies appear for only a few weeks each spring. Exotic plants, grazing, and development have caused the lupine plants on which they depend to decline dramatically. I went to one of the few places where they survive and spent many hours trying to make a definitive shot of these creatures, which land very briefly.
(Sewell—Nikon N90, 80–200mm f2.8 lens, SB-25 flash, Fuji Velvia)

Hikers at Cataract Falls, Mount Tamalpais Watershed; 1995 p. 82

I visited these falls on Marin Municipal Water District lands several times to make photographs. On this winter day, two hikers resting on a rock beside the falls, rushing from recent rains, provided the missing element I had been searching for.
(Sewell—Nikon N90, 24–50mm f3.3 lens, Fuji Velvia)

Aerial view of continuous forest north of Mount Tamalpais; 1995 p. 83

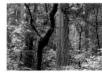

I chose this composition looking west over Pine Mountain Ridge to depict the extent of unbroken forest in Marin County. The land is in the Marin Municipal Water District, with parts of Kent Lake barely visible. The Bolinas Ridge section of the Bay Area Ridge Trail follows the ridge crest just behind the lake.
(Rowell—Nikon F4, 85mm f2 lens, Fuji Velvia)

Sword ferns above Cataract Creek, Mount Tamalpais; 1995 p. 84

When the creek was in flood after heavy rains, I leaned out over this bank of ferns with a wide-angle lens to capture a visual sense of flow toward a vanishing point—not, I hoped, my own.
(Rowell—Nikon N90s, 20mm f4 lens, Fuji Velvia)

Northern spotted owl, Point Reyes Peninsula; 1995 p. 85

To get good detail without the red-eye effect, I carefully set a flash with a portable soft box on a tripod about ten feet to the side of this surprisingly tolerant bird perched in a dark forest. When I backed up and shot with a long telephoto, the bird did not react to the flash.
(Rowell—Nikon F4, 500mm f4 lens, SB-26 flash, Fuji Velvia)

Pileated woodpecker, Point Reyes National Seashore; 1996 p. 85

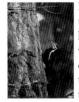

I was scouting for this uncommon bird in a known woodpecker area when I heard its loud, distinctive call. I followed the sound until I located this one; finally, after many visits to the area, I got a close-up photograph with good lighting.
(Sewell—Nikon N90, 200–400mm f4 lens, SB-25 flash, Fuji Velvia)

Coast redwood and bigleaf maple, Muir Woods National Monument; 1996 pp. 86–87

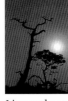

Rather than repeat typical photographs of clusters of redwood trees, I sought out fall colors on a misty day and used a telephoto lens from a distance to avoid convergence when looking up at the trees.
(Rowell—Nikon F5, 80–200mm f2.8 lens, Fuji Velvia)

Moonrise at Point Reyes National Seashore; 1996 p. 88

I was driving home after photographing a coastal sunset when I noticed living and dead cypress trees profiled against a moonlit sky. My family waited in the car while I jumped out and made this 15-second exposure.
(Sewell—Nikon N90, 80–200mm f2.8 lens, Fuji Velvia)

Northern spotted owl in flight, Mount Tamalpais; 1995 pp. 88–89

After weeks of watching this owl come and go from the same tree, I set up two flash units and prefocused my camera in front of the branch it always landed on. Using a remote trigger, I was able to catch it in flight as it ascended to the branch.
(Sewell—Nikon N90, 24–50mm f3.3 lens, 2 SB-25 flashes, Fuji Velvia)

Black-tailed buck at night, Mount Tamalpais; 1994–1995 p. 90

I designed a remote system to document a mountain lion and to see what types of animals used this wooded trail. This buck, one of many deer that crossed the infrared beam, triggered the camera and flash mounted in a waterproof container.
(Sewell—Nikon N2000, 50mm f1.4 lens, 2 SB-24 flashes, Fuji Velvia)

Gray fox at night, Mount Tamalpais; 1994–1995 p. 90

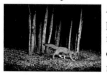

A fox in search of prey triggered the infrared beam during its nightly rounds. The previous year, on Mount Diablo, another fox had learned to take self-portraits, intentionally using up dozens of frames. When the film ran out, he tried to outsmart me by chewing up the wires that powered the unit.
(Sewell—Nikon N2000, 50mm f1.4 lens, 2 SB-24 flashes, Fuji Velvia)

Black-tailed jackrabbit at night, Mount Tamalpais; 1994–1995 p. 91

I checked my remote camera monthly, never knowing what to expect when I processed the film. The camera recorded numerous small mammals, including wood rats, deer mice, squirrels, and bats—evidence that the forest comes alive at night with nocturnal animals.
(Sewell—Nikon N2000, 50mm f1.4 lens, 2 SB-24 flashes, Fuji Velvia)

Striped skunk at night, Mount Tamalpais; 1994–1995 p. 91

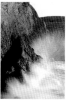

This is one of many skunks that crossed the path of my remote camera. After several active months, the camera produced images of animals I'd otherwise never see, documenting the rare spotted skunk and the most southern known coyote since their eradication from the Marin peninsula in the 1940s and 1950s.
(Sewell—Nikon N2000, 50mm f1.4 lens, 2 SB-24 flashes, Fuji Velvia)

Scrub jay on clover, Mount Tamalpais State Park; 1995 p. 92

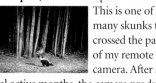

While hiking around to photograph spring wildflowers, I composed this scene with wild clover in front of rolling green hills and San Francisco Bay. After I had taken a few shots, this jay landed briefly, and I quickly took two more before it flew away.
(Sewell—Nikon N90, 24–50mm f3.3 lens, Kodak Lumiere)

Northern Pacific rattlesnake on Bolinas Ridge; 1996 p. 93

As I searched for a location to photograph the sunset overlooking the ocean, I spotted a rattlesnake on a nearby rock. I set up my camera and tripod before moving closer and made this photograph to the sound of maracas at sunset.
(Sewell—Nikon N90, 20mm f2.8 lens, SB-25 flash, Fuji Velvia)

Misty dawn on Bolinas Ridge, Mount Tamalpais; 1995 pp. 94–95

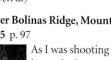

As first light struck the distant ridges of Point Reyes National Seashore, I focused on the foreground as rivers of fog flowed down ravines toward the sea in a reverse flow back out of San Francisco Bay over Bolinas Ridge.
(Rowell—Nikon F4, 80–200mm f2.8 lens, Fuji Velvia)

Wave crashing at sunset, Marin Headlands; 1995 p. 96

At the end of Rodeo Beach in the GGNRA, I aimed my camera away from the sunset at a dark rock and waited for waves to crash against it. With the camera fixed on a tripod, I shot a roll of 36 exposures at varying speeds around 1/4 second to capture the sense of chaotic motion.
(Rowell—Nikon F4, 80–200mm f2.8 lens, Fuji Velvia)

Fog at dawn over Bolinas Ridge, Mount Tamalpais; 1995 p. 97

As I was shooting long telephoto views into the mist, I noticed the bigger picture of soft, white fog lacing the left side of a shadowed ravine as the first crimson rays of sunlight touched the other side, with the ocean framed through the gap.
(Rowell—Nikon F4, 24mm f2.8 lens, Fuji Velvia)

Iceplant *(Carpobrotus chilensis)* and coyote bush *(Baccharis pilularis)*, Marin Headlands; 1995 p. 98

On a foggy fall afternoon when grand landscapes were out of the question, I tried to symbolize typical coastal habitat by singling out a coyote bush in bloom—the Bay Area's most common shrub—surrounded by a carpet of iceplant with cypress trees in the background.
(Rowell—Nikon F4, 24mm f2.8 lens, Fuji Velvia)

Gray fox, Mount Tamalpais Watershed; 1994 p. 99

Michael Sewell used the call of a rabbit in distress to lure this native fox close enough for me to photograph. As indicated by its curious expression, it never detected that we were human, disguised as we were by camouflage gear and drips of skunk scent.
(Rowell—Nikon F4, 500mm f4 lens, Fuji Velvia)

Iceplant *(Carpobrotus chilensis)* at sunset, coastal bluffs of Marin Headlands; 1991 p. 99

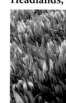

I used a macro lens to capture the texture of this common succulent backlighted by the setting sun above the ocean. Though other species of the sea fig family were definitely introduced, botanists believe this one grew here on the coast before the first explorers arrived.
(Rowell—Nikon F4, 55mm f2.8 lens, Fuji Velvia)

Sunset on sea stacks, Rodeo Beach, Marin Headlands; 1995 pp. 100–101

I had been taking workshop groups to shoot the abstract forms of these offshore rocks at sunset for years. One evening, it all came together and I found just the right spot to integrate the black shapes with a unique pattern in the clouds at the height of their sunset color.
(Rowell—Nikon F4, 35mm f2 lens, Fuji Velvia)

Stormy sunset from Tomales Point, Point Reyes National Seashore; 1996 pp. 102–103

I used a telephoto lens to juxtapose my hiking companion, Wilford Welch, with a beam of sunlight over the Pacific Ocean on a blustery spring evening.
(Rowell—Nikon N90s, 80–200mm f2.8 lens, Fuji Velvia)

Dawn over San Francisco Bay from Mount Tamalpais; 1996 p. 106

What especially drew me to capture this broad view of the Bay just before sunrise on a fall morning was the realization of how wild the overall scene looked. With their lights off, the cities were nearly invisible in the deep morning shadows of Mount Diablo and the East Bay hills, on the skyline.
(Rowell—Nikon F4, 55mm f2.8 lens, Fuji Velvia)

Black-tailed buck in fall velvet, Mount Tamalpais State Park; 1994 p. 112

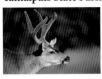

I first photographed this buck with a herd and then changed my position to create an uncluttered portrait with a clean, bright green background.
(Sewell—Nikon N90, 200–400mm f4 lens, Fuji Velvia)

Egret at sunset, Rodeo Lagoon, Marin Headlands; 1991 pp. 112–113

As I was leaving Rodeo Beach after sunset, I noticed a lone egret in the lagoon beside a bridge. I parked and tiptoed back to capture the bird silhouetted against the crimson reflection of the sky.
(Rowell—Nikon 8008s, 55mm f2.8 lens, Fuji Velvia)

Surf rainbow, Marin Headlands; 1992 p. 114

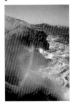

Knowing the physics of rainbows, I made this one happen before my camera by seeking a position near sunset where the breaking surf would be 42 degrees away from my shadow— the antisolar point. I had to crawl far out on a rocky ridge to get the correct angle and wait for the right wave.
(Rowell—Nikon F4, 35mm f2 lens, Fuji Velvia)

Ron Kauk climbing Endless Bummer, Mickey's Beach; 1990 p. 115

As one of the world's best rock climbers ascended this continuous overhang (rated 5.13b) entirely on handholds and footholds, with a rope for safety only, I set up my camera to profile him in the middle of a critical move.
(Rowell—Nikon F4, 24mm f2.8 lens, Fuji Velvia)

Starfish and octopus in tide pool, Palomarin Beach, Point Reyes National Seashore; 1996 p. 116

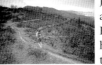

In evening light at low tide, I used a graduated neutral-density filter to open up the exposure on the dark foreground in a pool where I had discovered an octopus.
(Rowell—Nikon F4, 20mm f4 lens, Fuji Velvia)

Evening at Sculptured Beach, Point Reyes National Seashore; 1996 p. 117

I used my own long shadow in the last hour of light to symbolize the feeling of being all alone on this spectacular section of Drakes Bay, several miles from the nearest road.
(Rowell—Nikon N90s, 35mm f2 lens, Fuji Velvia)

Point Reyes Beach, Point Reyes National Seashore; 1996 pp. 118–119

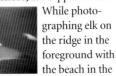

While photographing elk on the ridge in the foreground with the beach in the distance, I stopped to make a straight landscape image of the dramatic approach of a storm on a windy spring evening.
(Rowell—Nikon N90s, 80–200mm f2.8 lens, Fuji Velvia)

Aerial view over Tomales Point, Point Reyes National Seashore; 1996 p. 120

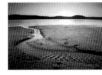

From the open window of my wife, Barbara's, Cessna 206, I framed this image of the northern end of the Point Reyes Peninsula looking over Tomales Bay. The Tomales Point Trail can be seen traversing the spring meadows.
(Rowell—Nikon F4, 85mm f2 lens, Fuji Velvia)

Backpacker on the Woodward Valley Trail, Point Reyes National Seashore; 1996 p. 121

Just a few months after the huge 1995 Point Reyes fire had burned across the park from Inverness to the sea, I found greenery already sprouting on the blackened lower slopes of Mount Wittenberg, the park's highest point. The backpacker was on her way to spend the night at Coast Camp.
(Rowell—Nikon N90s, 24mm f2.8 lens, Fuji Velvia)

Point Reyes checkerbloom (*Sidalcea calycosa*), Point Reyes National Seashore; 1996 p. 121

On a cold winter morning, I focused a macro lens on frost crystals coating the leaves of this rare and endangered species, listed by the California Native Plant Society for future official designation. The plant occurs only at Point Reyes and along the Sonoma coast.
(Rowell—Nikon F4, 55mm f2.8 lens, Fuji Velvia)

Sunset over the foggy Pacific Ocean behind a Monterey pine, Mount Tamalpais; 1995 p. 122

As the sun began to set over an extensive fog bank, I positioned myself on a steep hillside where I could line it up with an especially fine tree (also seen on page 28), wait for it to touch the horizon, and compress the scene into simplicity with a telephoto lens.
(Rowell—Nikon F4, 80–200mm f2.8 lens, Fuji Velvia)

Sunrise at Drakes Beach, Point Reyes National Seashore; 1996 p. 123

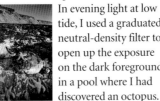

I scouted this location beforehand and decided to return at sunrise and use a 20mm lens to include the entire western half of Drakes Bay.
(Sewell—Nikon N90, 20mm f2.8 lens, Fuji Velvia)

Sunrise over Tomales Bay near Inverness; 1996 pp. 124–125

I found this scene where a freshwater stream merges with the narrow estuary at low tide and waited for the moment of richest predawn sky color to reflect off the waters and damp earth.
(Rowell—Nikon F4, 20mm f4 lens, Fuji Velvia)

Tule elk bull at sunset, Tomales Point, Point Reyes National Seashore; 1996 p. 125

After photographing a herd of elk against a green hillside in perfect afternoon light to show full detail in the animals, I returned at sunset to make this long telephoto view of a single elk silhouetted against the reflection of an orange cloud over the ocean.
(Rowell—Nikon F4, 500mm f4 lens, Fuji Velvia)

Baker Beach and the Golden Gate, GGNRA; 1996 p. 126

Knowing that the name "Golden Gate" was given to the Bay's entrance nearly a century before the bridge was built, I sought a wholly natural foreground with golden hues. I found an image to symbolize the name when the eroded sandstone of this wild beach below the Presidio of San Francisco took on the vivid color of a Pacific sunset.
(Rowell—Nikon F5, 24mm f2.8 lens, Fuji Velvia)

San Francisco in fog from the Berkeley Hills; 1995 pp. 128–129

I made this image about half an hour after sunset on a foggy evening with an extreme telephoto lens from the edge of Tilden Regional Park beside Grizzly Peak Boulevard, near the intersection of South Park Drive. On many other attempts to capture the feeling of the city in fog, I have never caught this shrouding of the city in twilight colors.
(Rowell—Nikon F4, 500mm f4 lens, Fuji Velvia)

Aerial view of the Presidio of San Francisco, GGNRA; p. 130

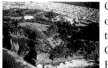

Only from the air or atop the south tower of the Golden Gate Bridge is it possible to get an overall sense of how vast and spectacular the 1,480 acres of the Presidio really are. I framed this view from my wife, Barbara's, Cessna 206 as we approached the bridge from the southern coast.
(Rowell—Nikon F4, 85mm f2 lens, Fuji Velvia)

Endangered Presidio manzanita (*Arctostaphylos hookeri* ssp. *ravenii*), Presidio of San Francisco, GGNRA; 1996 p. 130

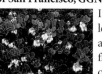

I used a macro lens and a slight amount of fill flash to bring out the winter blossoms on this exceedingly rare plant. Five of six known wild occurrences of the shrub have been destroyed by urbanization, leaving only the site in the Presidio itself.
(Rowell—Nikon F4, 55mm f2.8 lens, Fuji Velvia)

Cypress grove, the Presidio of San Francisco; 1996 p. 131

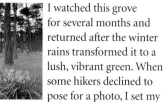

I watched this grove for several months and returned after the winter rains transformed it to a lush, vibrant green. When some hikers declined to pose for a photo, I set my self-timer and stepped into the frame.
(Sewell—Nikon N90, 20mm f2.8 lens, Fuji Velvia)

Aerial view of Golden Gate Park and Ocean Beach, San Francisco; 1996 p. 132

From my wife, Barbara's, Cessna 206 I framed a very formal composition to emphasize the strong architectural lines of this designed and planted urban greenbelt as well as to give it a sense of place, sprawling eastward from the sea to form one of the nation's truly great city parks.
(Rowell—Nikon F4, 35mm f2 lens, Fuji Velvia)

California sea lions at Pier 39, San Francisco; 1996 p. 133

Shortly after dawn on a winter weekday when few tourists were out on Pier 39, I set up my tripod and long telephoto to capture these well-known denizens of the pier in relative solitude.
(Rowell—Nikon F4, 500mm f4 lens, Fuji Velvia)

San Francisco greenbelts from the air; 1996 p. 133

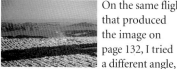

On the same flight that produced the image on page 132, I tried a different angle, with Golden Gate Park in the foreground, to give pictorial meaning to the word "greenbelt." Behind the urban park are the preserved GGNRA lands of the Presidio and, on the opposite side of the bridge, the Marin Headlands. Angel Island State Park stands out to the right in the Bay.
(Rowell—Nikon F4, 35mm f2 lens, Fuji Velvia)

Sunrise on Southeast Farallon Island; 1996 p. 134

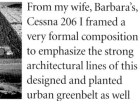

As I approached the island in a boat, I asked the captain to circle until I could catch the first flush of dawn. I used a fast wide-angle lens to combat the rocking of the boat and the low light and to get the moon in the composition.
(Rowell—Nikon F4, 35mm f2 lens, Fuji Velvia)

Breaching humpback whale, San Francisco coast; 1994 p. 135

From a boat on a crisp fall morning, I saw this migrating whale breach several times. The choppy sea made it necessary to hand-hold my camera.
(Sewell—Nikon N90, 80–200mm f2.8 lens, Fuji Velvia)

Northern right whale dolphin, San Mateo coast; 1994 p. 135

I was fortunate to observe this rarely seen dolphin on its annual northern migration. Using a polarizer to reduce reflections, I photographed it from a boat while it rode a wave off the bow.
(Sewell—Nikon N90, 80–200mm f2.8 lens, Fuji Velvia)

Western gull over Southeast Farallon Island from Shubrick Point; 1996 p. 136

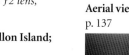

From a blind perched atop a high ridge, I decided to stop photographing individual birds with a big telephoto lens long enough to make an overall landscape image. With birds constantly in the air, the task was not easy; I shot a roll of 36 exposures to get this simple image with one prominent bird above the cove.
(Rowell—Nikon F4, 55mm f2.8 lens, Fuji Velvia)

Aerial view of the Farallon Islands; 1984 p. 137

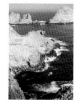

I made this photograph out the window of my wife, Barbara's, Cessna 206 on her flight over the crippled tanker SS *Puerto Rican* near Southeast Farallon Island. It caused a "minor spill" before its tanks were drained and it sank. "Only" about 5,000 birds died.
(Rowell—Nikon F3, 85mm f2 lens, Kodachrome 64)

Farallon Islands at sunset; 1996 p. 138

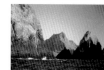

In this view through offshore islets from a boat off Southeast Farallon Island, the lighthouse on top of the island can be seen, 348 feet above the sea. The narrow vertical slit on the right is an odd angle of view through the Great Arch, a broad hole cut into hard granite by eons of wave action.
(Rowell—Nikon F4, 35mm f2 lens, Fuji Velvia)

Western gull on nest, Farallon Islands; 1996 p. 139

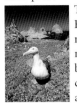

This nest in endemic Farallon weed juxtaposes most of the islands' major rock features in the background. I set up my camera and hid behind a nearby rock. The gull returned to the nest within five minutes, and I made this photograph using a remote trigger.
(Sewell—Nikon N90, 20mm f2.8 lens, SB-25 flash, Fuji Velvia)

Murre colony on Southeast Farallon Island; 1996 p. 140

From a high blind, I focused a telephoto lens on a major nesting area for the islands' 40,000 common murres. Their historical population was probably more than 300,000 before gold rush egg collectors and modern oil spills took their toll.
(Rowell—Nikon F4, 80–200mm f2.8 lens, Fuji Velvia)

Brandt's cormorant on nest, Southeast Farallon Island; 1996 p. 141

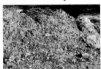

From the blind mentioned in the previous note with 1,000mm of lens (500mm plus 2X converter), I focused on a nesting bird and waited for the right moment to catch the sun on its vivid blue throat patch.
(Rowell—Nikon F4, 500mm f4 lens, Ektachrome 100S)

Western gull in flight, Southeast Farallon Island; 1996 p. 141

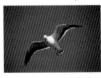

From the summit of the island, I was able to use an autofocus telephoto zoom to catch many single birds in flight as they swung in for a landing in the nesting area below.
(Rowell—Nikon F4, 80–200mm f2.8 lens, Ektachrome 100S)

Common murre courtship, Southeast Farallon Island; 1996 p. 141

This photo was taken from a cliff blind overlooking the largest murre colony on the islands, where thousands of birds displayed flamboyant wing flapping and beak-to-neck-rubbing courtship behavior. I took a light reading from the nearby rocks and chose an exposure that kept detail in both the dark and light feathers.
(Sewell—Nikon N90, 800mm f5.6 lens, Fuji Velvia)

Tufted puffin in breeding plumage, Southeast Farallon Island; 1996 p. 141

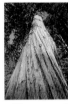

This photo was taken from a blind atop a cliff overlooking a murre colony. I noticed a pair of puffins approaching from the distance and positioned my 800mm lens for their arrival. For a correct exposure on the dark bird, I took a spot meter reading from the rocks in the background.
(Sewell—Nikon N90, 800mm f5.6 lens, Fuji Velvia)

Adolescent male elephant seal, Año Nuevo State Reserve; 1995 p. 142

During a guided tour, I searched the refuge for a seal that wasn't covered with sand and noticed this one in an inland pool. He bellowed at the tourists just as I made this photograph.
(Sewell—Nikon N90, 80–200mm f2.8 lens, Fuji Velvia)

Sparring bull elephant seals, Año Nuevo State Reserve; 1996 p. 142

I caught these huge creatures in a dominance battle on a mainland beach beside Año Nuevo Island, where northern elephant seals began breeding in the fifties after coming close to extinction around the turn of the century.
(Rowell—Nikon F4, 80–200mm f2.8 lens, Fuji Velvia)

Dawn at Pigeon Point, San Mateo coast; 1996 p. 143

While looking for a good landscape photo depicting Año Nuevo State Reserve, I drove out the road to Pigeon Point before dawn and walked to the beach to capture this sea stack in front of Año Nuevo and Franklin Points.
(Rowell—Nikon F4, 55mm f2.8 lens, Fuji Velvia)

Coast redwood, Big Basin Redwoods State Park; 1995 p. 144

After walking through several groves at Big Basin, I decided to focus on a single old-growth tree reaching for the sky in direct light—a powerful visual symbol of the stupendous height and breadth that make these trees true natural wonders.
(Rowell—Nikon F4, 20mm f4 lens, Fuji Velvia)

Hiker at Berry Creek Falls, Big Basin Redwoods State Park; 1996 p. 145

On a brisk winter day following a heavy rainstorm, my friend Chris Gill took me to the Bay Area's largest waterfall. Moments after we arrived, the morning sun broke through the trees, casting unphotogenic dappled light. We waited the entire day for the sun to pass over the canyon, bathing the falls in soft, even light.
(Sewell—Nikon N90, 24–50mm f3.3 lens, Fuji Velvia)

Aerial view of El Corte de Madera Creek Open Space Preserve, Santa Cruz Mountains; 1996 p. 146

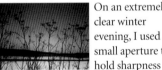

My wife, Barbara, circled low in her Cessna 206 so I could capture this expanse of wild redwood and Douglas fir forest with the urban South Bay on the horizon. The illusory bright spot of light, known as the Heiligenschein effect, is caused by the lack of shadows at the point opposite the sun combined with reflections from moist vegetation.
(Rowell—Nikon F4, 35mm f1.4 lens, Fuji Velvia)

Duveneck Windmill Pasture Area, Los Altos Hills; 1995 p. 147

I hiked past this scene near the Duveneck family's Hidden Villa summer camp in 1952 and came back with my camera 43 years later, after the family bequested 430 acres for an open space preserve. It took five stops of graduated neutral-density filters to equalize the tones of the shaded meadow and sunlit stormy sky.
(Rowell—Nikon F4, 35mm f1.4 lens, Fuji Velvia)

Fennel on the edge of San Francisco Bay at sunset, Coyote Hills Regional Park; 1995 pp. 148–149

On an extremely clear winter evening, I used a small aperture to hold sharpness on both the foreground plants and the distant Santa Cruz Mountains of the Peninsula.
(Rowell—Nikon F4, 55mm f2.8 lens, Fuji Velvia)

Palo Alto Baylands Nature Preserve, Palo Alto; 1996 p. 154

I climbed up on the railings of a boardwalk and used an extremely wide-angle lens to capture the dramatic line of this pathway through restored salt-marsh wetlands.
(Rowell—Nikon F4, 20mm f4 lens, Fuji Velvia)

Aerial view of Lower Crystal Springs Reservoir and San Francisco Watershed lands; 1996 p. 158

Most often seen from Highway 280 or from flights into San Francisco International Airport, Crystal Springs Reservoirs and the vast San Francisco Watershed lands appear invitingly wild in this image shot from my wife, Barbara's, Cessna 206. Exceptionally well protected, the lands are mostly closed to the public.
(*Rowell—Nikon F4, 35mm f1.4 lens, Fuji Velvia*)

Aerial view of Corkscrew Slough, Bair Island, San Francisco Bay National Wildlife Refuge; 1996 p. 164

On a flight my wife, Barbara, made for the Save San Francisco Bay Association, I used a telephoto lens to single out these healthy salt-marsh wetlands in the Bay near Redwood City. Just out of view on the island is a sudden demarcation into dry "reclaimed" land where a major development has been proposed.
(*Rowell—Nikon F4, 85mm f1.4 lens, Fuji Velvia*)

Endangered California clapper rail, Palo Alto Baylands; 1994 p. 165

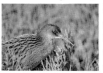

Clapper rails are brought to the top of their pickleweed habitat when an extreme high tide occurs. I used fill flash to enhance the details of this bird's feathers, which are set off by the red-and-green pickleweed.
(*Sewell—Nikon N90, 200–400mm f4 lens, SB-25 flash, Fuji Velvia*)

Osprey with chick on nest, Mount Tamalpais; 1994 p. 165

Prior to the nesting season, I set up a tree blind at a nest I was aware of, knowing the ospreys would probably return in spring. After observing the nest on several occasions, I returned to make this photograph after the chicks were hatched.
(*Sewell—Nikon N90, 800mm f5.6 lens, Fuji Velvia*)

Endangered San Francisco garter snake, San Mateo County; 1994 p. 165

This colorful reptile is on the brink of extinction. I made this photograph near a research site—one of the last locations where these snakes occur.
(*Sewell—Nikon N90, 200–400mm f4 lens, SB-25 flash, Fuji Velvia*)

California tiger salamander, San Mateo County; 1989 p. 165

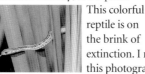

This declining species is difficult to locate, usually migrating during rainy weather. Its wet, rounded form didn't have any sharp edges to focus on, so I bracketed my focus slightly to make the image sharp.
(*Sewell—Nikon F3, 80–200mm f2.8 lens, Fujichrome 100*)

Black-necked stilts in flight, San Francisco Bay National Wildlife Refuge; 1996 pp. 166–167

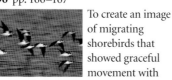

To create an image of migrating shorebirds that showed graceful movement with a dreamy feeling, I panned with a group of stilts as they flew by, using an aperture and shutter speed that gave the photograph rich color saturation while maintaining a sense of movement.
(*Sewell—Nikon N90S, 800mm f5.6 lens, Metz flash, Fuji Velvia*)

Black-necked stilt, Palo Alto Baylands Nature Preserve; 1996 p. 167

Just before first light struck a salt marsh, I set up my camera on a tripod with 1000mm of lens (500mm plus 2X converter) to catch this resident bird and its reflection.
(*Rowell—Nikon F4, 500mm f4 lens, Ektachrome 100S*)

Aerial view of the Diablo Range south of San Francisco Bay; 1990 pp. 168–169

When I took this unique telephoto view of the broad horizons of the South Bay, I did not have this book in mind. I composed it to symbolize our feelings of leaving home a few minutes after my wife, Barbara, had taken off before dawn from Oakland in her single-engine Cessna 206. We were bound for a three-month adventure in South America.
(*Rowell—Nikon F4, 85mm f1.4 lens, Fuji Velvia*)

Oak tree above Marsh Creek, east of Mount Diablo; 1996 p. 170

I silhouetted this lone oak against the clouds in an extensive area of oak woodland near the junction of Marsh Creek and Morgan Territory Roads. The trees have especially fine profiles in winter, when their leaves have dropped.
(*Rowell—Nikon F4, 24mm f2.8 lens, Fuji Velvia*)

Evening view from the Ohlone Wilderness Trail, Sunol Regional Wilderness; 1995 p. 172

The rolling hills and deep valleys of the Sunol Regional Wilderness are most beautiful in spring. I brought a large arsenal of camera equipment into the backcountry to make some definitive springtime photographs in evening light.
(*Rowell—Nikon F4, 80–200mm f2.8 lens, Fuji Velvia*)

Foggy morning on the Ohlone Wilderness Trail, Ohlone Regional Wilderness; 1995 p. 173

While running the Ohlone Wilderness 50km ultramarathon race on a spring morning, I stopped for a few seconds to photograph this mystical oak forest with a tiny six-ounce camera. The fog soon parted to reveal carpets of wildflowers; after shooting two rolls of film, I continued on to barely win my age group.
(*Rowell—Minox 35GL, 35mm f2.8 lens, Kodak Lumiere*)

Snow in the Ohlone Regional Wilderness from Calaveras Reservoir; 1995 p. 174

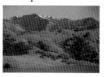

The morning after a late winter storm when the air was perfectly clear, I drove to Calaveras Reservoir to get this panorama of the green hills of Sunol and Ohlone Regional Wildernesses capped by snow.
(*Rowell—Nikon F4, 55mm f2.8 lens, Fuji Velvia*)

Spring wildflowers beneath black oak tree, Ohlone Regional Wilderness; 1995 p. 175

I used a wide-angle lens close to the ground to emphasize a foreground of spring wildflowers blooming in profusion on the crest of Valpe Ridge. The extensive meadows, dotted with black oaks, culminate in 3,817-foot Rose Peak.
(*Rowell—Nikon F4, 20mm f4 lens, Fuji Velvia*)

Wood duck and western pond turtle, Ohlone Regional Wilderness; 1989 p. 175

When I stumbled on this secluded pond while searching for feral pigs, a pair of startled ducks flushed from the water. Returning with a portable blind days later, I was able to make this photograph without being noticed.
(Sewell—Nikon F3, 200–400mm f4 lens, Fuji Velvia)

Evening fog behind oak forest, Ohlone Regional Wilderness; 1995 p. 176

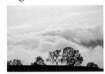

A telephoto lens emphasizes an approaching fog bank at twilight against a row of oaks on a high ridge of the wilderness area.
(Rowell—Nikon F4, 80–200mm f2.8 lens, Fuji Velvia)

Owl's clover (Orthocarpus purpurascens) at sunset, Ohlone Wilderness Trail, Ohlone Regional Wilderness; 1995 p. 177

I came across this vivid patch of purple owl's clover just before sunset and used a graduated neutral-density filter and fill flash to hold color and detail in both the deeply shadowed flowers and the sunlit sky.
(Rowell—Nikon N90S, 20mm f4 lens, SB-25 flash, Fuji Velvia)

Peregrine falcon, Sunol Regional Wilderness; 1995 p. 178

I took this wild bird's portrait moments before a biologist released it after trapping it in a net. He had taken a blood sample to check for environmental toxins and recorded its band number, which matched that of the captive-bred chick described in the following note. We were both gratified to learn that this successful breeding adult was the same chick I had photographed at the moment of its initial release on Mount Diablo five years earlier.
(Rowell—Nikon F4, 55mm f2.8 lens, Fuji Velvia)

Castle Rock at sunset, Mount Diablo State Park; 1995 p. 179

I made this photograph to complete the photo story described in the two preceding notes while returning from a mountain bike ride with my son, Tony, through Diablo Foothills Regional Park. Though the cave with the 1990 prairie falcon nest is not visible here, it is best not to reveal its exact location, in similar cliffs some distance away.
(Rowell—Nikon N90S, 135mm f3.5 lens, Fuji Velvia)

Peregrine falcon chick in prairie falcon nest, Mount Diablo State Park; 1990 p. 179

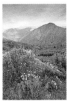

While doing an article on peregrines for the April 1991 *National Geographic,* I rappelled down a high cliff to help biologist Lee Aulman release this bird and photograph the event. We put the captive-bred chick into a prairie falcon nest containing four wild chicks in a cliffside cave. This photograph was not used in the story, but it gained new significance when I encountered the same bird as an adult on its own nest, 30 miles to the south.
(Rowell—Nikon F4, 20mm f4 lens, SB-24 flash, Fuji Velvia)

Oak tree on Rocky Ridge, Las Trampas Regional Wilderness; 1995 pp. 180–181

In the late afternoon on the 2,000-foot crest of Rocky Ridge, I used a very wide-angle lens to compose the pastoral curves of this spring landscape.
(Rowell—Nikon N90S, 20mm f4 lens, Fuji Velvia)

Wildflowers in Mitchell Canyon in front of Eagle Peak, Mount Diablo State Park; 1996 p. 186

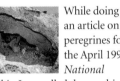

I spotted these flowers in harsh direct sunlight at one of the most rugged and remote areas of the park. Returning on an overcast day, I composed this scene when the light was soft and even.
(Sewell—Nikon N90, 24–50mm f3.3 lens, Fuji Velvia)

California poppies (Eschscholzia californica), Mitchell Canyon, Mount Diablo State Park; 1995 p. 189

While returning from a run up and down the mountain, I came across the most spectacular field of poppies I had ever seen in the Bay Area. The pattern of the poppies leads the viewer's eye across the green meadow and onto the wildest slopes of the mountain.
(Rowell—Nikon F4, 20mm f4 lens, Fuji Velvia)

Intersecting ridges in the foothills of Mount Diablo near Morgan Territory Regional Preserve; 1982 p. 193

On a perfect spring day when the rolling foothills were vivid green, I searched the landscape near Morgan Territory Road for the most aesthetic convergence of multiple ridges I could find. A telephoto lens compresses the perspective and brings the ridges together.
(Rowell—Nikon F3, 180mm f2.8 lens, Kodachrome 64)

Sharp-shinned hawk, Mount Diablo State Park; 1989 p. 197

I spotted this small hawk from my portable photography blind overlooking a secluded meadow on the north side of the mountain. Using a wide aperture, I isolated the pattern created by the dead manzanita from the rest of the background.
(Sewell—Nikon F3, 200–400mm f4 lens, Fujichrome 100)

Extreme telephoto view of Mount Diablo from Marin County; 1995 p. 197

While looking for wildlife above Tennessee Valley in the GGNRA on a very clear morning, I noticed how Mount Diablo and 35 miles of intervening ridge tops looked almost totally wild. I used 1,000mm of lens (500mm plus 2X converter) to single out the scene.
(Rowell—Nikon F4, 500mm f4 lens, Fuji Velvia)

Grazing lands in Mount Diablo foothills near Morgan Territory Regional Preserve; 1982 p. 198

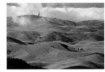

I made this telephoto view looking west from Morgan Territory Road on a morning when fog obscured the San Ramon Valley in the distance. I wanted to illustrate Bay Area agricultural lands as an important component of the metropolitan greenbelt. More than 8,500 farms, which produce more than $1 billion worth of annual output, currently hold back the flood of suburbia.
(Rowell—Nikon F4, 80–200mm f2.8 lens, Fuji Velvia)

Aerial view of Las Trampas Regional Wilderness and EBMUD lands; 1995 p. 199

On a flight with my wife, Barbara, I composed this scene of wild regional park and watershed lands stretching northward toward Walnut Creek. Without protection, development of this open space would have turned East Bay freeways into parking lots.
(Rowell—Nikon F4, 35mm f1.4 lens, Fuji Velvia)

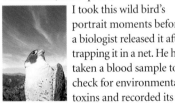

Mount Diablo fairy lantern (*Calochortus pulchellus*), Mount Diablo State Park; 1996 p. 200

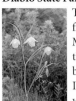

This rare, delicate flower occurs only on Mount Diablo and in the surrounding areas, blooming in large patches. I included other native wildflowers in this shot to give a strong sense of springtime on the mountain.
(*Sewell—Nikon N90, 80–200mm f2.8 lens, Fuji Velvia*)

Shooting stars (*Dodecatheon hendersonii*), Mitchell Canyon, Mount Diablo State Park; 1996 p. 201

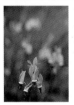

On a run up this wild canyon in spring, I stopped to set up a small tripod beside these spectacular blooms in morning light, throwing the background out of focus to isolate the flowers.
(*Rowell—Nikon F4, 55mm f2.8 lens, Fuji Velvia*)

Mule's ears (*Wyethia glabra*), Mitchell Canyon, Mount Diablo State Park; 1996 p. 201

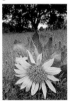

High in the canyon on a cloudy-bright morning in soft light, I used a wide-angle lens at ground level to show not only the flower but also the oak woodland.
(*Rowell—Nikon F4, 20mm f4 lens, Fuji Velvia*)

Coyote in brush, Mount Diablo State Park; 1989 p. 202

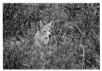

I sat in full camouflage gear against a large oak with outstretched legs and started predator calling, imitating the sound of a wounded rabbit. After less than a minute, I heard something approaching fast from behind. A coyote came around the tree in a full sprint, leaped over my legs, and landed ten feet beyond me, scaring both of us half to death. I grabbed this shot as it took one look back before disappearing into the bushes.
(*Sewell—Nikon F3, 200–400mm f4 lens, Fujichrome 100*)

Golden eagle and fledgling on nest, Mount Diablo State Park; 1989 p. 203

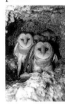

I secured permission from the chief ranger to photograph this historical nest site that dates back several decades. I set up my portable blind on a nearby hillside at night, when the eagle's vision is poor, and documented this huge five-foot nest over a one-month period. The chick fledged a few months before the Loma Prieta earthquake took the tree down.
(*Sewell—Nikon F3, 200–400mm f4 lens, Kodachrome 200*)

Raccoon couple at Bridal Nook picnic area, Mount Diablo State Park; 1990 p. 204

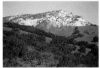

As I drove through the park, I noticed this raccoon couple standing in the picnic area. They appeared to be a mated pair in the middle of a minor domestic dispute.
(*Sewell—Nikon F3, 200–400mm f4 lens, Fujichrome 100*)

California red-legged frog, Morgan Territory Regional Preserve; 1988 p. 204

Since this photograph was made, the status of this frog has changed from "special concern" to threatened—only a step away from endangered, part of an ever-growing, sorrowful list. I moved in slow motion to get this shot without disturbing the pond's inhabitants.
(*Sewell—Nikon F3, 200–400mm f4 lens, Fujichrome 100*)

Alameda whipsnake, Mount Diablo State Park; 1989 p. 204

This rare and extremely fast-moving snake was trapped as part of a research project. Prior to its release, a friend, biologist Gary Beeman, kept the snake from getting away while I quickly made this photograph.
(*Sewell—Nikon F3, 80–200mm f2.8 lens, Fujichrome 100*)

Barn owls in cliff cave near Morgan Territory Regional Preserve; 1990 p. 205

I stood on an extension ladder, holding the top rung with one hand and balancing the camera in my other hand while I photographed these owls huddled together. A week later, someone with a gun killed them for "fun." The cave was used again the following year by another group of barn owls.
(*Sewell—Nikon F3, 24–50mm f3.3 lens, SB-16A flash, Fujichrome 100*)

Snow-capped summit, Mount Diablo State Park; 1994 p. 206

I had a good view of the snowy summit from Knob Cone Point Road on this clear, crisp winter morning and took advantage of a rare photographic opportunity in the Bay Area.
(*Sewell—Nikon N90, 80–200mm f2.8 lens, Fuji Velvia*)

View from near the top of Mount Diablo, Mount Diablo State Park; 1994 p. 207

I hiked above Juniper Camp on Mount Diablo on a snowy day and composed this close-up of snow-covered brush overlooking Walnut Creek and Lafayette.
(*Sewell—Nikon N90, 24–50mm f3.3 lens, Fuji Velvia*)

Gray fox, Mount Diablo State Park; 1988 p. 208

I lured this adult fox using animal calls while waiting in full camouflage gear in a secluded meadow near Prospectors Gap. After a few minutes, he popped over the rock and quickly darted around in search of my sounds, disappearing into the brush just after I made this photograph.
(*Sewell—Nikon F3, 150–500mm f5.6 lens, Fujichrome 100*)

Hiker and Mount Diablo from Vollmer Peak, Berkeley Hills; 1994 pp. 208-209

Use of a telephoto lens makes Mount Diablo appear to rise directly over a hiker by compressing the width of the valleys of the East Bay Interior. Two trail systems, each over thirty miles in length, connect this location on the crest of the Berkeley Hills with the distant summit.
(*Rowell—Nikon N70, 80–200mm f2.8 lens, Fuji Velvia*)

Mountain lion (captive), Coast Range; 1989 (not shown in main text)

Despite sporadic reports of Bay Area lion sightings, I spent four years maintaining a weatherproof remote camera beside wildlife trails on Mounts Tamalpais and Diablo without getting a photograph of one. Though I found fresh tracks near both locations, neither Galen nor I has seen more than fleeting glimpses of these largest remaining Bay Area predators in the wild. Because of our decision to use only unmanipulated images of wild animals taken in the Bay Area, this photograph, which does not appear in the main text, is shown here to symbolize a significant and elusive form of wildness we were unable to capture on film.
(*Sewell—Nikon F3, 80–200mm f2.8 lens, SB-16A flash, Fujichrome 100*)

221

A C K N O W L E D G M E N T S

My wife, Barbara Cushman Rowell, to whom I am deeply indebted for conceiving the idea for this book, insists that I thank N735LY. Her Cessna 206 not only provided her with a vision of Bay Area wilderness as a whole but also gave me a means of communicating that vision through aerial photography. I owe Barbara another debt of gratitude for enduring the months of focused seclusion I gave to writing. The combination of fatigue and satisfaction I now feel reminds me of the sensation of taking a pack off my shoulders for the last time at the end of a once-in-a-lifetime exploration.

When I literally shouldered a heavy pack to explore remote corners of the Bay Area, it was often at the invitation of Michael Sewell, who paved our way by obtaining special permission, where necessary, for us to photograph wildlife in sensitive areas. I wish to thank him—both for including me and for sharing his techniques of wildlife photography. Together, we explored Point Reyes, the Marin watershed, the Farallon Islands, Big Basin, Año Nuevo, Ohlone, and Mount Diablo.

Michael extends his thanks to me, for sharing my techniques of landscape photography, and to his wife and business partner, Denise Sewell, for her encouragement and assistance throughout the project. He would also like to thank those biologists, researchers, and preserve managers who assisted him in finding certain species and photographing them at close range as well as those who permitted him to set up blinds or call in wildlife to document their area's natural heritage. Readers of this book who are aspiring wildlife photographers are cautioned to check the regulations of each preserve before attempting to attract or closely approach Bay Area animals, especially those that are threatened or endangered and thus protected by law.

Michael and I would like to extend our thanks to the local organizations that supported our efforts, including those that appear on the facing page. Special mention is also due Audubon Canyon Ranch, the California Bat Conservation Fund, the Golden Gate Raptor Observatory, the National Oceanic and Atmospheric Administration, the Oceanic Society, the Point Reyes Bird Observatory, the Santa Cruz Predatory Bird Research Group, and the University of California.

Among the individuals who have made a difference in the North Bay region are Dennis Becker, Bob Bodarocko, Lisa DeGeronimo, John Dell'Osso, Allen Fish, Lou Garibaldi, Gordon Hasler, Angus "Buzz" Hull, Mike Johnson, Robin Leong, Casey B. May, Barry Nelson, Don Neubacher, Wallace NeVille, Brian O'Neill, Tim "Watertight" Parker, Steve Phelps, Toney Rowell, Christine Scott, John Shoemaker, John Takekawa, Edward Von der Porten, Landon Waggoner, Austin Wedemeyer, and Patricia Winters.

Individuals who have made a difference in the Peninsula and South Bay region include Frank Balthis, Sandy Elder, Chris Gill, Dan Howard, Marge Kolar, Tim Lane, E. Breck Parkman, Jim Sayer, Mary Jane Schram, Gary Strackin, Bill Sydeman, Edward Ueber, and John Wade.

Because of the overlapping jurisdictions of the East Bay Regional Park District and the East Bay Municipal Utility District, credits need to be combined for the East Bay and East Bay Interior regions. Here, we wish to thank Seth Adams, Dick Arnold, Christine Arnott, Steve Barbata, Reg Barrett, Gary Beeman, Thomas V. Bernardo, Steve Bobzien, Jim Bond, Bibi Chapman, John Cole, Joe DiDonato, Bob Doyle, Larry Ferri, Chris Franklin, John Ginochio, Diana Granados, Larry Hyder, Jerry Kent, Brian Latta, Barry Nelson, Bev Ortiz, Jenny Papka, Jerry Powell, Dale Sanders, Pat Solo, Robert L. Todd, Steve Van Landingham, and the late Bob Walker.

Special mention is due David R. Brower for writing the foreword for this book and relating his puppyhood experiences in the Berkeley Hills; to the select group of Bay Area environmental activists profiled on these pages—Mary Bowerman, Bob Doyle, Nonette Henko, Catherine Kerr, Sylvia McLaughlin, Brian O'Neill, Edgar Wayburn, and Peggy Wayburn—who not only gave their time for long interviews but also provided valuable comments on parts of the manuscript; and to my trail and adventure companions who appear in some of the photographs—Lee Aulman, Jib Ellison, Ron Kauk, Brian Maxwell, and Wilford Welch.

Almost all the photographs in this book were made with Nikon 35mm camera equipment. Both Michael Sewell and I would like to thank Nikon, Inc., for technical support. Thanks are also due Iris Photographics, Marin Photo, the New Lab, and Seawood Photo. Both Sieg Photographics and Professional Color Laboratory made fine prints for a *Bay Area Wild* exhibition shown during 1996 and 1997 at Mountain Light Gallery in Emeryville, California, coordinated by Ryan Baldwin. (For information on an expanded traveling museum exhibit, contact Ryan at Mountain Light Photography; the address is given at the bottom of this page.)

We wish to thank Peter Beren, director of Sierra Club Books, and his editors, Erik Migdail and Jim Cohee, for a great working relationship during packaging of this book by Mountain Light Press. I served as editorial director for the project, while Pat Harris handled primary text editing and Jennifer Barry did primary photo editing and design. Kristen Wurz completed the computer layout. Kim Pogorelsky did research and text transcription. Gary Crabbe and Inger Hogstrom worked with transparencies and scanned images. Janet Vail of Sierra Club Books oversaw the book's production.

Quotations are reprinted with kind permission from Harold Gilliam, Malcolm Margolin, and T. H. Watkins, full attributions appear on the copyright page. Manuscript readers who provided valuable comments about parts or all of the text include Mary Bowerman, Bob Doyle, Suzie Eastman, Blake Edgar, Dorothy Frye, Pat Harris, Nonette Henko, Catherine Kerr, Sylvia McLaughlin, Marilyn Moffitt, Brian O'Neill, Kim Pogorelsky, Denise Sewell, Michael Sewell, Candace Ward, and Edgar Wayburn.

We wish to thank Greenbelt Alliance for granting us permission to adapt its great digital map of threatened Bay Area greenbelt lands (page 18). Special thanks are due cartographer Louis Jaffe for reworking the map to fit our special needs. Jaffe, of Greenbelt Alliance/GreenInfo Network, also created the trail map on page 106 and the regional icon maps on the opening pages of the exhibit sections. We highly recommend Greenbelt Alliance's unparalleled graphic database of Bay Area environmental information to any publisher or organization in need of special maps or charts (415/543-4291).

No photograph in this book was altered or manipulated beyond normal digital prepress procedures, and all animals that appear on these pages are wild Bay Area creatures. Temporary captivity or control is revealed in the caption or in the photographic note in the book's final section. Exhibition prints or stock use of any of Galen Rowell's photographs that appear in this book may be obtained through Mountain Light Photography, 1466 66th Street, Emeryville, California 94608 (510/601-9000) (http://www.mountainlight.com); for Michael Sewell's photographs, contact Visual Pursuit, P.O. Box 811, Forest Knolls, California 94933 (415/488-1850).

AGENCIES AND ORGANIZATIONS

A select list of Bay Area environmental contacts

Regulatory Agencies

California Coastal Commission
Adopt-A-Beach Program
information 800/262-7848

California Department of
Parks and Recreation
Box 942896
Sacramento, CA 94296-0001
916/653-6995

East Bay Municipal Utility District
500 San Pablo Dam Road
Orinda, CA 94563
510/287-0459

East Bay Regional Park District
2950 Peralta Oaks Court
Oakland, CA 94605
510/635-0135; park info 562-7275

Golden Gate National Recreation Area
Fort Mason, Building 201
San Francisco, CA 94123
415/556-0560

Marin County Open Space District
Civic Center Drive, Room 417
San Rafael, CA 94903
415/499-6387

Marin Municipal Water District
220 Nellen Avenue
Corte Madera, CA 94925-1169
415/924-4600

Midpeninsula Regional
Open Space District
330 Distel Circle
Los Altos, CA 94002
415/691-1200

National Marine Sanctuaries
Fort Mason, Building 201
San Francisco, CA 94123
415/556-3509

Point Reyes National Seashore
Bear Valley Road
Point Reyes Station, CA 94956
415/663-1092

San Francisco Bay National
Wildlife Refuge Complex
P.O. Box 524
Newark, CA 94560
510/792-0222

Santa Clara County Parks
and Recreation Department
298 Garden Hill Drive
Los Gatos, CA 95030
408/358-3741

Environmental Organizations

American Land Conservancy
456 Montgomery Street, Suite 1450
San Francisco, CA 94104
415/403-3850

Bay Area Ridge Trail Council
26 O'Farrell Street, 4th Floor
San Francisco, CA 94108
415/391-9300

The Bay Institute
625 Grand Avenue, Suite 250
San Rafael, CA 94901
415/721-7680

Bay Keeper
Fort Mason, Building A
San Francisco, CA 94123-1382
415/567-4401

Committee for Green Foothills
3921 East Bayshore Road
Palo Alto, CA 94303
415/968-7243

Greenbelt Alliance
116 New Montgomery Street, Suite 640
San Francisco, CA 94105
415/543-4291

Headlands Institute
Yosemite National Institute
Golden Gate National Recreation Area
Building 1033
Sausalito, CA 94965
415/332-5771

Marin Conservation League
55 Mitchell Boulevard, Suite 21
San Rafael, CA 94903
415/472-6170

The Nature Conservancy
201 Mission Street, 4th Floor
San Francisco, CA 94105
415/777-0487

Peninsula Open Space Trust
3000 Sand Hill Road, Building 4,
Suite 135
Menlo Park, CA 94025
415/854-7696

Save Mount Diablo
P.O. Box 5376
Walnut Creek, CA 94596
510/947-3535

Save San Francisco Bay Association
1736 Franklin Street, 4th Floor
Oakland, CA 94612
510/452-9261

Save the Redwoods League
114 Sansome Street, Room 605
San Francisco, CA 94104
415/362-2352

Sempervirens Fund
2483 Old Middlefield Way, Suite 110
Mountain View, CA 94043
415/968-4509

Sierra Club Bay Chapter
2530 San Pablo Avenue, Suite I
Berkeley, CA 94702
510/848-0800

Sierra Club Legal Defense Fund
180 Montgomery Street, Suite 1400
San Francisco, CA 94104-4209
415/627-6700

Sierra Club Loma Prieta Chapter
3921 East Bayshore Road
Palo Alto, CA 94303
415/390-8411

Tamalpais Conservation Club
870 Market Street
San Francisco, CA 94102
415/391-8021

Trust for Public Land
116 New Montgomery Street,
4th Floor
San Francisco, CA 94105
415/495-4014

Urban Creeks Council
1250 Addison Street
Berkeley, CA 90702
510/540-6669

Previous Books by Galen Rowell

The Vertical World of Yosemite (anthology); 1974

In the Throne Room of the Mountain Gods; 1977

High and Wild: A Mountaineer's World; 1979

Many People Come, Looking, Looking; 1980

Alaska: Images of the Country (text by John McPhee); 1981

Mountains of the Middle Kingdom; 1983

Mountain Light: In Search of the Dynamic Landscape; 1986

The Yosemite (text by John Muir); 1989

The Art of Adventure; 1989

My Tibet (text by the Dalai Lama); 1990

Galen Rowell's Vision: The Art of Adventure Photography; 1993

Poles Apart: Parallel Visions of the Arctic and Antarctic; 1995

Design and photo editing by Jennifer Barry, Sausalito, CA
Computer-generated layout by Kristen Wurz
Text editing by Pat Harris and Galen Rowell
Text composition by Kim Pogorelsky
Sierra Club Books production by Janet Vail and Susan Ristow
Duplicate transparencies by Iris Photographics